W9-BTN-875

Jambo, Mama

Melinda Atwood

Cypress House
155 Cypress Street
Fort Bragg, CA 95437
1-800-773-7782
www.cypresshouse.com

Library of Congress Cataloging-in-Publication Data

Atwood, Melinda.
Jambo, Mama / Melinda Atwood.-- 1st ed.
p. cm.
ISBN 1-879384-38-8
1. Nairobi Region (Kenya)--Social life and customs. 2. Kenya--Social life and customs.
3. Atwood, Melinda. 4. Kenya--Description and travel. 5. Africa, Eastern--Description and travel. I. Title.

DT434.N3 A89 2000
967.62'5042 99-86959

Cover design: Robert Aulicino
Cover painting by Ole Kolii Paul
Author's photograph by Charmian Reading

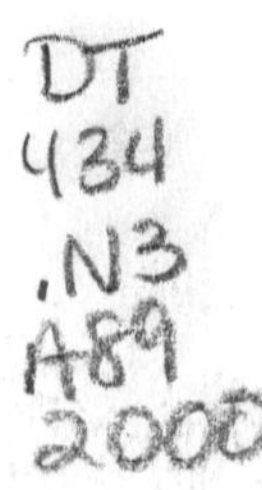

Manufactured in the United States of America

For Jake

Acknowledgements

I never dreamed of writing this book. It was not my idea to start with, and left on my own, I never would have started it, finished it, or ever seen it in print. I owe all that to others.

It began with my college pals, Eleanor and Peter Nalle. I had been writing long letters to Ellie, and thus, Pete, from the day I moved to Kenya and after several years of this back and forth, they encouraged me to put all these long tales into a book. I had no idea how to do that, so I wrote a few short stories, printed up three copies for Christmas presents, and that was that.

When I moved back to New York in 1992, I was urged to give it another try. That took me another two years and I only got half way done.

Then my son Jake took over. He decided to post one chapter every month on his web page, Bwanazulia.com. He had the expertise to do the Internet part, all I had to do was email each chapter to him, add a few pictures, and up they went. By the time the unwritten last chapters were finally due, I was working full time at a theatre in New York City and about to get married. That gave me the excuse of being too busy. But Jake kept pestering me. He also forwarded me all the email he received from our readers. There were people 'out there' asking for, and sometimes demanding, the next chapters. I was shamed into finishing.

And so I want to thank Ellie and Pete for their original idea, and their encouragement and faith in the early days of this project. I also thank them for the many wonderful times we had as we traipsed all over Africa together. Our little traveling threesome has somewhat disbanded now, but we'll always have Swakopmund.

I want to thank my dear friend and surrogate father, Douglas Sackfield. Douglas lived through every one of my tragedies and triumphs, either through the letters I wrote home or, God help him, in person. During all my years in Kenya, and for many thereafter, he listened to my endless tales of Ah-frica. He held my hand when I needed it and pushed me forward. He always believed, when I did not, that I could do this. Dearest D.

Jake is such a part of this story that it seems odd to thank him, but my life has been immeasurably richer just for his being in it. Our times together in Africa were indeed the best of times. And none of this would have happened had he not decided to post *Jambo, Mama* on the Web. He talked me through many of my doubts along the way and he kept me going, one chapter at a time. He is, as he has always been, what I am most proud of.

XXXXXXX Y.A.M.

And Billy. The day I met him my life changed quite dramatically, and for the better. Billy altered the way I looked at the world. And I never could, nor did I ever want to look back. Asante, Bwana Kidogo. Saaaaana.

I want to thank all the people out there in cyberspace who read each chapter as we posted it and then took the time to email me their encouraging words. It was an unexpected pleasure and a true gift to receive so much support from people, from all over the world, whom I had never met. They made me feel good and they carried me forward. They also kept asking me when it was going to be available in hard cover. Well, here it is.

And my love to my adorable and very patient husband Jean-Francois, just because he is who he is. He gives me the room, and very often the reason, to fly.

MSA

New York City
January, 2000

Contents

List of Illustrations

All photos taken by the author unless otherwise noted

Prologue

I have been asked, many times, why I went to live in Africa. After stumbling over the answer, equally as many times, I came up with a few quick sound bites. These ranged from wisecracking about being on the lam from the IRS to tossing off lines like, "It seemed like a good idea at the time." Or I might say that the opportunity arose and I took it. "Why Africa?" "Why not?" I had been there a few times before, had a few friends in Kenya, and what better place? If pressed really hard for more details, I might have mumbled something about recently going through a very bad time. But I always wanted it to sound as if this all occurred in a moment of pure whimsy: that I simply packed my bags one summer morning, grabbed my pith helmet, and hopped the first available flight for Nairobi.

My main objective, with all these answers, was to steer the conversation, as quickly as possible, away from the complicated and far more painful truth.

I did not know, when I lit out for Africa in 1987, that I was running away from home. I actually thought that I was off on a lark. A grand adventure. But I know now that I was running away from my family, running from all that had just happened, and away from what was looming ahead. And I was running away from what I feared was surely my destiny: ending up as my mother had.

My mother was a very wealthy, beautiful, charming, and accomplished woman who led a privileged and quite glamorous life. She had a large family, several homes, social position, numerous husbands, and friends who truly cared about her. She was also desperately unhappy. Her depression was probably clinical, it had surfaced many times before, and she had tried, on several occasions, to take her own life. But when she was diagnosed as having Lymphoma, it never occurred to me that she might view this as a very dramatic, and yet totally respectable, way out.

I didn't read the sign posts correctly. Maybe I should have made the connection between her previous desire to end her life and how she would deal with having cancer. I should have seen a rather exceptional woman who, after four husbands had come and gone, would still accept nothing but the opinion of some man as a reflection of her worth. I should have known that after having five children, in rapid succession, she had spent the rest of her life living out someone else's idea of what a "good mother" should be. I certainly should have seen that her money brought her countless material things, but little real happiness. But I did not. I never connected those dots. She was my mother and I loved her. I didn't see the woman she really was until almost the end.

Before she became ill, it was also not clear to me that her relationship with her children was as precarious and potentially explosive as it was, either. Granted we had always had to actively vie for our mother's affection. There were five of us, after all, and her attentions were in short supply. We all learned at a young age that the best way to get Mother's attention was to land in some kind of trouble. It needn't be big trouble, just more than the other four were currently in. But I was too close to that to see where it might, one day, lead.

There was also the very complex issue of her considerable wealth. We certainly enjoyed the benefits of growing up as we did; there were summer camps and fancy cars, private schools and trips to Europe. As we got older, however, money came to mean power to our mother, but to us it had come to represent love. Hers. It could be handed out in prodigious amounts, if you were in Mother's good graces, but it could also be cut off just as swiftly. We all rose and fell from those graces with considerable regularity, but, up until then, there had always been another day. We knew our number would come up again.

For most of my younger years, my little halo was securely in place. But once I decided to be less of a carbon copy of my mother, the more disfavor I found myself in. Much of what I did, beyond my nineteenth birthday, was not as my mother would have had it. She dismissed the career in dance, and later the theatre, that I pursued, by simply ignoring its existence. The dissolution of my two marriages, one at twenty-one and the next at twenty-seven, was further proof of my shortcomings. Although it seems to me that going through two husbands before the age of thirty was following quite closely in her footsteps, it didn't win me any points.

As far as my son, Jake, was concerned, the fact that he was the brightest star in her personal heaven apparently had nothing to do with how I was raising him. I never understood how he turned out to be such a great little fellow, if I was making such a mess of things. But my mother disapproved of almost everything I did with him and our relationship had been stormy and hurtful for many years.

Then she got cancer.

My ending up as her "significant caretaker" came about by default. Within mere weeks of hearing that she had Lymphoma, we received the next bit of numbing news: her husband of that decade, Step Dad Number Three, an artist with less serious talent than club house affability and a nose for a good opportunity, had bolted for the nearest exit. He was out the door and into the waiting arms of a woman my age before the second syllable of the word "cancer" had been pronounced. Not only was this a shattering blow to my mother, but it left the job of emotional support system unfilled. My younger sister, Christina, had been killed in a car accident in 1976 and my three brothers felt, and not without some justification, (the first diagnosis of her disease was not fatal) that Mother was making more of her illness than was absolutely necessary. That left me.

But I signed on not because I was faced with the prospect of becoming the companion of someone who always flew first class and ate in five star restaurants, but by the much more tantalizing possibility of intimacy.

During the three years that she was ill, I felt as if I had finally slid into love's home plate. There was a new light in my mother's eyes that appeared the minute she saw my face. The more time I spent with her, ultimately shelving my life in New York to be with her full time, the higher my star rose. I recognized how far this was from the many years that had gone before, and how circumstantial. I was neither a different nor a better person, but she thought I was. That feeling was not totally convincing, but it had been a long time coming and I wanted to hold on to it for as long as I could.

It is every child's worst nightmare that something terrible might happen to its mother, and by the spring of 1986, something terrible was happening to mine. She was dying. All through her illness, I had honestly believed that if I tried hard enough, if I could just infuse her with even a small part of the abundant energy I have always had, she would live. But she didn't want to live. This was not the face she showed the world at large, outwardly she was 'fighting the good fight.' But I knew how utterly despairing she was. It wasn't the cancer that was killing her; it was her inability to find any reason to go on living.

In April of that year, after surgery, chemotherapy and other more unconventional methods had failed, Mother attempted the last thing available: radiation. She was already weak from a recent surgery and the chances of this new regime making her more so were great. But she was determined. After only two treatments, something simply blew apart. I had just returned to New York from her home in South Carolina when I got the call to come right back. By the time I arrived there, she had slipped into a coma and I was told she would not live through the night. It had been my promise, one that she had extracted from me countless times, that she would die in her own bed, free of the tangle of tubes and drips, and that I would not let her die alone. Nor would I allow her to suffer. I took her home.

She could no longer communicate with me, but I chose to believe that she knew I was there and taking care of her. The doctors had told me that it was impossible to tell how much pain she was suffering, and increasing the dosage of morphine would further depress her breathing. But I could not sit there, knowing that she might be in the pain that she so feared and that I had promised to protect her from. It was a terrible choice, but I sent the doctors away and hired private nurses. I told them to do whatever was necessary to make sure my mother was comfortable.

And then I just sat by her bed, listening to her breathe, listening to her struggle to let go, and I waited. I changed her diapers and I talked to her. I told her that I loved her and I held her hand. And I waited. I knew she was not going to regain consciousness, and I tried to encourage her to go where I believed Tina would be waiting for her.

"It's okay. You can let go now."

On the fourth night, when she finally stopped breathing, the ensuing silence was stunning. I had never been that close to a death before, and as hoarse and grating as the sound of those last days had been, that stillness was far worse.

Then there was her funeral. And then they read her Will.

Mother had divided her considerable estate into four very unequal pieces with me, the current favorite, receiving the largest piece. She had gone even further to insure that I could not, after her death, divide my portion more equally among the four of us: she had put it into an irrevocable trust.

No one misunderstood her message. To our mother, I was the one who had taken care of her for three years, my brothers had not. They had their reasons, I am sure, but their lack of attention to her during her illness had hurt her deeply. This was her way of getting even. Although this news was not unexpected, it was, as far as my brothers were concerned, totally unacceptable. They instituted a lawsuit to overturn her Will with me as the target. I was accused of "undue influence."

I sympathized with the enormous punch to the gut that had just landed on each of them, but I did not support their decision to go through with this. A protracted legal battle with my own brothers was the last thing I needed, and I knew they would not win. Not only had I never asked her to do any such thing, but everyone knew that our mother only did what she wanted to do.

But it didn't matter what I felt, it was her Estate's legal obligation to defend her Will. I could not change that even if I had wanted to. Nonetheless, the months after her death were filled with bitter and acrimonious phone calls, tears, letters, shouting matches and horrible accusations, on all sides. But they were going to proceed.

There was no question of my fighting, I was going to flee. As soon as I knew this lawsuit was going ahead, I made plans to get as far away as possible. From this terrible confrontation with my brothers and, even then, from my mother. She was still there, pulling me into a situation I didn't want to be in. Forcing me, in some strange way, to stand in for her. To support her decisions. To be like her. I did not want to do it. I had just spent three years hearing how miserable much of her life had been and I had seen how sadly it had ended. Would I end up, when I was dying, with nothing but money, four ex-husbands and a badly broken spirit? Would I never know my own worth except in the eyes of some man? Any man? Would I, one day, be unable to find even one good reason to live? That terrified me more than the idea of battling my own brothers in court.

Of course, none of this came to me in clear, linear or even rational thought. It was all just a reaction. I felt, somewhere deep down in my gut, that if my mother had gone right, I should go left.

And so with all the lawyers jockeying for position and everyone's teeth bared, I set about clearing the decks to leave. One significant financial problem that had to be sorted out first was finding the money for Jake's tuition. Mother had always paid for his private schooling and had provided for this in her Will. But when a Will is contested, all assets are frozen until it is settled. Nothing can be disbursed. Not the money for Jake's tuition, not this great "inheritance" I was to receive, should anything be left after the lawyers were through, nothing. I couldn't have it, I couldn't borrow against it, and I couldn't get an advance.

And so I went down to the wholesale jewelry district in New York City and, after several humiliating hours of having my mother's things pawed over and scrutinized, I sold her diamond watch and a large pearl brooch. I felt like a pregnant hooker raising money for an abortion and I cried all the way home on the bus. But I had a large check in my wallet that was posted to Jake's school the next morning.

Then, on the twenty-sixth of July, 1987, I turned my back on my life as it was and boarded that British Air flight for Nairobi. I was sick at heart and scared senseless, but I was also somehow hopeful. I was finally starting to look ahead and, even better, I was going back to Africa.

one

Ah-frica

I had a hangover, and a significant hangover it was. I certainly knew better than to drink so much on long flights, but back in New York, where this journey had begun, it had seemed 'just the thing.' But two days later, at the unholy hour of six in the morning, it was painfully clear to me that there had been some flaws in that reasoning. Stumbling off the plane in Nairobi, I was more than sorry for my intemperance, I was truly repentant. Gathering up my hand luggage, I made sweeping promises to whatever deity might be listening:

"I promise I will never drink again, if I can just get through this day."

I had a reasonable, albeit generic, excuse for all that alcohol: nerves. I had waited months for this day to arrive and I was thrilled about moving to Africa, but I was also scared to death. All that summer I had managed to keep the major goblins at bay by sustaining a frenetic activity level. Or simply sticking my head in the sand. Avoidance was something I had developed some real expertise in that year. I had also taken full advantage of the attention my proposed new life had received. All those raised eyebrows were, at the very least, diverting. I had even managed to keep my sense of humor when confronted with the endless warnings about Death and Disease and The Dangers that Lurk in Far Away Places, that people kept wagging in my face. I waved them all aside. I announced that there was nothing to worry about because "I had a fah-rm in Ah-frica," doing my impression of Meryl Streep doing her impression of Karen Blixen.

But there comes a time when all that packing, planning and heavy denial can no longer hold up against the onslaught of reality. One day "Oh, Golly, Gee whiz! Isn't this just thrilling?" simply curdled into " Oh my God, what the hell am I doing?"

As the day of my actual departure approached, those sharp little edges of dread were getting ever sharper. Everyday, the gap between my clever remarks and the reality of a year alone in Africa grew wider. And on the morning of my flight, I woke up, no longer sassy, witty and brave, but scared to death and sick to my stomach. Not only did I not want to go, but I had no idea what had inspired me to consider such a hair brained stunt to begin with.

Once at Kennedy Airport, I started to feel marginally better. As the airplane doors locked behind me, having no way out felt oddly soothing. I am sure it was akin to the calm a condemned man must feel, trudging towards the gallows, but I was grateful for even that. Thus the champagne; it seemed appropriately celebratory. Never a person to have just one glass of champagne when two are clearly better, I kept these festivities going for the entire trip. British Air kept pouring and I kept celebrating. Never really drunk, but never completely sober either, I was jolly and slightly numb for the two days it takes to get from New York City to Kenya.

When I finally arrived in Nairobi, the combined effects of jet lag, no sleep, fifteen hours of air travel, and an approaching nervous breakdown, all joined hands and slammed into all that champagne. This crashing headache then met up with the problem with the air in Kenya. Nairobi sits at five thousand five hundred feet above sea level and the oxygen deprivation at that altitude renders the hardiest of souls light-headed, or just mildly stupid, for days. As that day was just barely beginning, my already precarious situation was going down hill, rapidly.

The next big hurdle to contend with was Jomo Kenyatta International Airport. JKI has to be one of the top ten airports in the world that are best avoided. It has been highly renovated in the recent past and is now marginally better, but back in 1987 it was cold, dark, badly designed, and inhospitable. Nothing more than a vast, decaying hangar, it was a triumph of peeling paint, patchy linoleum, flickering florescent lighting, and bureaucratic hassles. I already knew I was in for at least two very unhappy hours from the time I left the plane until I retrieved my luggage, if it weren't already on its way to Johannesburg.

Clearing passport control always took awhile. There were never enough officials to deal with the hundreds of arriving passengers, and those that were around were moving slowly. "There is no hurry in Africa," I repeated to myself as I waited in line. That was one of the many little sayings I had picked up in my travels and used to quote to my friends back in New York. It was meant to make me sound insouciant while, at the same time, the savvy world traveler. It was not, on that particular morning, having the desired effect.

Once through passport control, I descended a steeply pitched staircase to arrive in the main hall. There I stood watching the ancient conveyor belt rumble around in circles, hoping to spot my luggage. I had more than enough time to address the one question that kept going through my mind, "Why, Melinda? Why did you do this?"

Wasn't it just a few years ago that I was the happy, divorced mother of a sweet little, eleven-year old boy, living in New York? I had a job in the Off Broadway theater. I had friends and family. I had a nice boyfriend. How did I end up here, sick, tired, scared, and alone, and about to set up residence in some Third World country? How did I get here?

How indeed.

I first traveled to Africa with my son, Jake, in 1985 on a photographic safari. I had always longed to go to Africa, and was even booked to do so soon after Jake's birth. While I was complaining my way through the last few months of my pregnancy, my mother, in her usual escapist approach to personal problems, had planned just such a safari. As soon the new baby could spare me, my husband, David, and I were to join her and my future stepfather (Numero Tres) for a month in Africa. David was taken ill a week before we were to depart and when our scheduled flight to Africa was flying over the Sahara, I was home with a new baby and David was in surgery having fifteen inches of his intestines removed. Ever since then, I had carried a kind of personal IOU in my heart. Going to Africa always loomed large.

When, in 1985, long since single, I decided that Jake and I would finally make this journey, the excitement was palpable. And it came at a point in my mother's battle with cancer when a break was much needed. There had been a huge family fracas that Thanksgiving and, although far from unusual, it had convinced my mother that gathering her children around her sickbed was not such a good idea. There had been a nasty battle of words and, with no guarantee that it wouldn't happen again at Christmas, she sent me and my three brothers packing.

Jake and I went to Africa, and naturally enough, had a wonderful time. I think everyone who goes on safari in Kenya has a wonderful time, it is a very special place. But I felt that something more significant had occurred. Granted, almost anyone in my situation, coming from two and a half years in cancer wards, would have appreciated the freedom and wide open spaces of a place as profoundly beautiful as Kenya, but I believed it was more than that. I was convinced that I had just found the one place in the world where I truly belonged. When Jake and I left Nairobi after two weeks there, I cried for fifteen hours straight, all the way back to New York. There was certainly some regret about going back to what I knew I would be facing at my mother's bedside. But it felt exactly the way it feels to leave your new lover behind, just a bit harder to explain.

Most of my friends felt that that was precisely the problem; that I had left my new lover behind. They felt that this love sick state had less to do with leaving Africa and more to do with leaving young William Winter, our handsome young safari guide. It was true, to some degree. While I was busy living out my fantasies of being Karen Blixen, Billy had done a fair imitation of Denys Finch-Hatton. Our affair, although brief, had done nothing to diminish the pleasures of an African night.

Billy was bright, charming, wonderful company and, to me, utterly unique. Born and raised in Kenya, he had all the macho trappings of a "man of the bush," coupled with a great sensitivity. He could strip down his Range Rover in half an hour or lead me through the bush in search of rhino tracks in the dirt or lions in the grass. We would sit on a bluff at sunset looking out over the plains while he pointed out the beauty of a certain flower. He taught me to listen to the sounds of the night, to look for shapes in the underbrush, and to smell the rain coming, things I had never even thought about before. He took me to places he knew to be special, and introduced me to a country more beautiful than I had ever imagined. His being fourteen years my junior and bearing more than a passing resemblance to Mel Gibson didn't hurt either. It had all been very intoxicating.

But if Billy was very young, I was not. At thirty-eight, I knew enough to recognize the effects that campfires, handsome young men, and moonlight can have on one's better judgment. It was not totally sensible to throw my entire life away and dash off to Africa to chase some young thing around the thorn trees. I probably was in love with Billy, but my desire to move to Africa went deeper than that.

Although my mother's death, six months later, was more or less expected, I was utterly stunned by the loss of her. And even more stunned by my brothers lawsuit. For months, I could not pull myself together. I had been cut adrift. The previous three years had been consumed with caring for my mother, living almost every day with my heart in my throat. There had been frenzied dashes to emergency rooms, endless chemotherapy traumas, and countless medical horrors played out in as many hospital rooms. For three years, that had been my life. I had lived on hope, high drama, and adrenaline, while every day growing closer to a mother who, up until then, had never quite approved of me. I had become all too used to both the horrible drama of it and a newfound closeness with my mother. Then she was gone. And there was nothing. But an ugly legal battle with my three brothers.

Rearranging what used to be my life in New York held no special appeal and I had no real life left in New York anyway. I had been out of that loop more than I had been in it for three years and New York City is unforgiving in that way. I had long since packed in my love life, my social life, and my business life. Even Jake was no longer there. He had been in boarding school for over a year so that I could be with my mother full time. He was doing well, was happy, and it made no sense to bring him back to New York City just to give me a reason to get out of bed in the morning. All of the tethers of my old life had been cut; there was nothing holding me anymore. Knowing that added to my sadness, but it had an unexpected side effect. Being so unattached gave me a new kind of freedom.

For years, I had been needed and totally responsible for my mother. Now I was neither. I could slip out the back door without many people either noticing or being too greatly affected by my absence. And I coud get away from the confrontation that was looming on the horizon. It was one of those windows in time when there was no good reason to stay and one very good reason to go. And the freedom to do just that. I had the chance to run away, always a strong desire in times of pain, and I took it.

Was it brave? Not really. My sense of survival, combined with a good case of shell shock, were far greater players than real bravery. Was it selfish? Probably. I thought more about what I needed than I did about how this would affect anyone else, most particularly Jake.

He and I talked about it a great deal and he was enthusiastic about the chance to visit me on his vacations, but neither of us knew just how far away I really would be. And it was "only for a year," after all. Was it blind? Absolutely. I thought very little about what I was heading into, only that I needed to go. Many times, I heard "You can't run away from your problems." Well, I was going to make a damn good effort to run away from mine. I was stubborn, determined, and conveniently myopic. I had the bit in my teeth and I was going to go. Frankly, I would have gone to China or Antarctica had I had a few friends there. I consider it pure serendipity that I had been to Africa and had met Billy. It gave me a wonderful place to run to.

After my mother died, I made several more trips to Kenya. I was going back because I loved it, but also to see if it would still hold me in its thrall. It did. With each safari, I was more convinced that Africa was where I wanted to be. Even after Billy and I settled into a far more sensible friendship, I was still obsessed with Africa. There is an expression: "Once you have Africa in your blood . . . " Well, I sure had it in mine and in March of '87, I decided to make the leap. To live there. Although my friends understood my desire to run away, they were not as convinced as I, that this New York City girl "belonged" in Africa. They pointed out that I was under an enormous amount of stress and that this was not a particularly good time to be making such large decisions. I listened, or pretended to, but I could not be deterred. I did allow myself to be talked out of selling my co-op on Riverside Drive and unloading everything I owned on the Salvation Army. I settled on renting a house in Nairobi for a year. Once the decision to go had been made, things moved along quite rapidly. All of a sudden, or so it felt that terribly hung-over morning in July, there I was, in Ah-frica.

Having finally collected all my bags, I headed for the Customs desk. I was trying to keep a low profile, always a good idea in foreign lands, but I was far from successful. I had with me, along with the usual luggage, five large duffel bags. Why so much gear? I had brought all my household goods with me. The house that I had rented, or more correctly, had been rented for me by Billy's parents, Bill Sr. and Barbara Winter, although technically a "furnished rental," was coming to me without any manner of household appurtenances. I thought this quite inconvenient, but as the owner was Daniel Arap Moi, the President of Kenya, I chose not to make too big a fuss. The President had many houses, (as many as he liked, I should imagine,) and this was not an unusual situation for him, but it was for me. Another reason for going through with this domestic arrangement was the fact that I had already paid the entire year's rent in advance. By the time I found out that I had to purchase every can opener, the check had cleared.

Barbara and Bill had advised me to bring as much as I could with me. The quality of household goods in Kenya is decidedly inferior and far more expensive than what I could purchase in the States. I did as I was told. I was carrying bed linens for two queen sized and two twin beds. I had sheets and duvets and mattress covers. I brought all the blankets and bath towels for the bathrooms. I had bath mats. Not only was it bulky, but it weighed a considerable amount and, piled on to the ancient luggage cart at JKI, it was all but unmovable. To make this scene all the more ridiculous, my leather soled shoes kept slipping out from under me every time I tried to move this tonnage along. I felt like one of the Three Stooges. "Moe, Larry and Curly Go On Safari." Whenever I did manage to achieve any traction one of the four decrepit wheels would invariably slip into a divot in the linoleum and everything would tumble to the floor. The cart was careening out of control and about to tip over for the third time when I finally made it up to the Customs desk.

I handed the man my passport and currency form and smiled as broadly as I could.

"Jambo, Mama," he greeted me.

"Jambo, Bwana."

I was being obsequious, bwana is an old colonial term for master, but I did not want those bags opened and was willing to try anything. It was one more lengthy procedure I didn't want to face and I had real contraband stashed among my linens. I had with me a clock radio, a small typewriter, a cassette player, and two rechargeable flashlights. Such goodies were not allowed into Kenya without paying a significant duty, usually 200% of whatever arbitrary value the Customs chap decides to slap on. It can be a huge bother getting around this. I later learned how to bribe my way out of these situations, finding that if I talked very loud and fast, while pressing a few hundred shillings into the man's hand, I would be waved on through. The combination of attracting attention, creating confusion and money always worked. But back in '87, I thought everything was just as it is in the USA and who would even consider bribing a U.S. Customs officer? I also had no Kenyan currency on me and, nor had I acquired the bravado or perfected the sleight of hand these transactions require. I was counting on the man's good will.

"Jambo."

"How long will you be staying in Kenya?"

"Oh, just two weeks."

I was hoping that I could pass myself off as the average tourist, in Kenya for the standard two-week safari. Maybe he would consider me a lousy packer and a spoiled American and let it go at that?

"What have you brought for your friends here?" He had spotted the previous Kenya Entry Visas in my passport. No one returned to Kenya without presents for their friends. So many things could not be purchased that to return from abroad without tapes and books and new cassette decks was unthinkable.

"Nothing, mzee *(an elder person),* I have nothing. But I am choka sana. *(very tired)*. Kabissa. (*Truly)* I made a face and slouched dramatically over my luggage cart.

"Safari kubwa, bwana. Mimi choka sana." (*It was a long trip. I am very tired.)*

He didn't overreact to my sudden linguistic skills, but I had apparently aroused his pity. Thank God for the African's infinite sympathy for conditions they consider only a white man's problem, like jet lag. A great majority of the Africans never get on a train, let alone an airplane. It made perfect sense that such a preposterous journey, half way around the world in a metal box, would make anyone, at the very least, tired.

"Pole Mama. Choka sana. Pole." (*Sorry, very tired. So sorry.)* He stamped my passport and with a look of great concern, handed it back to me.

"Asante sana," (*Thank you very much)* I gasped out, my health failing by the minute. I took my passport and limped away.

As Billy was off leading a safari, Bill Sr. and Barbara were outside the gates to greet me. They piled me and all my luggage into their Land Cruiser and off we went. We were bound for Karen, the suburb that lies twelve kilometers to the southwest of Nairobi and where I was to be living for the next year. As we drove from the airport past the thorn trees and the occasional giraffe that poked its head out of Nairobi National Park, I could smell that familiar scent that always made my pulse quicken. The air at that altitude is wonderfully clear and thin and smells of wood smoke and lush vegetation. Even in Nairobi, with diesel fuel belching out of buses that never get inspected, and masses of humanity everywhere, there is something inexplicably sweet about the air. At that early hour, the streets were already teeming with the thousands of Africans who walk into Nairobi proper to work each day, and the traffic was beginning to back up. We drove past Wilson, the smaller commuter airport, past the main gates to the National Park, and out the Langata Road towards Karen.

two

Don't Worry, Melinda

We were barely past the city limits and Bill Sr. was already into his lecture on what I was to do to get myself organized. I was way beyond sensory overload and wasn't really listening. But my inattention did not slow him down. Nothing could stop Bill once he was on a roll.

William Henry Winter was a transplanted Englishman who had lived in Kenya for the past thirty-five years. Movie star handsome in his youth, he still had a dazzling smile, sky blue eyes, and silver hair that waved back off his forehead. At fifty-five, with a growing paunch, and a pronounced limp (a gift from a hunting client's wayward bullet that was meant for a Cape Buffalo, but shattered Bill's leg instead,) he had enormous panache and great charm. He had come to Kenya during "the Emergency" (the Mau Mau uprisings) as a policeman and had since been a game warden and a professional hunter. Until that bullet shortened his leg by three inches and his career by many years.

Bill was a world class raconteur. He had done just about everything exciting there was to do and had the tales to tell about it. He would sit by the fire at night and tell of stalking leopards through thick bush and of runaway African warriors. His eyes would glisten as he recounted the time, "back in my hunting days" when, while following a wounded elephant through high grass, he lost sight of it until the old bull doubled back and tripped over him. As with most of Bill's stories, that one ended with a joke on himself. He was essentially a self taught man, as widely read as anyone I ever met. He could discuss the theater in London or the politics of Sweden with as much authority as he could the lion tracking techniques of the Maasai. He was also, and this was pivotal to his personality, usually right. He had a vast store of knowledge, trivial and otherwise, and of all the bets I got suckered into waging against Bill Sr. in the years I lived in Africa, I recall only one that I won. (Liza Minelli did not sing "New York, New York" in the movie of *Cabaret*.)

Bill's greatest joy, if not mission in life was giving advice. He readily acknowledged himself as an authority on almost every subject, and was more than happy to impart his every thought to anyone within earshot. He never thought twice about any listener's desire to hear it all, he assumed they were grateful for his help. He had found the perfect pigeon with me. I was a female, new to Kenya, younger than he, and, worst of all an American, a category of people that he always singled out as particularly arrogant, ignorant and in definite want of his instructions. I am sure that he had decided, long before I arrived in Africa, that he was going to set my new life on the right track. If I had any sense at all, he told me almost hourly, I would follow his advice to the letter.

His "instructing" very often crossed the line from giving advice to browbeating, but he meant well and he usually had a laugh lurking somewhere behind his preachings. Even when he angered me the most, insulting my intelligence, my gender, or my nationality, he could make me laugh. Once, after I had been living and driving a car in Kenya for over a year, Bill Sr. announced, just once too often, that the steering wheel of the car was on the right. I had better heed his advice and stay on the correct side of the road. I couldn't believe he was still telling me that.

"Just what is it about me Bill, that makes you think I am so stupid?" I howled. "Is it because I am a blond, a woman, or an American?" He looked me straight in the face and, without dropping a beat, announced, "All three." We both burst out laughing.

Bill Sr. initially overwhelmed and frightened me, but I came, years later, to see that a great deal of his bluster masked his real tenderness.

As we drove out to Karen that morning I was trying to ignore him and just take in the sights. I was thrilled to be back in Africa and I didn't want to hear all his friendly advice. But that never bothered Bill. He started with the weather and my very ill timed entrance.

"It's bloody miserable weather now, Melinda." He informed me. "You shouldn't have come now, you know. September would have been better. But never mind." He then moved on to lecture me on how I was going to have my throat slit or my hand cut off if I didn't put my jewelry away immediately. That took him to the need for strict security measures in my new house and how I must learn to lock all the doors and never tell anyone in my employ where I was going. Never keep any money in the house and be sure to hide all keys.

"You don't know how these thieves are, Melinda. Bloody swine I tell you. Now you take the advice of W.H. Winter and get a safe to bolt to your closet floor. Which reminds me, the gates at your new nyumba *(house)* are just not suitable. Not suitable at all. We must call Ultimate Security and have them come 'round and install your alarm system. Panic buttons in every room, that's what we have, isn't that right Barbie? You just push the tit and the mobile unit will be there in three minutes. But don't you worry Melinda, we will get everything sorted out. You aren't alone here, you know."

That got my attention. Panic buttons? Alarm systems? I thought "the Emergency" was over. I was nervous enough about the year ahead of me without hearing how endangered my life was about to become because I wore a watch or kept five dollars in loose change in the house.

But when I attempted to ask him just exactly how bad this crime wave was, he had moved on to the topic of my staff. He was listing all the help I would need, house girls, guards, cooks, gardeners, and a driver. "A grand lady from New York has to have a driver, Melinda."

I didn't want a driver, but no one was listening to me. He then moved on to the problems with the house. It seemed this presidential palace had no power and no major kitchen appliances.

"But don't worry Melinda, we will get in touch with His Excellency and get you all kitted out. And I know a chap, old gray bollocks Jamblin, nice old mzee, who will rent you a cooker and a fridge. You see, Melinda, W. H. Winter will look after you. You have nothing to worry about."

Well, that was a comfort. Of course, had Bill not been so busy pointing out all the things I didn't need to worry about, I probably wouldn't have worried about them, but I didn't say that. I didn't say anything. Not only was interrupting Bill impossible, but as his list of things I needed to address grew longer, I had been terrorized into silence. If Bill had meant to frighten me and he very well may have, he had achieved his goal. As he went on and on, I began to have the distinct feeling that I couldn't possibly cope with all this. By the time we pulled into the Winter's driveway in Karen, I was on the verge of tears. In the forty minutes that it took to drive from JKI to Karen, Bill had wiped out what little courage I even thought I had left. And all his Don't Worry, Melindas were not helping. As we parked the car and Bill started to give endless advice to the gardener unfortunate enough to be standing there, I bolted for the house. I slammed the bathroom door behind me and let the tears fall. Moments later, looking at my now even puffier eyes in the mirror, all I could say was "Well, Melinda old girl, this is a fine mess you've got us into."

After splashing water on my face, I took a deep breath and ventured out. I made my way to the dining table (it was only eight AM) and faked my way through breakfast. A medicinal Bloody Mary would have been more to my liking than the fried bacon, fried eggs and fried tomatoes the Kenyans so love. But I pushed the food around on my plate, making little designs with the greasy traces, and pretended to listen to Bill's further dissertations. Barbara, a black-haired, Tanzania-born beauty, and Bill's wife of thirty years, was busy organizing her kitchen staff, giving only a cursory nod to every one of Bill's, "Isn't that right, Barbie." Barbara was a woman never short of her own opinions, and, like her husband, willing to give them to you whether you asked for them or not. This was not the time. Barbara was, as I found most of the women born and bred in that part of the world to be, strong minded, outspoken, and extremely independent. But thirty years of conubial bliss with W. H. Winter had taught her to save her breath when Bill was on one of his rants.

There was never any mention of my dalliance with the younger Winter. It was not like either one of them to tread lightly on any subject, or to just keep their mouths shut and so I never felt it was a matter of deference to the delicacy of the topic or my privacy. I am still convinced that they were just so relieved that Billy hadn't gotten serious about this 'older American woman,' that they put the whole horrid thought out of their minds.

But back in July '87, as we drank our coffee, Bill Sr. had moved on to what were his absolute favorite topics, his mantras, especially when speaking to Americans: the correct voltage in Kenya and the correct side of the road to drive on. He was pounding this point home.

"You Yanks never get it through your thick kichwas (*heads*) that the voltage in Kenya is 240. I can't tell you, Melinda, the safari clients who have sent me things that are as useful as tits on a bull. And you have got to remember that one drives on the left hand side of the road. You will get yourself killed, Melinda, mark my words. You listen to me and stay on the bloody left."

But, Bill assured me, again, I had nothing to worry about. Keeping herself out of the cross hairs, Barbara just smiled at me conspiratorially, shaking her head and rolling her eyes.

Once we had concluded our breakfast, we set out to find my new house. All I knew was what Bill had told me over the crackling international telephone lines; it had a breathtaking view of the Ngong Hills. I should have paid more attention to the fact that it was the President of Kenya's house, but I had no idea what that signified. The only private home in Kenya that I had ever been in was the Winter's. It was a sprawling white washed stone dwelling with a cedar-shingled roof, set on ten beautiful acres of flowering trees and shrubs. It was elegant and warm, in a British colonial sort of way. Bill's constant exhortations to the many garden bibis (*wives)* he employed made for well-tended flower beds and immaculate lawns. The interior had white plaster walls and wide planked wooden floors. Overstuffed chairs were covered in English chintzes and there were cut flowers everywhere. The sun streamed through small paned windows that were secured with brass latches and flowering vines crept up the sides of the house and over the chimneys. The fireplace mantelpiece in the main sitting room was carved out of a large slab of wood Bill had carried on his back out of the Meru forest. He loved to tell of this deed of youthful derring-do. A bronze statue of an elephant captured in full charge faced off with another of a Cape Buffalo pawing the ground. A pair of elephants tusks, reminders of the time before there was a ban on all such ivory, were mounted on the wall. The Winter's home was enchanting and colorful, and spoke of the many adventures of its larger then life owner. I was hoping for something just like it. To be more precise, I had my heart set on it.

I had spent the months before heading to Africa pouring over books on Kenya, to say nothing of wearing out my copy of the videotape of *Out Of Africa.* Not only had I memorized all the best dialogue and had Meryl Streep's accent down pat, I had also fashioned a very romantic image of my future life in Kenya. I wanted to live in, if not the Winter's house, then Karen Blixen's. It had to be quaint and colonial and perhaps, if I was lucky, a slightly run down, thatched roof cottage. I wanted atmosphere, history, and the air of foreign intrigue. The house I was to live in was a major player in my fantasy life that summer. It was with a nervous, but eager heart, that I climbed back into the Toyota and set off with Bill, driving through Karen, to see my little "cottage."

Karen sits at 6300 feet above sea level and the most striking feature about it is that it doesn't look anything like Africa "should" look. Karen resembles Carmel, California far more than a desert or the set of Ramar of the Jungle. And the climate is superb. Because of the high elevation and its location only five hundred miles south of the Equator, the weather is almost perfect year round. It's sunny, warm and dry eight months out of the year. There are two rainy seasons, the short rains in November, and the long rains in March, April and May, but even then it feels dry. The rain is so desperately needed in most parts of Kenya that everyone is grateful for every sprinkle. There are days in July and August when it gets quite cold, but that just seems a relief from the otherwise endless perfect days.

The soil is rich and red and the vegetation lush. Flowering trees such as nandi flame, flamboyant, and jacaranda grow tall and elegant. When they flower in October their crimson, purple and flame red blossoms are spectacular. There are bottlebrush trees with whimsical red flowers and cape chestnuts with blossoms that resemble orchids. Bougainvillea and poinsettias bloom year round, and rose bushes thrive with minimal attention. Ripe avocados will drop from the trees and hit you on the head if you don't pick them quickly enough.

Driving around Karen one might get the impression that it is a farming community. It isn't really; it's just that there are always herds of cows and goats on every corner. The Africans regard their livestock as money and on most afternoons, you can catch a small boy or old man dozing in the shade of a thorn tree while their four legged bankrolls munch on nearby grass or wander off. As the Africans walk everywhere, there isn't a road in town without several footpaths worn into deep ruts running parallel to it. People heading to or from work walk in pairs or small groups. The more fortunate catch a ride on the back of a bicycle pedaled along by a willing, and more affluent, friend. There are young mothers everywhere, each with a baby strapped to her back. They knit as they walk, while another child, never any older than three, stumbles along behind.

Equally as common are the old ladies, the mama mzees, who carry large bundles of firewood on their backs. They are secured by a strap across their foreheads. These old mamas were long ago bent low by the weight of their burdens. Many people simply sit by the side of the road watching the world go by. Not only is there no hurry in Africa, there is not enough employment either. Sitting by the side of the road is not considered loitering in Karen, it is just what a great many people do on any given afternoon.

Large and formidable gates guard all the homes of any consequence. There is often a guard sitting nearby, ready should a visitor wish entrance to the compound. It is another of the many forms of security that are so important in Karen. The gap between the "haves" and the "have-nots" is wide and petty crime is endemic. Landowners in Karen are almost exclusively European, the local colloquialism for Caucasian, and their attempts at securing their property against break ins and robberies have escalated greatly over the years. Not wanting to be the weak link in the neighborhood chain, each home is equipped with gates and guards, dogs and alarm systems. There are bars on all the windows. No one but the police is allowed to carry a gun, but the guards hired to protect the grounds wield spears and bows and arrows. Private security firms have sprung up and flourished. There are mobile units parked at almost every major crossroad in case a radio-transmitted alarm is sounded. All those gates and guards made Karen seem like an armed camp to me those first months in Kenya, but as the years went by, I barely noticed them.

I knew my new address was Mbagathi Ridge and as we turned a corner and headed up that street, I started to pay full attention. As we drove by each house, I peered through the gates wondering which one was mine. I don't know if Bill heard me gasp (probably not, he was busy expounding on his plans for the planting of new bushes and the weeding of my garden,) but as we pulled into the driveway, I could feel first my jaw, then my heart hit the floor.

"Pretty grand, wouldn't you say, Melinda?"

I didn't answer that.

"Barbie and I almost bought it ourselves a few years back, but . . . "

I still said nothing. I was too stunned by the sight of this structure to reply. This wasn't Karen Blixen's house. This was not a thatched roof cottage and it would never be described as quaint or colonial. What I saw standing at the end of the long driveway was a pale green, two-story cement block with a flat tiled roof. It was huge, oddly shaped, and homely. There were massive carved wooden doors in the white and gold tiled entranceway and wrought iron curlicues covering every window. The Poinsettias, bolted to ten feet high, gave the whole place a distinct air of southern decay. The grass was growing knee high and everything that wasn't overgrown was dead.

"We will get some bibis in here tomorrow to sort out your garden, Melinda. Don't you worry." I didn't answer that either. I was trying to decide if the whole scene was more reminiscent of the Addams family, or Tara, after the Yankees had swept through Georgia, when Bill shut off the car and led me into the front hall.

As the large doors slammed behind me, I could see nothing, temporarily blinded by the sudden darkness.

"Now this isn't all bad, would you say, Melinda?"

No, it wasn't all bad. It was worse. As my eyes adjusted, what I saw was the interior of a monastery. We were standing in the middle of a thirty square foot entrance hall with dark gold silk drapes pulled across every window. The furniture was all upholstered in brown velvet, the wallpaper was mustard brown silk, and the wainscoting stood shoulder high. It was very dark in there. There was a working fountain in the middle of the hall with a blue floodlight suspended above it, but even that failed to lend any sorely needed levity. The carpeting, also brown and wall to wall, was all that kept our footsteps from echoing as we walked from one room to the next, each more relentlessly cheerless than the one before it.

Bill was chattering on about how grand it all was and how wonderful and full my life was going to be, one day soon, when I was entertaining twenty people for lunch every day in my post Civil War garden. The only nod he gave to the very pronounced gloom of the place was when he said he was confident that it would all be much brighter soon. Once we located the keys that would unlock the metal gates that covered the sliding glass doors that lay behind the floor to ceiling drapes, that is.

We passed from the all brown dining room, complete with heavy chandeliers and wall sconces, into the kitchen. The most remarkable feature there was the two gaping holes where a stove and refrigerator should have been. Bill reminded me of his friend Jamblin, "old gray bollocks," who was going to rent me these appliances, and then strode merrily back out into the hall. I followed silently behind him.

We finished touring the lower story, complete with formal living room, den, and bath, and made our way up the stairs. Bill yanked aside the drapes that covered the window on the landing, and that lent us enough light to see that the staircase was set against the wall on a distinct angle that was not ninety degrees. Upstairs there were two bedrooms and another den, decorated, as was its twin below, ceiling to floor, in Kelly green. The main feature of the bathrooms was that they matched their attached bedrooms, tiled top to bottom in a matching pastel. Bill was still commenting on how grand it all was and how happy I was going to be when we arrived at the master bedroom. He was saving the best for last.

It was a symphony in pink and gold. Everything was covered either in pink silk or pink velvet or trimmed with pink fringe. The dressing table was white with gold flowers, but it did have a pink velvet stool. The bedspread and drapes pulled the whole scheme together: they were pink and gold cut velvet.

Bill was going on about my rosy future and the grandeur of this dwelling and paying no attention to me, which was a lucky thing as I was busy fighting back my tears of disappointment. It was clearly foolish of me to have planted the image of my little "settler's cottage" so firmly in my head, I know Bill had tried to please me and I will always be grateful to him for all the efforts he made on my behalf. But the truth was that this cathouse pink bedroom was so far away from what I had been dreaming about that I was heart broken. I was also much too tired to be too philosophical.

Bill then opened the side door of the bedroom and walked out on to a patio. I had missed its larger entrance of full sliding glass doors that opened from the upstairs hall, (they were behind all those gold drapes,) but this was the master bedroom entrance. As we stepped out onto the flagstone, Bill said once again "How's that, Melinda? Now that isn't all bad? Is it?"

I uttered the first words I had said all morning.

"No, Bill. That's beautiful."

There were the Ngong Hills. The four very distinct knuckles of the Ngongs rose before me in a 180-degree postcard view, the Africa I had been dreaming about. As I stood there looking at the Ngongs my spirits lifted. Maybe this was going to be all right after all. To hell with this pretentious house and to hell with all that endless velvet. If I could just sit on this patio and look at the Ngongs and smell the air in Africa, I just might live through the year I had signed on for. I would just never go downstairs again. Or I would redecorate. I suddenly didn't care. For the first time since I had arrived that morning, I was happy I had come. I could even remember what it was about Africa that had captured such a large part of my soul.

I had done a considerable amount of traveling in my day, had been almost around the world, and even I found it strange that I was as affected by Africa as I was. But Africa really is different. It is magical and many travelers before me have waxed rhapsodic on that subject. But when that sense of awe and wonder stuck me, I was utterly dumbfounded. Perhaps this is caused by the nearness of all the animals. Maybe being so close to the ancient rightness of Nature just moves us on some profound level. Or is it being in the land where man is supposed to have been born? Richard Leaky espouses the genetic memory theory. He holds that all our origins are buried deep within our DNA helices and that they just start to sing out loud when we set foot on African soil. Possibly. All I knew was that once I had been there I was obsessed with it. There was simply no other place on earth that I wanted to be.

The light on the hills at sunset in the Maasai Mara rendered me awestruck. The smell of the air in Nairobi, although cloudy with diesel fuel, was intoxicating. I was completely content, in the nearly insufferable heat of the desert, to simply be there. The colors of the Cherangani Hills at sunset, blue after blue after blue, one massive, granite ripple that faded into a hundred more shades of gray as they receded into the infinite space that so typifies Africa left me dizzy. I would lie in my tent, somewhere between frightened and thrilled, spellbound by the sounds of the night. The earth would shake with the roar of nearby lions, while baboons, shrieking at one another, swung through the branches of the giant fig trees overhead. The metallic ping of the Abysinnian Night Jars became the counterpoint to the barking of the zebras. It all formed a wildlife symphony that was performed under the canopy of the millions of stars in the African sky.

I noticed that when I was in Africa I liked me better. Everything felt clearer and cleaner to me, on the inside. My inside. I was brave where I had never before been brave. I was sure of things I had never even thought about. I was sure of myself and life made more sense to me. It was far more straightforward and simple than I had ever found it to be. When I was in Africa, I was comfortable in ways I had never been comfortable before: comfortable in my skin, comfortable in my clothes, and comfortable with myself. I was happy, and maybe for the first time in my life, at peace. Everything about Africa was foreign to anything I had ever known, and it suited me perfectly. (Maybe because it was so far from anything I had known.) Right from the start, I had no doubt at all that this was where I belonged. During the two years that I had been going back and forth to Kenya, I had experienced far more than a love affair with a man or even a whole country. I had begun to feel as if my soul was waking up.

"Look Melinda, ngombes."

Calling me back from my reverie, Bill indicated the cows in the adjoining back yard. "I always like looking at ngombes. Don't you?" I had never been wildly enthusiastic about looking at cows while living in New York, but I had found the joys of many new things on my previous trips to Africa, so maybe cows were the next things on the list.

I had been loaned two of the Winters' house staff until we could find some suitable people for me. Or until Bill could. Nyamburra was their house girl and Illiab their cook. When we arrived that morning, they were both busy dusting furniture and polishing all that dark woodwork. After running out of things to tell me about cows, Bill instructed Nyamburra to make up my bed, draw me a bath and then leave me to get some sleep. I was rather taken aback by the whole idea of having anyone draw my bath, and protested that I was quite capable of doing this myself. This elicited Bill's lecture on "How to Treat Ones House Staff."

Bill informed me, in a tone of voice that was a cut above his usual advice, that I was not to let my ridiculous, liberal American proclivities get in the way of doing things correctly in Kenya. This was Africa, not New York, and if I didn't do as he was telling me and handle my staff correctly, I would live to regret it. It all sounded very colonial and overbearing, even for Bill, and I inwardly told myself that as soon as he left I would do as I bloody well pleased. I had, after all, had household help before and I had never had a problem. I would treat my African help as I had treated the housekeeper I had when Jake was a baby or anyone else who had been in my employ in the States. This was one thing I did not need Bill Sr.'s advice on.

But I nodded to Bill, saying I was sure he was right and gladly let the whole subject drop. With that, he announced that he was going back to his house but would return in a few hours to collect me. We were going to Nairobi to rent a car for me and buy more things for the kitchen. I wasn't sure where I was going to find the strength to do all that, but I didn't fancy arguing with him either. I thanked him for all the trouble he had taken on my behalf and as he drove out of my driveway, I raced up the stairs to help Nyamburra make up my bed.

I spoke only a few select sentences of Swahili and most of those I had picked up on safari. They dealt primarily with animals and camp related matters. Nyamburra spoke no English at all and so we made do with hand signals. I was smiling more than I had smiled in days and saying endless thank yous for everything she did. She had to tear the dirty clothes out of my hands to stop me from being so helpful and I had most of my things picked up before she could get to them. She looked quite bewildered at my behavior, but I was sure that would pass, as she became more accustomed to my equal opportunity ways. Then I was left alone. I was supposed to sleep, but I was too tired and excited to even consider it. Sitting in my pink bathtub, I tried to collect my thoughts, but my mood kept swinging between panic, elation, and fear, topped off with a good case of sleep deprivation and Bill Sr.'s verbal overkill.

By five o'clock that evening, I was driving my newly rented Charade on the "wrong" side of the road back from Nairobi. The rush hour traffic was hopelessly snarled and the rules of the road nonexistent. His driver had gone ahead with his car and Bill was now "helping" by telling me when and how to shift with my left hand while pointing out every pothole, cow or old man on a bicycle that I had to look out for. He was also informing me, with every other sentence, that I was quite obviously going to be killed on these lawless roads of Kenya if I didn't pay stricter attention. He punctuated all of this by throwing up his hands and shouting "God, Almighty" whenever another vehicle cut in front of us. There were no turn signals or brake lights on most of the service vehicles and the hundreds of pedestrians all seemed to have a death wish. I'm not sure if even a New York City cab driver would be prepared for this particular test of nerves and driving skills, but I certainly was not.

We had just come from the Indian bazaar. This is a small section of Nairobi, primarily Biashara Street, where most of the shops selling household items and dry goods are located. They almost all consist of one front room, dusty and cluttered and all are dimly lit. Most are owned and run by Asians and staffed with young Africans boys that are shouted at to fetch this faster or carry that higher for the all-important customer. Bill and I had just spent several hours going from one shop to the next purchasing pots and pans and other kitchen necessities. Although I had managed to import all the bed linens, I had not purchased the heavier items. What I did bring had cost me a tremendous amount in overweight charges, but I don't think any amount of money would have persuaded British Air to allow me another one hundred kilos.

As we shopped, Bill conducted most of the transactions in Swahili. When not addressing the Asian shop owners, he made asides to Stephen, Bill's African 'Man Friday,' who followed us about, agreed with everything Bill said, and carried all our purchases to the car. I had very little idea what was going on and even less to say about it. Bill did all the purchasing in shillings, a currency that made no sense to me at all. I had, in my past trips to Kenya, always been on safari with Billy. He had handled all the money and I never had to figure out what cost what. Even if I had, the value of the shilling against the dollar changes from month to month. Whatever quickie conversion formula I had used then would have been useless years later. I had been listening to six hundred of this and two thousand of that all afternoon and I couldn't do the calculations in my head fast enough to know what "we" were spending. I eventually learned to think in shillings, but for many worrisome months, every price tag was mentally translated into an exact dollar equivalency. At the end of that day, I owed Bill about twenty thousand something's.

I had dinner that evening with the Winters. Bill was still going full throttle about all the things we were going to get sorted out tomorrow, all the things he had neglected to tell me about today and the hundred other things I still didn't have to worry about. Barbara tried to get a word in every now and then, but it was hopeless. By the time I drove my little car back to my well-upholstered abode and unloaded all my utensils, I was in tears again. I sat on the upstairs patio looking up at the incredible stars that adorn the African night sky and tried to take several deep breaths. This had been one very trying week and probably the longest single day of my life. I didn't want to even think about what tomorrow might bring.

And yet, somewhere in the back of my shell-shocked brain there was a little spark of glee. Despite my exhaustion and pronounced insecurities about the situation I had just plunked myself down in, I knew that after all those years of waiting and dreaming, all the months of sitting in hospitals with my mother, and all the scheming and planning to get there, I had finally made it. I had left my old life behind and was about to start a new one. I had no idea what the changes would be, nor did I really think too much about it. I had my "Fahrm in Ah-frica . . . "Well, it wasn't exactly a farm, I don't think the cows next door counted, but it was definitely in Africa. And it was at the foot of the Ngong Hills.

three

You Know, Madame . . .

Having sorted out all my kitchen problems, including the rental of a cooker and fridge from old Mr. Jamblin, Bill launched himself into the more formidable task of hiring my household staff. I did manage to decline the offer of a driver, but that was the only one on the list that I was allowed to eliminate. Bill insisted that I have the full complement of staff members. Getting help in Kenya is not a problem, between overpopulation and the lack of jobs, all one need do is whisper into the wind that help is needed and a long line of people, willing to do just about anything, will instantly show up at your front door. The problem is, as in many places, finding good help.

Although our first hiring attempts were not disastrous, they were not all that successful either. There was a rapid succession of people who came for a few days and then, once paid, left in the night. Newly hired workers are paid as kibarua, (*casual, daily labor*) for a trial period of several weeks and it is their privilege to leave without notice if things don't work out and your right to let them go. No strings attached. But I was always surprised to wake up and find that the very smiling Mary or Mwange had failed to return. Although Bill tried to convince me that it had nothing to do with me, I was sure that something I had said or done was why they had beat such a hasty retreat. The truth was probably that they didn't get along with someone else in my employ, tribal differences were always an issue, or that they just wandered off. Or forgot to come back. Or changed their mind. It probably didn't have anything to do with me, but if I didn't scare them to death, I certainly confused them. I had all these very American habits that must have seemed quite peculiar to them-especially my pronounced unwillingness to allow them to do their job.

Where I come from, we are very solicitous of our help. We don't overtax them or ask them to do anything they would prefer not to do. In my mother's house, we routinely cleaned up before the cleaning lady came to clean up. We are extremely friendly towards the people who work, and often live, in our homes, always noting that they are "just like a member of the family." And we pay good money for the privilege. Not in Kenya. As the saying there goes, "It is better to be feared than loved."

In Africa, the help is treated with a formal deference and the class distinctions are firmly drawn. You needn't be particularly friendly and you never mix socially with the staff. You do not discuss your personal life or your thoughts and feelings except as they relate to the job being done. You are always firm, and usually, but not necessarily, polite. The average wage was, and this was under government guidelines at that time, about fifty dollars a month. For this meager sum, you never hesitated to ask a staff member to perform any task, no matter how odious. You never washed a dish or picked up a sock, carried out the garbage or waxed the kitchen floor.

I did all of those things. Or tried to. Along with feeling that I was living in a fishbowl, I was always one step ahead of my staff when it came to cleaning up. I was not used to so many people hovering around me and I was raised to pick up after myself. It is surprisingly easy to get used to being waited on, and I managed to adapt very nicely, but in the early months, it went against my grain. What I didn't understand was that they really did want to scrub the floor, just not for the reasons I thought. I was initially very impressed by everyone's industry and by how quickly people snapped to when things needed to be done. But this was not so much their predilection for hard work as the need to keep their jobs. Jobs are scarce in Kenya, and extremely cushy jobs, like working for a newly transplanted American, are rarer still. Should they be made useless, either by someone else taking over their duties, or by my doing too much for myself, they would then become redundant. That is the word that is used in Kenya when you let someone go; you say they are being "made redundant." I didn't understand that all the hustling around my house was to show me how essential they were. I just felt guilty that it took so many people to look after me.

After a few bad starts, Bill managed to hire a few people who did stay on. Some, like Stephen Karanja, my shambaman *(gardener),* and the afore mentioned Nyamburra, were with me until I left Kenya. Nyamburra did not come to work for me until later, as she was quite pregnant when she and Stephen moved onto my compound. Jotham, son of Illiab, the Winter's mpishi (*cook*) was to become my askari (*guard*) and he worked for me until the end. The in-house staff was a bit trickier and there were several comings and goings before we found Mildred and Daniel.

They came to me as a married couple; Daniel was to be the cook and Mildred, arriving a few days later, the house girl. Although "married" is often a euphemism among the Africans, I didn't know that then, nor would I have cared. Daniel had previously worked for friends of the Winters and I was told that he was a very skilled cook. What I was not told was that the lady of the house had caught him reeking of her perfume one afternoon, a botched attempt to cover up the smell of liquor on his breath, and had sacked him. Bill considered this woman pretentious and high handed, and thought Daniel might merit another try. I was, at that stage, following Bill's lead quite faithfully. He was at my house at least once every day telling me what I needed to do and how to do it. If he said hire, I hired.

Daniel was a splendid cook and his English was almost fluent. He could take a recipe from any cookbook and recreate it exactly. The execution was perfect and the presentation flawless. He also took whatever messages I received, when the phone worked, and wrote them down, signing them 'Your Obedient Servant.' I did think that a bit unctuous, but having nothing to compare his behavior with, I let it pass. For several months, things went very smoothly and I had the fanciest cuisine in Karen. I was enjoying cheese soufflés for lunch and raspberry tarts for dinner. I thought I had located the prince of all manservants. But it turned out that Daniel's demons had gone underground only temporarily. He did indeed drink, usually my liquor, and when drunk he beat up on Mildred. He did not stay in my employ for too long.

Daniel was not fired for drunkenness, however, but for dereliction of his duties. While I was away one night and Mildred was on an authorized leave, he had left the house, with Jake in it, unattended.

He had already been warned about his drinking, but this was the final straw. The Winters were there to answer Jake's call, but Bill Sr. said I had no choice but to send Daniel packing.

The labor laws of Kenya were, for the most part, heavily slanted towards the employee. Granted the wage levels were paltry by American standards, but once someone worked for you, it was very difficult to get rid of them. Even a thief, caught walking down the road with your crown jewels had to be given all moneys owed him and probably severance pay. If someone hit you over the head with a stick you could sack them 'summarily,' but in cases like drunkenness or tardiness there had to be three written warnings handed out before the offender could be let go. In telling me exactly how to go about firing Daniel, Bill was trying to make sure I avoided any future problems with the Labor Board.

I did exactly as Bill had instructed me. I gathered all my staff together and made a long speech about the sanctity of the President of Kenya's house. It was not just I who had been let down and treated with such low esteem, but the owner as well. The careless disregard of the Presedent of Kenya's house was quite intolerable. (Jake told me later that I used the phrase "the President of Kenya" about fifteen times in as many minutes. But every time I said it all heads nodded. I knew I was scoring points.) I found the entire procedure frightening, but I stood in the kitchen and did as I had been told. Firing anyone is unnerving, but I added to this my concern that my staff think me unfair or cruel. I was too naive to worry about the far greater problem of having a disgruntled employee bring the bureaucratic wrath and interminable hassle of the Kenya Labor Board down upon me. (I would learn that hard lesson years later.)

I managed to get through my speech and Daniel off my property that night and when I awoke the next day, Mildred was making toast and all seemed calm and back to normal. How silly of me to have been so nervous. Wasn't it typical of Bill Sr. to overstate the problems with the Africans. That sentiment only lasted until I went to my safe to find that it had been cleaned out of all foreign currency. Daniel had apparently had my keys copied and had left me with this parting shot.

The day after I fired Daniel, Mildred was signed on to be the cook. Peter and Eleanor Nalle, old pals from college and their son, Graham, were coming to Kenya for their holiday. They were my first house guests and I had planned a great safari to show them this wondrous place I now called home. I was also looking forward to having guests without having to cook a thing, change a bed, or wash any dishes. The idea of having Daniel whip up little patisserie for tea everyday was most appealing and I had mapped out quite fancy menus for the duration of their stay. All I had to do was arrange the dozens of roses that I would put in every room.

Daniel was long gone by the time the Nalles' plane touched down in Nairobi. There was not enough time to hire another cook, and so Mildred got the promotion. When I asked her if she knew how to even broil a chicken, she replied, "Kidogo" (*a little.*) "Well Mildred old pal. I am going to teach you. You take the kuku, (*chicke*n), out of the fridge . . . "

Mildred was about thirty-two when she first came to work for me. I say "about" because many Africans note their age by age groups rather than years. We based Mildred's age on the age of her fifteen-year-old son. She had a moon shaped face, a radiant smile, and the high cheekbones and chocolate brown skin typical of her Abaluya tribal bloodlines. She was sweet and hard working, and, as far as I was concerned, utterly trustworthy. Although she initially spoke no more than four words of English, the vast social distance between us, a gulf that I was told could never be crossed, was a far greater barrier than language to our having any kind of a personal relationship. I had been told repeatedly the very strict dictates concerning the dealings with one's staff. I knew that getting chatty and personal with them was "simply not done." But seeing no point in that, I tossed that rule out straight away.

For whatever reasons friendships form and people gravitate towards one another, Mildred and I had a bond. We certainly did not have any background in common, although we did have sons the same age, but we seemed to understand each other. I appreciated her warmth and the fact that she seemed to be looking out for me. I, in turn, took care of her. She also had the enormous good sense to laugh at my jokes, or at least smile at all the right places. Mildred was the first person I saw every morning and the last one at night, and I came to be honestly fond of her. I felt she liked me as well, or at least I hoped so. What my staff thought of me should not have mattered as much as it did, and Bill Sr. told me many times that I was a "bloody fool" to be so familiar with my help, but it did matter. I wanted them to like me. Especially Mildred.

Our early conversations were linguistically very limited, resembling charades more than an intellectual exchange. But as the months went by, we developed our own style of conversing that was halfway between the two languages. I learned more Swahili and Mildred picked my Americanisms. I would repeat her expressions and she mimicked mine. We had short cuts and hand signals and, when it was all put together, it worked.

An example of Mildred's progress is to be found on a tape that I recorded one day. I had just returned to Karen from a short safari and was making a tape to send to Jake. Audiotapes were one of the ways Jake and I had found to breach the gap of my being so far away. As I was recording, I asked Mildred to say a few words. She did: "We are happy now. Your Mommy is here and we are happy. We are very happy. Now we are happy."

The most significant reason for my getting chummy with Mildred was that I was lonely. I am naturally quite gregarious, but in times of stress, the need to talk to someone becomes even more pronounced. I was far away from home, Billy was out on safari most of the time, Bill Sr. was a far better talker than listener, Barbara had little tolerance for what she viewed as my very American emotionality, and I didn't know anyone else. I turned to Mildred. Try explaining the emotional intricacies of moving to a new country, leaving everything in your old life behind, being scared and alone, and still in heavy mourning using three words and your hands. But Mildred very patiently listened to all my tales and always nodded at the right times. She, in turn, told me all kinds of arcane African tidbits. She instructed me on how to end an unwanted pregnancy with either ice cubes or herbs, and what salve to put on my feet to keep the "skin from wearing out." Mildred ran my house and she worried about me. I know that it had a good deal to do with my being her current source of employment, but I also felt that Mildred looked out for me. She could take one look at me and tell if I had eaten my breakfast. "You are not eating very nicely, Madame. This is not good. You will get Malaria."

She even enlightened me on the finer points of the traditional African legal system. When I tried to explain to her the idea of taking someone to court to right a wrong, something I was all too familiar with, Mildred just shook her head. This made no sense to her at all. It was, she informed me, not the African way of doing things. "You know Madame," (When she wanted me to pay particular attention to what she was about to say she would begin with those words.) "You know Madame, this is not Africa way. In Africa we do not do like this. If it was me, I would get someone to kill you. Or take your things."

Those early days in Africa were like being pitched into a parallel universe. Other than the clothes I had brought with me and my own face in the mirror, (Jake was not to arrive for several weeks) there was nothing around me that I had known before. Everything was different. Almost every detail, from the cereal I had for breakfast, (to say nothing of having it served to me on the patio,) to the lack of television at night was different. The air was different, the trees were different, and the climate was different. Better, but different. Every label on every bottle in every little shop was different. Interesting, but different. Even the language was different. I expected Swahili to be unfamiliar to me, but I wasn't prepared to have trouble understanding English.

The English the Europeans in Karen spoke sounded nothing like the language I was raised with. Not only did they use British words for things, 'lorry' for truck and 'jumper' for sweater and 'flat' for apartment; these folks took it even further by peppering their speeches with little Swahili phrases. I had a hard time keeping up with most conversations, and I was never in on the joke.

All these changes kept me too off kilter to spend much time dwelling on what I was feeling. It was one day at a time. There were the negatives, phones that didn't work and power cuts several times a day. The water pump failed regularly, cutting off all the water to the house. The mail never seemed to have anything in it for me, when it arrived, which was never. And I was alone most of the time. In those early months, I didn't have anything constructive to do. My daily routine, something I clung to in New York, was nonexistent. I was lonely and vaguely frightened a good deal of the time.

But then there were the pluses, like having tea brought to your bedroom every morning and filling the house with roses from your own garden. The fact that the phone didn't work meant that no one I had come all the way to Africa to avoid could reach me. My past couldn't reach me. The air smelled inexplicably sweet, the birds seemed something out of a surreal dream, and there were monkeys in the trees. Most of all there was the excitement of being right in the middle of a grand adventure, in Ah-frica. The sense of "Yes, I can" that each day brought went a long way to filling the holes I still had in my heart. Those early months in Africa were some of the most bizarre I ever lived through. At the same time, they were enormous fun.

Some days the surprises took the form of unannounced visitors. One morning during my first week there, while standing in my Kelly green den, I saw the gates open and a parade of African women glide up my driveway. Each was carrying a basket of flowers on her head. I counted at least fifteen as they made their sinuous way towards the house. These were the bibis Bill had promised to send. Along with the baskets full of cuttings from his garden, they were a gift of labor. I was surprised to see so many people attacking my garden, but even more, by how they went about it. Once the flowers were all unloaded, they started to dig holes in the earth using small branches they had broken from the trees. They were planting the grass blade by blade.

They would pull up select sections of the existing grass in large hunks, then divide them up into smaller pieces and proceed to plant these individual stems into whatever bare spots they found. No grass seed and no seed spreaders here, this grass was planted by hand, blade by blade. Once well watered, the remarkably tough, drought resistant root system of this "kikuyu" grass would take hold and spread rapidly. In a matter of a few weeks, one could cut back the top growth to reveal a beautiful, even lawn underneath. Of course, a man swinging a panga, (*machete*) always did the cutting of this grass. Lawn mowers were scarce, usually imported, and didn't work nearly as well as a man with a panga. This was one of my first lessons about how things were done in Kenya: always use manpower. Electric equipment was expensive and, as the power went off all the time, unreliable. Manpower was plentiful, fairly steady, and cheap.

Several weeks later, I was surprised to see another column of visitors coming up my driveway. Twenty men in what appeared to be white shorty pajamas marched into the compound, followed by another in uniform carrying a machine gun. The sight of a man in uniform sporting a rifle was not all that odd, the Kenyan traffic police all carried AK 47s, but I was surprised to see him heading toward my front door. Mildred greeted the officer at the door. She then came running to inform me that they were a gift from His Excellency, the President. They were prisoners who had been let out for the day to pull the weeds out of his/my gardens. The PJs were their prison uniform.

About one month later, I had an even less expected visitor. While again sitting in my upstairs office, probably writing one of the thousands of letters I wrote home, I saw a large blue Mercedes Benz cruise up the drive. As it pulled to a stop, I could see that there were two Africans inside, both wearing a suit and tie. Even I knew that these had to be Government people. Not only were the coat and tie a tip off, but most of the Mercedes in Kenya were owned by government officials. I rushed to pull myself together and ran down the stairs to open the front door. Stepping out into the driveway, I shook both men's hands and then started making nervous small talk. I was, I hoped, dividing my attentions equally between the two.

I thought I was handling the situation quite well when Mildred came racing from behind the house. It was only after she had led one of the two away that I realized my mistake. It had not occurred to me that everyone in the government had a driver. I had made a serious faux pas by not recognizing which one was the driver and which was the more important passenger and the tribal differences as well. I would have fumbled even further by continuing to stand in the driveway and talk to the remaining man, had Mildred not rescued me. As she led the one fellow away to the kitchen, she announced that she would bring some tea to the sitting room as soon as it was ready. That was my much-needed cue to invite him into the house.

As we sat and talked, I still had no idea who he was, other than someone in the government. I had even less idea what he wanted. He asked me many questions about why I was there and what I did back in the States. He was very polite, but not being exactly clear what the purpose of his visit was, I wasn't sure what I should say-or not say. I did get the feeling that I was being checked out, this was the President's house, but nothing was clearly stated as to why he was there.

He finally told me that if I needed anything at all, I was to call the State House and he would see to it that I was taken care of. He handed me his calling card. It stated his name, one that I later found out was well known to everyone in Kenya, except me of course, accompanied by Kenya's Presidential seal in gold. The words, "Special Assistant to the President" were embossed on it. He wrote his personal phone number on the back, saying that if I couldn't get through to the State House, I should just call him directly. As he got up to leave he added that if I ever wanted to import anything, a car, a container, he could arrange that too. He just happened to have an import /export company. I assured him I would keep him in mind.

Hearing the front door open, Mildred quickly sent his driver back to the car. After shaking my hand again, they got back into their blue Mercedes and drove off. Once they had gone, I turned to Mildred and slapped my forhead and made a face, indicating what an idiot I felt like. I couldn't believe I had mixed up the presidential envoy and the driver. I had further embarrassed myself with all that business about serving tea. But again, I had just followed the rules as they existed in the USA.

In New York City, if you bump into someone on the street you chat for a minute and then go on about your busy way. If you live in the suburbs and someone pulls into your driveway unannounced, it is assumed that they are there to ask a quick question or drop off something vital. No one stays for tea. No one would expect you to go to all that trouble, especially when they show up without being invited. And who in America serves tea anyway? In Kenya, however, you invite everyone in for tea. It isn't considered putting anyone to a great deal of trouble. It isn't any trouble. You don't do anything, your staff does it all. No one expects you to call ahead because the phones never work. No one worries about interrupting what you were doing because you probably weren't doing anything all that important anyway. Certainly nothing that couldn't be done the next day just as easily. And even if you were right in the middle of something utterly vital, anyone with even a drop of British blood in them would quite happily put aside their own funeral for a cup of tea.

Jake followed me over to Africa in early August. Very much in his grandmother's bloodline, he adjusted very quickly to having a lot of household help. What could be better than having servants to pick up all your clothes, make your bed, and tidy up behind you so quickly that your mother never sees the teenaged mess you created?

Jake had also inherited my love of travel. It was something we did very well together and gave us many good times to counter some of the bad ones that come along when raising a child alone, particularly during adolescence. As my mother's illness progressed and I was more absent from home, Jake had suffered. He needed his mother, but I was too pulled by my obligations to mine to give him my attention. Odd as it sounds, my moving to Africa did a great deal to repair some of that damage. There were no road signs for this kind of parenting, I had no idea how to be a Long Distance Mother. And that was the saving grace. I couldn't do what I had been raised to do. I couldn't be the kind of mother my mother had been, something I knew I didn't want to repeat. Jake and I had to find a new way. Our way.

Although totally supportive of my move, the reality of it had caused Jake many unhappy moments. He had already been in boarding school before I left, a necessity when I could not be home to care for him properly and living with his father was not an option. But being as far away as Africa was an entirely different thing. We had not yet learned how to be good letter writers and the phones, so much a part of every day life in the USA, barely functioned in Kenya. The crackling of the lines and the fading in and out of any sound made phoning more frustrating than it was worth. The reality was that I was halfway around the world and I could not get there quickly if he needed me. That separation was one price for this great African adventure that we had not thought about and one that we both paid. He, I am afraid, more than I.

Jake loved Africa almost as much as I did, and came over every holiday and for all his summer vacations. It was a great adventure for a young boy and having his home address listed as Nairobi was much 'cooler' than being from some humdrum spot like New York. When he was there, we spent our every waking moment together, far more time than we ever would have back in the US. We didn't retreat to our rooms after dinner to watch our own TVs. We sat together and watched some ancient video, when they were available from the dukas. Nor did we go our separate ways each day. We had no one but each other and so we stuck together. We ate together. We shopped together. We played cards together. We played endless trivial pursuit together. We went on safari together discovering this marvelous new country. We had great adventures. Together. It was as if we belonged to a special club that no one else could join because no one else would have understood. It was just the two of us. Jake and me. Out there in Ah-frica.

I honestly believe our time together in Africa all thoughout Jake's teenage years made it possible for us to be the very great friends we are today.

My mornings were usually taken up with dragging out every task for as long as I could. I had nothing to do and no where to go and so I took as much time as I could to do the very basic things. Like eating breakfast. Or reading a magazine for the twentieth time. Breakfast was served on the patio outside my bedroom so I could sit and look at the Ngongs. I had managed to curb Mildred's desire to cook me fried eggs and bacon every day, but she made up for what she considered my bad eating habits by putting absolutely everything I had ever indicated I ate for breakfast on the tray. Every day. After stalling as long as I could I would move onto my next mission of the morning: "doing my Jane Fonda."

By the time I left Kenya there were a few health clubs, but in '87 there were none. I had brought a workout videotape with me. My going through this ritual always sent Mildred into gales of giggles. "Madame is doing ex-cise," she would inform anyone who might ask, not making the slightest effort to conceal her mirth. None of my staff members could understand why anyone would purposefully put themselves through all that physical labor when they were perfectly free to sit and do nothing all morning. I am sure they wrote this strange behavior off as yet another one of my weird American traits. Should someone drop by, as it was Bill Sr.'s wont to do, I had to stop what I was doing and order up the usual tea and biscuits. Bill did not consider it rude to interrupt my efforts to stay in shape, quite the contrary. I think he considered it self-involved of me, and certainly very "American." No one in Karen, except a few American ex-pat ladies I later met, paid the slightest attention to their heart rate, their cholesterol count, or their fat gram intake. I found that quite astounding at first, but increasingly soothing as the years went along. I had spent my whole life staring at myself in ballet studio mirrors, and listening to my mother agonize over her waning youth. At forty years old, it was a pleasure to let some of that obsessive behavior go and Kenya was just the place to do it. But in the beginning, I still had all that American energy, drive and guilt and I "did my Jane Fonda" every morning. I also didn't have much else to do.

After doing my "ex-cise," bathing and finally getting dressed, I would call Mildred to find out what it was that we needed in the kitchen. As the months went by, she was able to write out a list for me, but deciphering what she meant was still a source of great merriment to Jake and me. She did not write English very well and spelled phonetically, so these translations were very creative. Kish. Sufly. And ahchoks. (quiche, soufflee, and artichokes) or be-cons, littis, fol peper, bred, hem, jeez. When she had no idea what to call something, she would just copy down the exact words that appeared on the label of the item needed. It took Jake and me the better part of a day to figure out that Kangestan was the brand name for the paper that went on the bottom of the canary's cage.

My favorite linguistic misstep was the one that Mildred took the most ribbing about. It had to do with her pronunciation of both peas and beans. She could say either peans or beas, but could not reverse them. I could never figure out why that was. If you can say peans or beas, why can't you rearrange all that and say it the other way round? It is rather like the reversing of "L" and "R" that the Africans also do. How is it that one can say Loan and mean the Antelope, or Roan and mean the monetary transaction and, yet, not be able to get those two correctly reversed. Whatever the reason, Mildred had a problem with peas and beans.

"What vegetable should we get for dinner tonight, Mildred? Beans or peas?"

"Peans. No, beas."

"Well, which one is it? Peas or beans?"

"Peans." Shaking her head. "Beas."

"Which one?"

"Beas. No, peans."

She was trying to get it right and I was not really helping. It was something we did weekly and it always struck me as funny. It became a set routine, our own version of "Who's On First." Mildred would finally give up, laugh, and hold up her fingers and say:

"You know Madame, the little ones."

"Oh, Okay. Now I understand. Peas."

"Yes, Madame. Beas."

four

The Karen Dukas

After my morning chat with Mildred, the next chore on the list was shopping. The house on Mbagathi Ridge was only four kilometers from the center of Karen, but as I pulled out of my driveway each day, I always wondered if I was going to make it back alive. Driving a car in Kenya is about as close as you can come, without actually pointing a loaded revolver at your head, to playing Russian Roulette.

Aside from the obvious difficulty of having to drive on the left-hand side of the road, the greater hazard was that all the roads in Kenya, with the possible exception of the ones the President frequented, are abysmal. They are badly built and even less well maintained. In the dry season you have to cope with dust and the maze of pot holes, some of which are a good three feet deep. When you hit one of these large divots, even if moving at a reasonable speed, you can blow out a tire, smash your sump guard, or destroy your universal joint.

The rainy season adds a whole new twist, the potholes all fill with water. As you approach what appears to be a wet spot, you have no idea if it is just a slight depression in the road or a large crater. You have to avoid the potholes and the puddles and the people on bicycles on your side of the road while keeping an eye on the oncoming vehicles that are doing a similar tango on the other side.

And watch out for all the goats and cows on the roads. They don't make a habit of running right in front of you, but occasionally one gets skittish and races out under the wheels. You do not want to run over someone's goat. Aside from not wanting to kill innocent animals, it will take all day to soothe the owner and then pay him for the damages. And you will be stuck at the scene of this crime until nightfall, surrounded by a throng of unhappy, but very vocally helpful, local folks trying to sort things out. You do not want to be out driving after dark either. Not only do the roads not improve with the setting of the sun, but there are no street lights and darkness lends cover to thugs and thieves. It is an old trick to scatter nails on the back roads and, having disabled several tires, jump the driver. Driving is a dangerous business in Kenya, but it is a big country and if you want to go anywhere, you have to drive. You just learn the rules, such as they are, and do the best you can.

In my early days in Africa, my heart would start to pound when I picked up my car keys from the hall table. I eventually became so cool headed that I could avoid the pot holes, swerve around any goats, down shift with my left hand while I groped for a lipstick behind the passenger seat. All the while fending off the attack of my German Shepherd who was trying to claw his way over the back seat and into my lap while on his reluctant way to the vets. In the rainy season. On my earlier vehicular forays, however, I just kept talking out loud to myself, "The line is on the right," and driving very slowly.

The actual town of Karen is nothing more than a dusty X on a local map. It's a dirt path of five hundred yards, along which sit a few funny little shops. To the people who live in Karen this little grouping of stores is called the Karen dukas, duka meaning 'shop' in Swahili. If you say you are going to 'town', you mean Nairobi proper. If you only need a carton of milk, you run down to the dukas.

Karen was named for it's most famous resident, Baroness Karen Von Blixen, aka Isak Dinesen. In the early part of the century she owned about forty thousand acres there and when she left Kenya she sold it to a Dane by the name of Remy Martin. He divided the land into twenty-acre plots and, in turn, sold them off. Karen has since been sub-divided into some minimum five acre plots, a sign of progress that very few residents applaud, and has grown considerably since the Baroness' day. But it still looks and feels like a nineteenth century outpost. No longer are there horses and hitching posts outside of the dukas, but it would not be at all surprising if there were. It is not just the feeling of timelessness, it is the reality. Nothing changed at the

Karen Dukas. Year after year, it was always the same.

I usually parked my car in front of what was the center of most of the activity: the Karen Provision Stores. This resembled what a General Store probably looked like back in America's youth. Out front, two rusting gas pumps were always surrounded by at least a dozen small children who were, very quickly, at my car door begging for a shilling. I had been told, repeatedly, by Bill Sr. not to encourage this behavior. I told them hapana, *(no)* but they never took hapana for an answer. I ignored them by concentrating on all the posters in the dusty windows, but that wasn't very successful either. These were a persistent lot and not easily deterred. A child begging is never a good thing in any society and the people who feel sorry for them and give them money only exacerbate the situation.

I took a few minutes to peruse the scores of handwritten messages tacked to the front doors. They announced someone's search for a short-term let, or the availability of someone else's house servant. Cars were offered up for sale and children's outgrown clothing or pony saddles could be obtained. Many people and possessions change hands via the Karen Provision Stores bulletin board.

These messages were written in Kenyan English with it's unique mixture of British expressions and Swahili. It was many months before I would start calling trucks 'lorries,' and everyone 'chap,' but longer still before I was so fluent as to add the more local flavor of throwing bibi, (*wife*,) and mzee, (*older person,)* and fundi, (*handy man*,) into my every utterance.

Inside, what little sunlight spilled through the door was suffused with dust. Fine layers of dust covered everything in Karen, even during the rains. Then you had mud on everything outside and still a layer of dust on the inside. Because the earth in Kenya was so red, this dust lent a rosy glow to the light.

Almost everything of life's basic needs could be found at the duka. If Yogi Patel, the owner, did not have what you wanted today, he would get it for you tomorrow. Yogi is what is referred to in Kenya as an Asian, and is, as are most of the shop owners in Nairobi, an enterprising and hard working Kenyan of Indian descent. (There are three distinct classes in Kenya: the Europeans, also called mzungu, which covers almost all Caucasians, the Asians, and the Africans. Anyone who is an actual citizen of the country, regadless of color, is a Kenyan. It is a very class conscious society and the hierarchy becomes clear to anyone who lives there for more than a few months. The Asians were often looked down upon by the Africans and the Europeans considered themselves superior to everyone.)

The Asians came to Kenya in the 1800s to work on the construction of the railroad, The Lunatic Express, that was to cross East Africa from Mombassa to Uganda. After the work was completed, thousands stayed on to make Kenya their permanent home. Although they are not always held in high social regard, they own and run a substantial number of the small businesses in the country. The Asians make many of the mercantile wheels go 'round.

Once inside the duka, I grabbed a diminutive shopping cart and started my trek through the narrow aisles. The Karen Provision Stores (there is only one, 'stores' meant storage area) was a one story, wooden, 100 x 75 foot room, with every inch of space utilized. The shelves were stacked to the ceiling. There was maize meal, a major staple in the African diet, and local sugar packed in with chocolate dipped Macadamia nuts. There were mosquito coils and post cards on a rusty, rotating stand had been there since Uhuru, (Kenya's freedom from British rule more than forty years ago.) There was milking salve, paintbrushes, and flea dip alongside all the fresh produce. In the next aisle there were black Wellington rubber boots piled on top of coils of rope, firecrackers, small plastic toys and bottles of imported and locally made wine. There were video tapes to rent and rows of tinned (canned) soup. Although there was everything you might need there wasn't much choice in each category. There was only one brand of butter (KCC), one brand of tinned tomah-toes (Kenylon), and one brand of toilet paper (Roses.) Roses had an unrefined quality but it was available in pink, blue, and green. The third aisle contained over the counter medications. There were familiar items like Vicks Nasal Spray and aspirin, but there were also worming medicines and other tinctures in oddly shaped bottles. Worms and malaria and ailments I had never even heard of were treated with medicine that could be purchased in a "super" market.

If I couldn't find something, asking for it was not much help. If they were not called by their Swahili name, such as maiai for eggs, unga for flour, (dog food was unga kwa mbwa, a phrase that got a chuckle out of me for almost six years), they simply had different names. Corn was not corn but maize and potato chips were potato crisps, which left french fries to be called chips. Papaya went by pau pau and hamburger meat was mince. Buying something as simple as bacon was further complicated by the fact that there were many different kinds. There was strip bacon and back bacon and side bacon and sizzling bacon. I had no idea which was which and I still don't. Most of the vegetables were initially unrecognizable to me. And should I be so foolish as to try to help myself, the young girl who was attending this area always made it clear that this was her job.

If the power went off, as it did about once a day, no one even blinked. The cash register kept right on rolling. It was cranked by hand.

Bill Sr. had introduced me to the Patel family and an account had been opened in my name. Yogi manned the front checkout desk and remembered everyone who had run in, grabbed a newspaper, and said that they would be back later to "sort it out." He cleared off the counter top between every transaction, wiping an ever-spreading hole into the gray linoleum and wrote your bill out by hand. Yogi thanked everyone by name.

The most consistent factor to all the goods at the duka was that they were locally made. Imported goods could be very expensive ($8 for a box of Kellogg's Corn Flakes), and did not sell very well. What is made locally, and the list increases every year, is vastly preferable. Kenyans are very enterprising folks and if one wants Camembert cheese than one had better figure out how to make it oneself. It is certainly not going to be flown in on Air France. Even if it were, it would probably end up sitting in the sun at the end of the runway for three days, mishandled or mislaid. It might be the tiniest bit over-ripe when it finally reached the duka shelves.

This is what usually happened to the wine. Once off-loaded at JKI, if it made it past the many pairs of well greased palms, it was very likely to sit for hours in the sun. This treatment does nothing for the bouquet and the consuming of imported wines was not a big local pastime. It is fortunate that proper spirits, whiskey, vodka, and the like, stand up to a fair amount of abuse. Kenyans are fairly serious drinkers—I knew some with rather astounding capacities—and the ruination of a good Scotch would not be well received. It was not a country of hopeless inebriates, but people did drink their fair share. A slower pace of living and a warmer climate add to this propensity, to say nothing of having staff members at home doing all the things one would do for oneself in the States. Should you have of a glass of wine too many at lunch you can always go home and take a little nap and the children will still be picked up at school and dinner will be on the table on time.

Abstinence is not really considered too great a virtue, either, whereas being a good fellow and joining in the fun and the spirit of the moment is. In fact, it is considered rather bad form to be too rigid about anything. Kenyans are not interested in hearing how many sit ups you did, nor how virtuous your diet has become since you stopped eating red meat. When everyone is having another round of gin and tonics, "I will just have a soda water" is greeted with boos all around. The inference is that you are being a bore and a prig. However, the announcement that one is suffering from a hangover, "feeling rather frag-ile" or that one's car "climbed a tree" on the way home last night is never met with raised eyebrows and stony silences, implying that you should consider a visit to Mrs. Ford's clinic. It simply means that you had a good time. The only caveat you would hear would be that the next time you are in similar circumstances, "you really should consider calling for your driver to transport you home."

Kenyans are hearty folks. The white man only settled there a few generations ago and most of the Europeans come from that stock. And it is pioneer stock. The bloodlines go back, usually to the British, but certainly to people with that quirk in their character that would bring them out to such a wilderness in the first place. Many that went to East Africa, a British protectorate, were adventurers, gamblers, or desperadoes. It also attracted the lovelorn and the loners. People who wanted to try their luck at something new or run away from everything old ended up in Kenya. These were folks who had the courage to make that long journey and then, the even greater courage to stay on. Kenya is a country where the faint of heart and weak of body did not, and still do not, last very long. It is a profoundly beautiful country. There are areas where the land is vast beyond description, the climate superb, and the living rather luxurious, given the abundant labor force. But there are also places where one will be dead in two days without water and the rain washes out all the roads in three hours. The lions, and the "shifta," (*bandits*) will attack. It is not a country for a sissy. Nor for anyone without a sense of humor.

Humor is essential. If you cannot laugh at a great many of the things that go on every day you will never last. There are so many daily hitches and flaws in the system that only a sense of humor keeps you sane. In my second year there, I met a man who worked for AT&T. He had come from Scotland and had only been in Kenya for a few months. He was trying to organize a labor force to install some underground cables. The night we ran into him at the bar at the Norfolk Hotel, he was tearing his hair, hysterical with frustration. He wanted things to work as they do in Europe. He wanted order and the speedy completion of tasks. He wanted people to show up for work. What he had, instead, was Ah-frica. All of us, standing around the bar, just smiled and shook our heads.

We laughed at his stories of mishap and mismanagement. We enjoyed his lamenting about the employee who didn't come to work because his uncle had been run over by a Matatu, a small van, and how the dead mans possessions, including his very valuable goats, which were on the matatu with him, had been stolen. This fellow had then gone to fetch his mother from yet another village to get the papers so that they could get her dead brothers goats back. And the body ofcourse. But it had rained that night and there was no transport and then, once the bus was back in service, it broke down and while everyone was waiting for the spare parts to arrive, he had all his money, and the goats and the body, stolen from him. But, he could not understand why this Scotsman was so irate. He was there wasn't he? We all thought that was both amusing and typical. This A T& T fellow did not. He left Kenya shortly thereafter.

It was funny. Many things are funny. The zebras and wildebeests hovering all over the airstrips in the Maasai Mara during the annual migrations have to be chased with cars before anyone dares land a plane. It wreaks havoc with the Airkenya schedule—or the planes wing should all that shooing fail—but it is quite entertaining to watch. When the power goes out just five hours before Thanksgiving dinner is to be served to twenty guests it must be greeted with humor. What else can you do but head down to Rolf's and order up large amounts of pizza? And even larger amounts of drinks. Everyone understands about the power cuts and just has another beer and laughs about it. There are always problems with your staff, problems with the phone company, the abominable roads, or the mail that never arrives. These things happen every day, and if you didn't laugh about it, you too would soon be on your way "home."

Having a good sense of humor is essential to living in Kenya and so, it seemed to me, is having an affair. There is a saying that goes back to the Colonial days, "Are you married or do you live in Kenya?"

implying, of course, that being married doesn't mean too much in Kenya. Extramarital affairs abound. It has evolved that way for several reasons. The first, which took me years to understand, is the institution of the British Marriage. The British think we Americans are all divorce happy, and I suppose we are, but they approach marriage very differently than we do. We think about love, they think about presentation. I knew many people in Kenya who could not stand to be in the same room with their spouses and yet they stay married. They simply put up an appropriate social front, and then came up with some weak reason why one of them lived back in Britain. She lives in London, he lives in Karen, and they have affairs.

Then there is the sheer size of the country. You could go off to get supplies and not return for weeks. The men who lead the tourists around on safaris are out in the bush ten months out of the year, probably hopping into bed with all the Karen Blixen wannabes from New York. A girl at home in Karen can get lonely and bored when left with the kiddies.

Having time on ones hands is a constant and it too accounts for much of the hanky panky. There is no TV to speak of, even less theater, no gyms, certainly no movies or opera to attend, and no Bloomingdales. What does one do with all those long afternoons, and longer nights, when staring at the trees and appreciating the quality of the air isn't enough? One has an affair with someone else's husband. And ones own husband, should he be around, is probably involved with the neighbors wife down the road. The big deal is not the doing of it, everyone does it, the trick is not getting caught.

Karen is a very small town and everyone knows everyone else. You know where they live and what they are supposed to be doing all day. Everyone knows everyone else's car and license plate numbers. They can identify it when it is parked at the Heron Court Motel in neighboring Hurlingham, (the only motel in town where one could rent a jacuzzi by the hour,) when one is supposed to be in Mombassa:

"Isn't that Mike McIntires Range Rover over there? KQP 487? I am sure he told me he was going to the coast today. No, hang on, that isn't Mike's car. He sold it last year to Ian Smith. And I know he is supposed to be in Tsavo. And his wife is in UK for a month. Why, that devil!"

One cannot go off on a "dirty weekend" without stumbling over four other couples from Karen hiding out in the same dive in

Zanzibar. It is too small a community, and your staff misses nothing, for anything to remain a secret for too long; someone always finds out.

Unlike Muthaiga, a spiffier suburb on the other side of Nairobi, most of the residents of Karen are Kenyan citizens, and there for the long haul. Muthaiga attracts the "two year wonders," the ex-pats who have been sent to Africa by Caltex or Citibank. They stay for two years, living on generous American salaries and a multitude of perks, before moving on to yet another remote and dangerous spot. Karen residents are almost exclusively Europeans. Most were born and raised there. There are some ex-pats, but they are apt to be long-term residents. My situation was not totally unique either. There were others who, like myself, came to Kenya, fell in love with either the country or somebody in it, and decided to stay. One of Kenya's top architects, my friend David Beglin, who still spoke with his native Irish brogue, had been in Kenya for almost twenty years. He maintains his home in Dublin and always talked about leaving, but his wife says he never will.

As tourism is a significant foreign exchange earner in Kenya, many Karenites work in the safari business. The local roads are full of Range Rovers and Land Cruisers. There are many safari support industries, as well, tent makers, travel agents and of course vehicular repair shops. No one works too hard though, and many take pride in that. Unlike the United States, it is considered rude to ask someone what they "do," but when asked, the standard reply is, "As little as possible, thank you." Everyone takes at least two hours for lunch and a swim, stops at ten and four for tea, and quits promptly at five PM. No one would consider working on Saturday or Sunday, and everyone can usually manage to have a standing golf game on Tuesday afternoons. Thursday afternoons is reserved for seeing ones mistress. There is always time for a chat while picking up a few things at the dukas or the children at the Karen nursery school.

Or the Post Office. The Karen post office is a rather spare wooden structure with three service windows, each designated for a specific business. You could buy stamps, if there were any, at one window and you could pick up any over sized packages at another. The third window was for paying your phone bill. You could not, however, get two things done at one window, the ladies behind the windows would not allow it. They did, however, allow cutting into the "queue."

There didn't seem to be much compunction about stepping in front of someone if one just wanted to buy a quick stamp with exact change or drop off a letter to be mailed.

The outside walls of the post office were lined with rusting private post boxes. You could count on running into someone there. The schedules of most people were very easy to track, and if you wanted to either see your lover or assiduously avoid his wife, you just had to pick the hour you went to the dukas to "collect the post."

The post office is run by Kenya Post and Telecommunications, which was also responsible for the hair tearing ineptitude of the telephone company. One is very lucky in Kenya if a letter arrives at its destination after weeks, or even months spent traveling from the neighboring town. More often than not, it never gets there at all. Stamps routinely get removed from envelopes, and there are always letters in your box that do not belong to you. If you are a nice guy, you take them back to the lady in the Post Office and tell her it is an incorrect box number. That guarantees that they will be back in your box again in about two days. Of course if you are not a nice guy, you just throw the damn things out and pray that someone is not doing the same with your mail. I learned very quickly that if I wanted something to get where it is going, without a snag, I had it hand delivered.

I did not, however, ever come to terms with a phone system that simply didn't function. If it rained, the phone went off. If you paid your bill, it went off. If someone thought you didn't pay your bill, it went off. Of course the KP and T was the organization that made it impossible for you to get the bill in the first place. When you didn't get it and the phone was cut off for non-payment, to whom could you complain?

Another significant stop in town was the Karen Chemist, which sat across from the gas station. In Kenya, you could buy just about anything over the counter without a prescription. There were no watchdog organizations like the American FDA, and you could get sleeping pills and antibiotics just by asking. You could buy codeine-laced cough syrup, Valium, diuretics, anti-anxiety drugs, and stomach remedies loaded with morphine. All kinds of birth control medications that have not even been considered in the United States were for sale. All were readily available and handed to you packaged in little brown envelopes, like veterinarians use in the States.

The down side of all this was, being such a small town, it was a very small shop. There was one room and everyone had to stand at the counter and ask in full voice for whatever it was they wanted. There were no fifty-foot long aisles to hide in while you very discreetly selected some potent body shampoo.

When I first arrived there was no bank in Karen. The nearest branch of Barclays' Bank was in Hurlingham, a twenty-minute drive. There was a good deal of restrictions on banking too. You could only cash a check for two thousand shillings, then about one hundred dollars, without having to pass a security check. That would entail scrutinizing a hand written ledger on which all your past transactions had been recorded. A few years later Barclays' opened a tiny spot next to the Karen Provision Store and there was always a line coming out of the closet sized lobby snaking around the gas pumps in front of the dukas. Doing your banking was another time consuming process and provided another chance to chat or flirt or drum your fingers. A few years later Barclays moved to a much larger building in Karen, but that did not change the way things were done, it only meant that there was a larger space to wait in.

The biggest gathering spot in Karen was The Horseman, the local eatery. It was the only restaurant in Karen, and for many years the only restaurant that side of Nairobi. Karen residents ate there at least one night a week. Saturday nights and Sunday, when most people let their staff have a day off, the Horseman was packed. On those nights the clientele was more varied. People came from all the Nairobi suburbs and the scene was very multiracial. There was food to suit everyone's taste.

In 1987, The Horseman was just one small restaurant, but by 1992, there were three more dining areas. There was what were locally referred to as "The pizza place," "the other new steak place," "the pub" and "the old upstairs place," all located in what used to be a dusty parking area. "The pizza place" was all safari chairs, brick floors, and wooden picnic tables that were painted white and steadied by match books. It was surrounded by banks of flowers and covered by a tarpaulin that leaked in the long rains. You could order from a leather bound menu that offered everything from several kinds of pizza, Chinese food, Indian dishes, and a variety of toasted sandwiches and 'chips.'

"That other new steak place" was an outdoor grill room. It was much larger, had a proper wooden roof, and sat in the center of this culinary crazy quilt. It was on a raised wooden platform that was outfitted with brass railings and horsy decor. You had to walk over a small bridge that crossed an artificial pond to get to the tables. There the menu was written on a wooden paddle and included steak, shrimp and chicken. They were cooked in front of you on a charcoal grill and served with a baked potato. They also offered game meats such as zebra and antelope from time to time. In each of these locales, you were supposed to order from the menu of the area you were sitting in. But everyone knew the owner and the African waiters would never dare turn down a request from a patron. If you didn't like what was on the menu where you were sitting you could order from one of the others. I think there was also some push to make certain areas more deserving of fancier dress, but that didn't work either. Not only would the head waiter never dare send anyone away, no one in Karen had any fancy duds to don.

"The old upstairs place" was the most visually unusual. A study in Laura Ashley chintz, with more brass railings and polo prints, one felt one had just stepped into a restaurant in Switzerland. It was a much more intimate space, with dark walls and candles on all the tables. It was the original restaurant in the complex and the most pretentious. The menu there was the same year in and year out, (as was the case with all of the restaurants,) but offered much fancier fare, squab and pates and interesting pastas. But there too, if you didn't see what you wanted on the menu you could have your waiter bring you a hamburger from downstairs and put it on your tab. One never had to have any cash in Karen, everyone knew everyone else and your word was good enough.

"The pub" was the latest addition and featured etched glass, even more brass railings and polo prints, and the dubious pleasure of karaoke nights. You could sit at the bar and drink all day and order from all the menus of the other three places. When choosing your spot to dine at the Horseman, what and who you wanted to look at was more important than what you wanted to eat.

The Horseman was owned by a very hefty, entrepreneurial German ex-pat named Rolf Schmidt. Rolf had as big a personality as he had frame. An institution in Karen, he was at his restaurant eighteen hours a day, walking around in his chef's hat, bellowing into his cellular phone, chasing his African staff about, and playfully propositioning all the women. He drove a 1969 Corvette, had a striking Muslim wife, wore a gold Rolex watch, and played a reasonable game of polo (which explained all the horsy decor and polo prints.) He also ran a pretty fair restaurant complex. The food was tasty, a rarity in Nairobi, and it was, although somewhat over priced, amusingly multinational. Everyone in Karen was forever griping about the food and the prices and the basic cleanliness at The Horseman. There were tales of rats behind the kitchen, dubious ingredients in the spring rolls, and food poisoning from the salad bar, but that never seemed to hurt Rolf's business. The Horseman was full every Saturday night and all day Sunday.

five

Foreign Tongues

With Jake's departure for the States at the end of that first summer, I was alone again. Having so many staff members should have offered some form of companionship, and in the USA it might have, but not in Kenya. In America, you might weep on the shoulder of your house girl or bend the ear of your cook, carrying on about how very good or terribly rotten things in your life were. That's Okay in the States, but in Kenya, staff members are staff members. They are not friends.

There is obviously the language barrier to contend with, but more importantly, the line between "master" and "servant" is one that is never crossed. Or so I was told. Which isn't to say that I didn't cross it, I did, especially with Mildred. But I needed friends, real friends, my contemporaries.

I saw a notice on the door of the Karen dukas, "For Sale. King Charles Spaniel Puppies" and a local phone number. Now there was an idea: get a dog. Man's best friend. I thought about it for a day or so, arguing with myself about the necessity of a puppy, then I made the call. The owner, another American woman, was away for two weeks. "Good," I thought, "I will probably get over this impulse by then." A puppy, although not a real friend, would provide much welcomed company. But what if I left after my year? Sure, this was easy, I had acres of land and lots of staff to care for a dog, but New York City would be another matter. Was I going to leave the dog at the Karen SPCA when I left? I tried to curb my pronounced tendency to immediately act upon every thought that springs into my head.

Two weeks later, half hoping that all the puppies would have been sold, I called again. The owner was back, and there just happened to be two puppies left. I dashed right over. It was a foregone conclusion that once I saw them, I would take one. It would be amazing if I made it out the door with only one. But I did manage, and he was adorable. He had the quintessential spaniel face, with sad eyes and droopy ears. He was white with brown spots, and a pedigree that went back to the Tudors.

We named him Kipele. It was Swahili for Spot. I thought that was most fitting : "Look Mildred, see Spot. See Spot run." We were all happy with our new arrival. I say "we" because I had become a "we." My staff and I were now "we." Everything that went on, or entered in, or belonged to the household was for "us." And now "we" had a puppy named Kipele, who was spoiled rotten.

He had had his own ayah, (*nanny)* since birth and she had fed him boiled chicken by hand since he was weaned. He refused to eat any other way, and only then if you practically chewed it for him. I refused to do that, and he refused to eat. He began wasting away. Mildred wanted to feed him by hand and was trying to wear down my resolve with odd looks. I told her I knew he would eventually give in, but I know she was mumbling things about puppy abuse behind my back. After a full week of this hunger strike, he finally consented to eat his chicken out of a bowl. It was then another month before we could progress to feeding him regular mince, (hamburger), and another few weeks before we could move on to dog mince, a local delicacy the contents of which I never had a desire to know. I knew I would eventually win this little contest of wills, but Kipele was one stubborn little chap.

Other than his eating habits, he was not much trouble at all. He slept through the night, stayed in his own basket, and never chewed anything he wasn't meant to. He was bright and sweet and followed me around with an adoring look on his face. He kept me company. I was growing quite fond of him when he rolled into adolescence and began to mark his territory. I knew that lions marked their territory and cheetahs marked their territory, but I had never heard of a Spaniel marking his territory. Kipele did. He peed on every single chair, couch leg, or curtain in the house. He didn't miss a heavily upholstered one. I am not sure how he made this decision, but Kipele avoided all the wooden chair legs, saving himself for the cut velvet. I tried to reason with him, and Mildred tried it in Swahili, to no avail. He was determined. No matter what we did or threatened, my dog peed all over the President of Kenya's furniture.

One of my daily rituals was to sit at night having a cocktail, watch the sun set and read the local paper. I tried to get the International Herald as often as possible, but it's arrival in Kenya depended on whether the government liked what was said about them that day, or not. It was only sporadically available. The local papers were hawked on every street corner and they were plentiful. There were at that time three dailies in Nairobi: the Kenya Times, The Nation, and The Standard and all three were printed in both English and Swahili. I read the English version of The Standard. Any mention of the international news was paltry at best. I didn't know about the stock market crash in October of 1988 until I was on a plane to New York four months later. Although I missed not knowing what was happening in my old world, I found the news that was printed in The Standard far more amusing. All I had ever read was the New York or London Times, both venerable, factual, and correct, but, compared to The Standard, they are dull, dull, dull. One may have been able to read what was happening in the world financial markets, but one never read any good stories about people falling into pit latrines. In Kenya, the daily paper was full of such fascinating tales.

I used to clip articles from the Standard to send to a friend of mine who was getting her masters degree in journalism at NYU. If she were stuck for a thrill factor, or just wanted to see if her professor actually read what she wrote, one of these stories would definitely help. One that I found quite interesting and rather thought provoking was about some young boys "genital" (sic) getting cut off. This was not that unusual. Every time I picked up The Standard, there was at least one article about someone's something getting cut off. Or falling off. Or going missing. Body parts in Kenya were forever either rotting or dripping or being severed from their owner. What made this particular story memorable was that it said that during this botched circumcision ritual "the section of the cut part disappeared mysteriously." It went on to add, "The whole of yesterday teenagers were busy looking for the lost part of the genital in the surrounding bush." Aside from the wonderful choice of words, there was the strong visual image of all these teenage boys on their hands and knees searching for the "cut part," suffering, no doubt, some form of sympathetic pains. It made me think: How big could this part be? What did they hope to do with it should they find it?

Then there were the ever-frequent stories about people falling into pit latrines. A pit latrine is a thirty-foot deep hole with a few planks placed over it and a small structure surrounding it. This should afford the latrine visitor some semblance of privacy. These are public toilets and people in Kenya were constantly falling into them. Or stuffing dead bodies down them. I could see the logic behind the latter, but how did the former occur? You have to recoil at the image of being in that familiar posture when you hear the ominous sound of wood splintering and the plank underfoot starts to shatter. Without benefit of hiking up your trousers, you are plunged into a thirty-foot deep pit. It was certainly a misfortune, and newsworthy enough to be reported in The Standard.

The very best thing about The Standard was a column that was printed every Thursday called "Ask Doctor Amref." Amref is an acronym used by the Flying Doctor's Society. It stood for African Medical Relief Emergency Fund. This was an organization of doctors and pilots who flew all over Kenya rescuing folks in difficult medical circumstances. Be it lion attacks or car accidents, shiftas, or malaria, the Flying Doctors came to the rescue. They saved many lives every year. They also contributed this wonderful column to The Standard every Thursday.

I have no idea who Doctor Amref was but I found him extraordinary in his sincerity. He answered everything in the most serious and professional manner. He was a Brit, I am sure. Who but the British could keep such a stiff upper lip? I don't think I was, in general, unduly drawn to stories about body parts, or to genitalia in particular, but it seemed that these were what the majority of these tales were about. There was a letter, Dear Doctor Amref, from a woman who claimed that she smelled bad. She bathed several times a day and she changed her clothes just as regularly, but she still smelled bad. Even her best friend agreed that she smelled bad. She was convinced it was "bad blood." What else would cause someone to smell bad no matter what they did? And she was most unhappy about this. Dear Doctor Amref, what shall I do?

Another tale was the week's leading story, "Losing Skin Color." "Dear Doctor Amref, I have this problem . . . " It seemed that this chap had a tiny white spot on his "organ" that was, a year ago, the size of a dot from a ballpoint pen. It had grown since then and now the white spot was covering the "whole head." He did not think that he had been infected with VD, at least not recently, but he was very worried that this discoloration could spread to his whole body.

He had acknowledged that he might have a skin disease, as the color on "the soft part" was going from, "black to brownish." He had, wisely, sought medical counsel and he had been advised that melanin, or the lack thereof, was what caused this problem. The pigment that makes skin either light or dark was missing. It needed to be jump-started. He had been told to expose his fading parts to sunlight. He had done just that, he told Dr Amref, for two hours a day. This was not easy, considering the part in question. And the fact that he was, as he put it, "uncircumcised."

One distinct advantage to having so much "spare" time was that I could devote my attentions to peripheral matters, like learning to speak better Swahili. After several months of living in Kenya I found that I understood only about one fourth of what Mildred said to me, but I wanted to be truly fluent. I had tried to learn it once before, most unsuccessfully.

When I first went to Kenya, back in 1985, I had listened to Billy chatter away with his safari staff for the two weeks Jake and I were with him, and I was enchanted with the sound of Swahili. While there, I mastered "Jambo," and "Asante Sana," but I wanted to learn it all. Swahili held Mystery, Foreign Intrigue, and Adventure in every syllable. I also felt that when I returned to Africa (which, after two weeks there, I was convinced was the land of my destiny), speaking the language fluently would help me to blend in better. I bought a set of Berlitz language tapes. "Kiswahili," it said, "The Lingua Franca of East Africa."

Not exactly. Kiswahili is proper Swahili, and is only spoken on the Coast of Kenya. What is spoken in Nairobi is a sort of "kitchen" Swahili. I did not know this, of course, and I spent hour upon hour for weeks endlessly repeating what the man on the Berlitz tape told me to say; "Hujambo mi bibi na ma bwana. U hali gani?"

I also learned my numbers from one to ten and repeated them to myself every day while doing my sit-ups at the gym. "Moja, Mbili, Tatu, Nne." I took to leaving clever messages on my friend's answering machines in Kiswahili. I am sure I said something like "Take the dog out and shoot it" when I was trying to tell someone to call me back, but no one knew what I was saying and so no one could correct me. The humor in all this was lost on everyone but me. My friends took it as further proof that I had contracted some tropical disease while "on safari" in Africa that rendered my thinking confused and humor aberrant. But I was a woman on a mission, and I pressed on. "Jambo mi bibi na ma bwana. U hali gani?"

I told Billy what I was up to on one of our many long distance phone calls. He was very enthusiastic. When I actually gave him a well-memorized sample of my new skills, however, he informed me that he had no idea what I had said. He didn't understand proper Kiswahili and no one else did either. I threw the tapes out.

The best way to learn any language is to be thrown to the linguistic lions. Survival is always a very persuasive motivation for learning. I had people working for me who picked up English, (Kiingareza,) far quicker than I learned Swahili. Africans are superior linguists. Everyone speaks many dialects and everyone is taught English in school. Although Mildred said she could speak English when first we met, she could not really understand a word I said; I spoke too fast. But even having to deal with my rapid fire speech patterns she became fluent in my language long before I was even passable in hers. I should have tried harder. It was vital to know what was going on in my own household. I listened to all the chatter in the kitchen at night and I think I would have known had an uprising been planned, but it was some time before I was comfortable speaking it.

Swahili is actually very easy. There are only about one hundred words that you need to know to get by. I would have had trouble discussing the finer points of neo-classic architecture, but I eventually could make myself understood in my daily circumstances. On safari, you talk about tents and food and hot water. And all the animals. The first full phrase I learned, a very important phrase to know when on safari, was "Lette pombe ingine, tafadhali" *(Please bring me another drink).* Around the house, one sticks to the appropriate topics. I could tell someone that my shoes were dirty, the water cold or that dinner was for six people tonight and should be served at eight P.M. Please.

The repetitive nature of many of the Swahili words is amusing. Sasa and bara bara, kati kati, mimi, wewe, sisi, *[now, road, middle, me, you, us.]* My favorite, lala salama, means sleep well, or good night, or sweet dreams. Pole was handy. Pole indicates sympathy. "I want you and your family to know that you have my very deepest and most profound sympathies for this great misfortune that has befallen you. I cannot tell you how sorry I am." Pole sana. (*Very sorry.*) But pole pole means slow, or slowly. How one gets from sorry to slowly, I have yet to figure out.

As Swahili is a spoken language, and was written down by the people who later arrived in Kenya, (primarily British), it is written as it is spoken. If you cannot think of the right word in Swahili, just say it with a British accent and attach an 'I' to the end. Witness the names of the objects that arrived with the first white men: blenketti, texi, footi, (*tapemeasure*), whiti, banki. For variety, there is mota ca (*automobile*). I hung on to this knowledge because when Mildred didn't know the English spelling, she would write things down phonetically. "Madame. Ledi qwa benki reng. She sed to kal bek. Is ujent. Wewe nataka unga kwa mbwa na frutes." (*We need dog food and fruits*).

One problem that does arise when trying to converse with Africans is that every tribe has its own dialect. There is Kikuyu or Maa, for the Maasai, or Abaluya and those are far more difficult to master. I had about thirty five Kikuyus working for me in my carpet business, and they tried for years to teach me how to say "hello" and "how are you." I couldn't wrap my tongue around most of it. I could understand what they were saying, when they were talking about carpets and measurements and wool, but, beyond that, I was lost.

The other very distinct feature of the dialects is the hundreds of different ways assent in indicated. Each tribe has about three different grunts to fit any occasion. There is just about every possible variation on the theme of "eh." It can go from eyeh, to ayah, to eeeh. It can have a lilt on the end or a dip in the middle. This can sound as four distinct syllables, or just one. It's one thing to proniunce it and a whole other to write it down. It is rather like trying to spell the sound of someone crying, or clearing their throat. All vocals. Every African exchange of dialogue has about ten of these per paragraph, like our "yup," or "yeah," or "uh-huh," It indicates that you are still listening and vaguely in agreement with what is being said. The sound of these vocal assents became almost backround noise.

I got into a jam once because of that casual attitude. I was on safari with Billy, up in the Northern Frontier District, in a tiny little town, a few camels along the river, called Kaputir. We were camped there for a few days, hanging out. The word had gone out that we were looking to purchase some local handicrafts. Within less than an hour after our arrival, there were lines of local folks pouring into camp, offering up their wares for sale. There were gourds and rungus, (African night sticks) appearing by the minute. The witch doctor had a pair of handmade bells on his legs that I was keen on taking back to New York with me. With every passing hour there were more people gathered around the kitchen tent, all looking to sell their belongings. The bargaining had begun.

Bargaining in Africa is an art form as well as being very time consuming. One can haggle back and forth for hours over twenty shillings. Everyone gets involved and it can become very lively. It is highly amusing to watch. In order for it to be a "good deal," however, everyone must end up satisfied with the outcome. Both parties must go away content that they got what they wanted and that all was mutually agreed upon, otherwise it is not binding.

There was, among the many necklaces worn by the women in the village, one that caught my eye. It appeared on the second day on the neck of the oldest and most wrinkled lady I had ever seen. It was unusual in design: black beads on white shells and about ten to twelve inches wide. We had been bargaining for hours every day and were acquiring quite a lot of merchandise, but this old Mama mzee would not part with her necklace. I was determined to have it. After trying unsuccessfully to talk this old lady into a sale, I decided that if she and I became pals, close friends, she might become more amenable to parting with this masterpiece of local craftsmanship. I struck up a conversation with her. Well, not exactly a conversation, more of a mutual grunting of assent.

I had been listening for days to the sound of this 'aiyeh,' the Turkana agreement sound and thought I had it down pat. I considered this just the time to use it. "Aiyeh." Nodding my head to everything, she said, I answered "Aiyeh." She was chattering away and I was nodding and saying "Aiyeh." She'd point at this or that and rattle off a long sentence. I would do my imitation of a Turkana agreement. Nod. Smile. Agree. "Aiyeh."

On the third afternoon, we were both standing on the edge of the bargaining circle. Every time Lambat or Esecon, the chief bargainers among our crew, would secure an object, they would pass it to me to hold. This old mama would then take whatever it was, beaded necklace, gourd or spear, out of my hands to inspect, and then say something to me. I assumed she was commenting on each item's artistic merit, and I would say "Aiyeh" and nod to indicate that I agreed with her superior taste and greater wisdom in these matters. Billy was not around for all this, probably off negotiating for the goat we were going to buy for a big ngoma *(party)* we were hosting that evening. He would have undoubtedly told me to watch what I was doing. But he wasn't there and the crew was too busy inspecting the items being offered. I was on my own.

I had been agreeing to any number of things for the better portion of the afternoon. I had probably agreed to marry her first born child and put up my New York co-op as the bride price. I had no idea what had been said and, furthermore, thought nothing about it. As evening came and the ngoma started we all left the bargaining circle and went on to the next event. As we parted company. I nodded and "aiyeh-ed" at whatever she said and went merrily on my way.

When we were to leave Kaputir, I was going without the necklace. Despite our newfound friendship (and pending in-law status), the mama mzee would not sell it. She did, however, come screeching down to the truck, as we were about to pull out. She stood in front of us, waving her arms and rattling on as if we were about to make off with her prize goat. There was a very rapid exchange of words between the old woman and Esecon that was then translated into Swahili for Bill. After a few more exchanges, Bill said something that calmed her down and then turned to me. With eyebrows raised and that familiar look on his face he asked me what I had agreed to. I had no idea.

Well, she certainly knew. I had agreed to pay her a very specific sum for every item she had "helped" me hold that previous afternoon. As she took each necklace or gourd from my hand, she was not only inspecting them, but weighing them to see how much she should charge me for her assistance in holding them. I had agreed, item by item, to quite a tidy sum.

Granted, I had no idea that I had done this, but I had agreed, every single time, and fair is fair. We had to pay it. Bill dug into his pockets and produced the necessary shillings. The old woman was mollified, and shuffled off in a cloud of red dust muttering to herself and glaring back over her shoulder. It was very clear, in any language, that she knew a welcher when she saw one. I had to face the fact that we were not really going to be friends after all. (The wedding was probably off too.)

Once she had gone, Bill turned to me and shook his head.

"Honestly, Memsaab, I don't think I can let you out of my sight. You must be more careful with these people up here. You have no idea the amount of trouble you can get yourself into."

I wanted to defend myself and explain what had happened. I wanted to tell him that the whole episode had just been a misunderstanding. But I said nothing. I knew he was right. And what could I say? Aiyeh?

six

Graham

Jake was to spend the Christmas holiday that year, 1987, with his father, and not relishing the idea of being alone for Christmas, I left for the States in November. I was conscious of being homesick, but the closer I came to packing my bags, the more excited I was about going back to New York. All I could think about was watching the evening news on 'real' television, going to the theatre, and the consummate joys of Enchiladas Suissas. I wanted to go to Zabar's and eat enough H & H bagels to make myself ill. I missed Cheerios and English muffins (the Kenyans had never heard of them), American popcorn and the New York Times crossword puzzle.

I told Jake that I would return to Africa, but I did not think I wanted to stay on after my "year" was up. We had toyed with the idea of my staying in Kenya longer and Jake was sorry to hear that I didn't think it was going to happen. As a form of inducement, he brought up the safari I was planning to take with Billy in February. But that was only for a few weeks, and even the most thrilling of safaris did not make up for living in Kenya, alone and idle, for the other eleven months of the year.

After the thrill of eating in all of New York restaurants faded, I started to find being "home" rather exhausting. It was Christmas and the weather, especially compared to the perfection of the climate in Karen, was horrid. But beyond that, the whole city moved too fast and was way too loud. I felt like a tourist. I had lost my New York edge. After a few weeks, I wanted to go back to Africa.

Returning to Kenya in January was an unexpected delight. The air was clean and fragrant and I was welcomed by Kipele, the Ngong Hills, Mildred and all my staff. They had made a sign and hung it over the front door. It read "You are truly welcome." They also commented on how fat I had become. This was a compliment, meaning that I looked prosperous and healthy. But I had, in fact, gained a few pounds in New York and didn't really want to hear about it. Nyamburra made it all the worse by grabbing her ample hips, nodding in my direction and pronouncing "Nyama mingi" (*much meat*).

Karen didn't feel so foreign this time. My ugly old house held a few memories and there was even a semblance of a life for me now. I was happy to see Bill Sr. and the Winters welcomed me back as a member of their clan. All the waiters at Rolf's asked about my safari and people I ran into at the dukas said Jambo. A few seemed to have noticed that I had been away, most notably Moses, my number one bag boy. I think he missed my heavy-handed tipping and the tales I told him of Jake. Moses called Jake the bwana mkubwa (*the big man*) and was fascinated by his life in America.

I don't know if it was because I was trying to focus on the positive, or if life in Karen really was becoming more comfortable for me. For whatever reason it felt better. Not quite "home," but better. As the first weeks of '88 rolled by, I started to believe that this might actually work for me. Maybe I would sort out some of the problems and find a way to stay there longer. Maybe I would make some new friends. Maybe I would "meet someone."

In February, Judy Spier, a friend from New York, came to visit me, and we went off on safari around Kenya. We traveled to Lake Baringo, the Aberdares, and Lewa Downs for a camel safari. I booked this particular event for Judy, knowing that, although it was a bit rugged for a first-time safari goer, she would enjoy it as much as I always had.

Before my first safari to Africa, my experience of adventure travel was dinner in the Princess Grill on the QE II. My ex-husband used to say that my idea of roughing it was sharing a bathroom in a five star hotel. As a child, I had suffered from a host of allergies and chronic asthma. The word 'sleeping-bag' made me wheeze. And no one ever called me "a trouper." But Africa seemed to be changing that. Each successive safari had been incrementally less cushy and I had become braver, stronger and more knowledgeable with each trip. " You are getting really rugged, Memsaab." Billy would tell me. I of course agreed with him, knowing that we were grading on a curve.

Every time I returned to Kenya, Billy had come up with something new to challenge me. I was very uncertain of my ability, never mind desire, to cope with these challenges, but I went along because I trusted him. The first time he suggested a camel safari, though, I almost refused to go. It sounded like some kind of Outward Bound endurance test. Definitely not for me.

"William, you know this is not my idea of fun."

"You will love it. Trust me."

"I do, but . . . "

"Have I ever led you astray?"

"No, but I think you have gone too far this time. I don't want to walk in the desert for ten miles a day. Or ride a bloody camel for that matter. Or sleep in a fly camp. What the hell is a fly camp anyway?"

"Just a small traveling camp. You will love this. You are going to fall down laughing you will be having so much fun."

"I doubt it."

But we did go and, regardless of Billy's many reassurances, I was scared to death that first night. Sleeping under a bush in a mosquito net was not what I was used to. How was I supposed to get any sleep, tucked into this thing, listening to all the snakes and bugs and I didn't even want to know what else prowling around in the leaves two inches from my head? I had images of attacking hyenas and bloodthirsty "shifta" sneaking through camp and seeking out my lily-white flesh. After our ten mile walk that day, I was exhausted, but too scared to sleep. Then there were the stars at night. An African night sky is spectacular and the show going on in the heavens was too fantastic to miss.

I got very little sleep on that camel safari, but with every day, as we hiked through the dust and the thorns and the burrs that stuck to my American Girl Cheerleader socks, chewing holes in my calves, I felt better. Every night I was less afraid, and after a week, I was delighted with myself. I had cuts and scrapes and blisters all over my body. From the knee down, I looked like a victim of a shark attack, but I felt capable and strong and I had had a wonderful time.

Arriving in Karen, after our camel trek, Judy and I found that we had just missed an exciting event. Nyamburra had had her baby. It hadn't gone smoothly though, and for hours, the placenta had refused come out. Mildred told us how Stephen, a first time father, had paced the floors until he had driven all the women in attendance crazy. Mildred finally gave him something constructive to do, sending him off to locate a specific herb in the garden. He found it, Nyamburra ate it, and the placenta came out. By the time we arrived, all was well. We welcomed baby Isaac into our little group.

A few days later we headed off for two nights at Governor's Camp in the Maasai Mara. The Mara, the northern extension of the Serengeti Plains, is the largest and most popular of all Kenya's game reserves. It has the greatest concentration and most photographically accessible game of all the parks. Whenever I had wageni (*visitors*), I saved it for last.

To get to the Mara from Nairobi one can drive a miserable seven hours over Kenya's notoriously pitted roads or one can hop on one of the fifty-minute "milk runs" that fly from Wilson twice a day. Airkenya and it's fleet of small aircraft take all manner of small packages, mail bags, emergency supplies and whoever is holding a ticket to the various game reserves, and drop them off at each lodge's attending airstrip. A few of these strips are just two tracks in the grass and the larger planes cannot land. Most are at least mud and gravel and only partially wash away in the rainy season. Musiara, serving Governor's Camp, and it's baby sister, Little Governor's, is one of the better ones.

As Judy and I got out of our plane and into the Range Rovers sent to collect us, I saw what I thought was an American male. He was built like an American and he was wearing desert boots, Banana Republic shorts, and a "Big Apple" tee shirt. I missed the navy blue socks. He was standing on the Musiara airstrip, aviation radio in hand, watching a single engine aircraft circling in the skies over his head. We caught each other's eye.

Big Governor's, one of the most popular camps in the Mara, has thirty tents, each equipped with proper flush toilets and showers en suite. It is a good place to bring timid travelers. Although a stay there is certainly not roughing it, the camp does retain enough of the atmosphere of the old time safari camps that the experience is not watered down to the point of being meaningless. Many of the newer tented camps in Kenya have taken the "luxury" idea too far, adding marble baths, electric lights, and overhead fans. Other than four green canvas walls, there is little left to remind someone that they are in a tent at all. Little Governor's, located just across a bend in the Mara River, was reached by means of a small boat. Other than that, it was essentially the same setup, only smaller by half.

After checking in, Judy and I were sitting at the bar, having a beer and looking out at the plains. Giraffes floated by and herds of zebras and wildebeests could be seen grazing on the nearby hills. There was also a troop of resident Baboons. After living near humans for most of their lives, they had become extremely bold. They had figured out what was where, and were very apt to dash through an unzipped tent flap, screech menacingly at anyone who stood in their way, and snatch up any available snacks that they saw. Or your Rolex watch.

As we were sipping our beers and watching Africa drift by, the man I had seen on the airstrip came striding in to the bar. He plunked down in a chair and introduced himself: Graham Elson. Tall and tan, he had strong features, graying, curly hair, an easy smile, and striking aquamarine eyes. I guessed he was between thirty-five and forty and he was definitely British. We started in with the usual safari chitchat: where have you been, what have you seen, where are you from, and how long are you staying, He was just beginning to capture my attention when he told us what he was doing there: he was a balloon pilot. A hot air balloon pilot.

"Oh, no." I thought. "Not one of Those."

I swung my legs over the arm of my chair, turning my back on this conversation, and went back to working on my New York Times crossword puzzle. I had no interest in any "balloon pilot," aquamarine eyes or no.

There were, at that time, about fifteen of these chaps in the Mara, spread among the different lodges and I had encountered them before. Known as "The Most Dangerous Animal in The Mara," you only had to be in Kenya for five minutes before you heard about them. One of them had been there for far too many years and his business card listed him as a balloon pilot on one side and a sex maniac on the other. One story goes that another pilot once took a Polaroid picture of himself in all his erect, male glory, and sent it to a woman's tent with a note attached saying, "Do you think you are ready for this?" And they usually were.

These men had women crawling into their beds, room keys stuffed into their back pockets, and notes left for them in the "guest book." The most infamous was "For the blow job of a lifetime, come to

Mara Buffalo, tent three, tonight at ten." It was a rite of passage that every female tourist felt she must experience, part of the "Complete Safari Experience," like a "welcome cocktail."

It should be written up in all the brochures:

"During your once-in-a-lifetime safari to Kenya you will experience the following things: perfect weather, two game drives a day in the worlds most beautiful game parks, all meals a la carte, transfers to and from the airport and all taxes and tipping prepaid. Regrettably, hunting is no longer permitted in Kenya and you may not take a lion home as a trophy, but, we can assure you that you will certainly be able to score with any one of the balloon pilots."

I could see where these fellows might have some limited appeal. They were a reasonably good-looking bunch, easygoing, usually tall and slim, and they all had blue eyes. And they were, for the most part, Europeans with those accents that American women find so irresistible.

The other salient ingredient in this easy seduction was that the very real danger of ballooning is a turn on. Once aloft in this contraption, you are hanging, powerless, hundreds of feet in the air, in a wicker basket, beneath a ten story piece of rip stop nylon. It is held together with nothing more than a few strips of Velcro. There is only Mr. Handsome Pilot standing between you and certain death. As you begin to relax a bit and listen to his wildlife spiel, you realize what a Sensitive Soul he has. He really Cares about the Land and the Mara and the Rhinos and Saving the Baby Elephants. He becomes more appealing with every bird species he identifies.

Getting a crush on a balloon pilot is very much like falling for a Great White Hunter, only quicker.

Upon a "sporting" but safe landing, you are handed a glass of champagne and one of his winning smiles. As you stand on the plains of the Mara with the sun barely up and all the glories of Africa surrounding you, breathless from the whole experience, he pours you another glass of champagne, crinkles his blue eyes at you, and says something witty. It can be very intoxicating.

I was wise to this. I lived there, after all, and was not some starry-eyed little wag (local slang for wageni, *visitor.*) I had already had my Great White-Hunter experience and I had no desire to carve another notch in my tent pole with a balloon pilot.

The balloon flights took off from Little Governor's and Judy and

I were there and ready to go at dawn the next day. Although Graham was at the launch site, strutting around in his black jumpsuit with his worldwide balloon meet patches on the sleeves, we were not assigned space in his balloon. He did, however, tip his Ray Bans to me as he walked over to supervise his crew. I think I yawned in response.

After the flight, we were all drinking champagne and getting ready for the outdoor breakfast they served. Known as the "Heart Attack Special," it consisted of fried eggs, fried mushrooms, fried bacon, fried sausages, and fried toast. It was fun to watch them prepare, as they cooked it over the burners used to heat up the air in the balloons, but the cholesterol level was record breaking. Graham came over and began to talk to me again. I don't know if it was the champagne, or if I was beginning to find him more attractive, but I was less rude this time. We talked about living in Africa, it was understood by then that I lived in Karen, and all the pluses and minuses of being an ex-pat. We talked about having to get away from Africa every so often for a dose of cultural stimulation. As we were launching into the topic of 'personal freedom', he said to me:

"So, where is your husband?"

"I don't have one. Where is your wife?"

"I haven't a clue. Lost track of her."

As we were piling into the Land Rovers for the drive back to camp, he invited Judy and me to join him for lunch. He would come to "collect" us. I thought this should round out Judy's safari in Kenya nicely.

Lunch was distinguished primarily by how little anyone got to say about anything except flying. Not only were all the balloon pilots at the table but three of them, Kenneth, Mark and Graham, were working towards their private pilots license in fixed wing aircraft. The flight instructor, Denise, an ex-pat American, who was as concerned with Jesus and handing out bibles to the local tribesmen as she was with airplanes, was down there that day teaching these three to fly. (Denise used to print up biblical sayings on balloons, regular toy balloons, and hand them around all the manyattas in the Mara.) The conversation never veered from the subject of flying. But I caught Graham's eye as he seemed to watch me and I could feel myself blush. I was surprised at my response, especially since I had already lumped him into the category of 'supremely undesirable.'

After lunch, Judy decided that she wanted to join a late afternoon game drive, and I stayed on at Little Governor's. Graham invited me down to the balloon pilots house and, as there were several of us going, I went along. It was a little cottage with a thatched roof and shaded veranda. There were creepers growing on a roof that was crowned with a broken airplane propeller. A retired balloon basket had been converted into an outdoor bar and there were hyena teeth marks on all the leather corners. The cottage was called Prop House and was atmospheric, if a bit frat-house in decor. Graham told me he had designed it himself. When I finally left for Big Governor's he said that he would try to get over for dinner that night. I thought to myself, "Don't start with this man, Melinda. A balloon pilot?"

He did not show up that night and I was disappointed. When he and Denise joined us at breakfast the next morning, after their lessons, he told us that there had been no boat to cross the Mara River and the hippos were too close to risk swimming across. When it was time for Judy and me to go, I took a deep breath and wrote my phone number on the back of a napkin. Making some nervous speech about returning the favor of the lunch, if ever any of them, (heavy emphasis on the plural) were ever up in Nairobi, give me a call. Graham jumped up, nearly knocking the table over, and grabbed the piece of paper out of my hand.

Five days later he rang up. He was in Nairobi for a few days and asked would I care to join him for " a meal?" I met him at the bar at the Norfolk.

The Norfolk Hotel, built in the early part of the century, is a landmark in Nairobi. It has been destroyed by fire and rebuilt many times but, at that time, it still retained that "Old Africa" feeling. There were stuffed animal heads mounted on the walls and always the feeling that hunters might come trooping onto the verandah at any minute. They would be covered in dust, streaked with sweat, with rifles slung over their shoulders. Followed perhaps by Teddy Roosevelt and his hundreds of African bearers, they would carry enormous tusks of ivory. No one would be surprised by any of this. They would sidle up to the bar, order rounds of gin and tonics, and settle in to tell their safari tales.

Back in the "good old days" shoot 'em ups occurred on a fairly regular basis at the Norfolk and the sight of horses being ridden through the dining room was not at all unusual. All manner of assignations took place there, then and now, and a reputation for holding one's liquor or losing one's virtue could be had on any given evening. You didn't really feel you were living in Kenya until you had been propositioned at the bar at the Norfolk.

Graham was his usual loquacious self and we talked about the things people talk about on a first date. After dinner, we drove over to the East African Aero Club for drinks. I wasn't sure if I was up for more flying stories, but it turned out to be a quirky little place right on the Wilson Airport compound. A bunker from the outside, inside it was right out of *West With The Night*. The walls were covered in broken propellers and photographs of Kenya in the early part of the century. Full of mementos of bush pilots and bi-wings, it embodied every boy's fantasies about flying. I liked the place, and, strangely enough, I began to think that I liked Graham as well.

Graham had traveled a good deal and had interesting tales to tell. He told me funny stories of flying balloons in Thailand and France and of doing stunts in dirigibles for James Bond movies. He had even taken a dare to do a "You Asked For It" for American TV. He had flown a single man balloon to the top of a ski lift and then skied back down the trail, only to do it all again. The fact that he had never skied before didn't stop him. The filming crew said they could edit out any mishaps and so he threw himself down the slopes. He could also order a good bottle of wine and he ate with the right fork. He was easy to be with. He was also all the things the balloon pilots were known for: witty, charming, and handsome. And married. "Separated" he said. He hadn't really lost track of his wife; she was living in Spain. I did manage to find out how long he had been in Africa without her and eight years sounded "separated" enough to me.

As many disparaging remarks as I made about what he did for a living, the truth is that his being a pilot was perfect. He was, at that time anyway, "my kind of guy." The first man I ever fell in love with was a pilot and it has been my experience that pilots, especially bush pilots or, in this case balloon pilots, march to a different drummer. They don't spend their days punching time clocks like some boring banker, nor do they put in long hours in law libraries. They are mavericks who push at the edges of societal norms. That appealed to me.

After we had arranged to have dinner again the next night, I dropped Graham off at his hotel. I invited him out to Karen this time, and when he kissed me goodnight, I all but fainted. Granted it had been about a decade since I had been properly kissed, but there was electricity there. This had "trouble" written all over it.

As there is no public transportation in Nairobi that anyone would really want to use, I picked Graham up the next night, and we drove out to Karen. On the way, we were driving behind Barbara Winter and her daughter, Heather. I knew that my being seen with a man would elicit a lecture from Bill Sr. on anything from inappropriate relationships to sexually transmitted diseases. Oh, goody.

During sundowners on the upstairs patio, I probed into his life as much as he would allow. Which wasn't much. Answering personal questions makes most Brits edgy, and it made this one apoplectic. If you asked Graham what he had for lunch, he would tell you it's none of your bloody business. But I didn't know that then, and so I plodded onwards. I was curious about him, and even more so about this wife of his. He was decidedly reluctant to talk about her but he did manage to satisfy me that they really were separated. They had never had any children and as there was no animosity between them and no real reason for divorce, they just lived apart. Or so he said. I didn't really care all that much, I had just met the man, and Spain sounded far enough away for me. As long as she stayed there.

I was attracted to his secretiveness. I have always been a sucker for a man who seems to have shadows across his heart. I warm to the investigative process, foolishly thinking that I can plumb his depths and then make their mysteries work in my favor. If Graham was withholding so much information, and he was, I assumed that there must be something fascinating there to discover. Still waters running deep and all that. It never occurred to me that his unwillingness to talk about a good many things might not indicate someone who was interesting, complex and profound, but someone who simply had a lot to hide.

We had dinner that night on the lower patio and when a storm blew in we ran back upstairs to sit under an overhang and watch the rain. The rain in Kenya is spectacular. Pouring out of the sky in tremendous sheets it can put on quite a display. It also brought out all the smells of the soil and the flowers. As we sat on the couch, snuggled up together, watching the rain, I thought, "I could probably tolerate a few more evenings like this."

The next day I drove Graham to Nairobi to catch his flight back down to the Mara. Things had gone quite smoothly and it had all seemed very easy. As we were having coffee, I started fishing for an invitation to visit him in the Mara. It took him forever to pick up on all my female hinting, which I excused as another English/American social difference. As we were leaving the coffee shop, he finally said "If you ever are in the Mara, drop by Governor's. I'm usually there." Drop by? The Mara? It was a seven-hour drive from Nairobi! How, pray tell, does one drop by? I didn't consider that a solid enough invitation and so, sucking up my courage, I said "Well, why don't you invite me?" And he replied, "I just did." That was his idea of an invitation? "If you are ever in the Mara, drop by?" Well, I guess this is not going to be quite as easy as I had thought. With that he kissed me goodbye at my car and walked off. Feeling more than a little confused, I drove back out to Karen to brace for my lecture from Bill Sr. and get ready for my safari with Bill Jr.

I knew all too well of my tendency to get all moony and stupid over men who give me even the slightest hard time. I was very grateful that I had a grand new adventure on my immediate calendar. I had missed some of the hints of the real problems to come, but I already had a sneaky feeling that there were some differences between Graham and me that went beyond his pronunciation of tomah-toe. Americans are more comfortable than the British when talking about feelings and emotions and Graham and I were extreme examples of each of these camps. There had been, in the past twelve hours, just enough snags to capture my interest. Going off on safari with Billy was the perfect diversion to keep me from spinning my romantic wheels. Once young Winter and I were out of Nairobi, I would forget all about the dubious charms of Mr. Graham Elson.

Many things in this life are put forth as being "better than sex," but going on safari is one I can personally attest to.

Billy

Jake and Melinda at the Equator 1985

President Mois house in Karen

The Ngong Hills as seen from the patio

David Duff and Bill Sr.

Mildred and Nyamburra outside Moi's House

Kipele

Post office in Karen

The new bank in Karen

Peter and Eleanor Nalle in Samburu

Melinda and Baby Isaac

Graham

The crew in the NFD

Kaputir

Mildred, Celestine and Fannis

Weavers at a loom

Virginia and a pile carpet

The Hippo carpet

A settler's cottage

The master bath at 141 Dagoretti Rd. —before

The cow sheds at 141

The work had started on the house

The living room is gutted

Melinda with Zeke and Rat

Jake at new factory

Jake and James with the ill-fated truck

Factory finished with our "high-tech" washing system

Melinda with the old Kufuma sign at the new location

seven

The Safari Kubwa

The idea had come to Billy and me one evening, a year earlier en route to Lake Baringo. Having left the Maasai Mara at dawn, we had been bouncing over Kenya's wretched roads all day. By five that night we should have long since been jarred into sullen silence. The terrain was barren, the temperature in the high nineties, we were sweaty, dusty, and tired and we had probably just vibrated our kidneys into premature failure. It had been a trying trip, even by safari standards, and yet, as the lake came into view Billy and I were talking about how beautiful everything was, and what fun we were having.

This was my third safari to Africa and I was, at this point, giving serious thought to living there. "If you like this part of the world, Memsaab," Billy said, using his pet name for me, "You will love the NFD. That is very special country up there. Only a few very rugged souls can brave it, though. What do you think about making that your next safari? An African badge of courage?"

"Sure. Whatever you say. What's the NFD?"

The NFD is the Northern Frontier District. Kenya has a varied terrain with mountains, forests and savanna grass lands all within a country the size of Texas. The NFD, officially renamed the North Eastern District after Independence, but still called the NFD, is the largest segment of the country. It is the uppermost part and is bordered by Somalia, Ethiopia, Sudan, and Uganda. It is untamed, unexplored, and for all intents and purposes, uninhabited. Other than the few nomadic tribesmen who spend their lives tending their camels, there are not many people in the NFD. Although an extremely hostile environment, it is also wildly beautiful with the quality of a surreal moonscape. Stretches of land end only at the mountain ranges that rise like mirages on the horizon. The vegetation, adapted through the ages to exist with minimal water, has taken on strange and magical shapes. The endless skies host a relentless sun all day and limitless stars at night. The colors, always filtered through the intense heat and ever-present dust have a shimmering, almost mystical quality. Everything feels muted. Everything except the heat.

Although the Equator cuts across the center of Kenya, the more populous towns like Nairobi and it's suburbs, are saved from the intensity of the heat by their elevation. As you head into lower altitudes, either towards the Indian Ocean on the eastern Coast or descend into the NFD the temperature goes up five degrees with every thousand feet. Temperatures at the coast are cooled by the sea breezes, but in the desert, it is not remarkable for the thermometer to read one hundred and thirty degrees Fahrenheit.

The other hostile element to contend with is the "shifta," the bandits that have infiltrated Kenya from its northern neighbors. In 1988, they were dangerous and armed with AK-47s (the left-over gifts of First World countries and senseless wars.) But more recently, the proliferation of gun bearing Somali refugee has made the NFD off limits to anyone other than relief organizations and the military. In 1988, the "shifta" were more apt to be poaching elephants and stealing cattle than shooting at unwanted visitors.

Under most circumstances being on safari with Billy was not rough going at all. Meticulous in every detail, he was incredibly observant of his client's needs. Billy never cut corners and he never took the cheaper or easier path. We also had very abundant labor at our disposal. It was nothing to have a staff of fifteen along to look after eight clients (and there is nothing like a staff of fifteen to smooth out those rough little edges at the end of the day.) We traveled with proper facilities: big, stand-up sleeping tents complete with real beds and mattresses. We had shower and private "loo" tents, and tea brought to your tent at dawn. We had no electricity, but dinner was set in the dining tent with the wine chilled (we had a generator) and the candles lit at eight sharp.

Billy believed that, after earning the requisite number of merit badges in the game parks, I was ready to take the next plunge: the Safari

Kubwa. (*The Big Safari)* The NFD. Billy had never been there either, it was far too inconvenient and dangerous a spot for tourists to visit, the climate was forbidding and supplies were a constant problem. But his inexperience struck me as a plus. I liked the idea of our being together, out on that limb of the unknown. We both agreed that this significant safari would celebrate my passage from being a "wag" to an official Kenya resident. It would also be a highlight of my "year" in Kenya. I was thrilled with the idea of this High Adventure. We would be "pioneers together," me and "the Great White Hunter," "like the good old days." "The Real Africa." I was somewhere between living out my Karen Blixen fantasy and simple thrill seeking.

Adrenaline, I had found, is a real rush. It's a fix. The more your heart pounds and the more terrified you are, the better it feels when it's over. It also means that you have to push down on that same pedal a little harder the next time. Going through these things with someone else is like great sex. I was starting to understand those crazed fools who jump out of airplanes or hunt big game on foot. I didn't have the faintest idea what the real hardships of this safari might be. All I could see was that it was going to be 'heart stopping,' 'life threatening,' and fun. I knew we would be in this together, I trusted Billy to take care of me, and that's all that mattered.

We had decided on February of the next year: three weeks in the desert.

It was going to be just the two of us and the ten in staff we were taking. At first I thought that to be a lot of crew members to have along, but an ex-game warden friend of mine, who had spent years up in the NFD before Independence, later said to me, "Only ten men? That was very foolish of you. What if half of them fell ill?" Their numbers were more for security than for luxury living, but I didn't really understand that at the time. I did recognize the need for the essential chaps, mechanics and drivers and cooks, but having Wairangu, from the Meru tribe, as my tent man seemed a nice little extra. As was the case with many of the crew, he had been on safari with us before and had already had the dubious pleasure of taking care of me.

Your tent man's job is to look after you exclusively. He brings you tea in the morning, drinks when you want them, fills your shower bag, changes your bed, tidies up the loo tent, and washes most of your clothes. (It was considered good manners that a ladies "smalls" be done by their rightful owner.) It is a very intimate relationship. Your chap is there to make you happy. He will learn your routines very quickly and know all your likes and dislikes as soon as he can. By the time we went into the NFD, Wairangu knew how I liked my tea, when to replace the loo paper, when I did or did not require a hot water bottle in my bed, how often I changed my clothes and where I put my chapstick at night. He knew when I was not feeling well, probably my menstrual cycle, and certainly my every mood.

Leaving all thoughts of this new British lover of mine behind, Billy and I left Nairobi in the last week of February, heading for Lake Nakuru where our first camp awaited us. We stayed there for a few days, looking for leopards, watching the flamingos, and getting re-acquainted. Since moving to Kenya, I had seen very little of Billy, as he was always out on safari. Whenever he did come through Karen, he never stayed longer than it took him to drop off one set of clients, change his clothes, re-supply his camps, and pick up the next set. Now that we were on safari together once more, I was looking forward to his company.

We spent a good deal of our time in Nakuru poring over maps and talking about what we were about to do. Billy sat by the fire at night and told me tales Bill Sr. had told him about the different tribes we would see and what I was to expect. He told me how dangerous it might get and how brave I would have to be. I was entranced and proud.

Although young Winter could hold court around any campfire, he was not the grand storyteller his father was. He didn't have Bill Sr's enormous need for an audience. Billy was quieter and gentler, more introspective, and much easier to get along with. I adored both of them and could spend hours with either, but Bill Sr. and I never made it past two hours without a verbal tangle. Billy and I never quarreled.

While in Nakuru, we were also double-checking all the staff and everything on the truck. Our plan was to quickly cross out of any routinely traveled areas into the NFD, and we needed to make sure that everything was in perfect working order. We were also acclimating to the heat. It was the end of February, the Long Rains were coming, and it was already extremely hot, especially to me, only recently back from Christmas in New York. Lambat, our headman, laughed whenever I commented on the temperature. He would grin at me and whisper "Lodwar." Lodwar was the Northernmost town that we would pass through, and the lowest in altitude. What Lambat was trying to tell me was, "You think this is hot? HA! Stand by kid. You ain't seen nothin' yet!."

"What's a little heat?" I thought. "How bad can it get?"

Lambat was from the Ndorobo tribe and had been a tracker for Bill Sr. most of his life. Now roughly in his forties, he was one of the best in the business. Lambat could see things hundreds of yards away that I wouldn't see until I sat on them. He had bionic eyes. He rode in the back of the car and kept a lookout for whatever struck him as either interesting or unusual. When we were in the game parks his job was to look for whatever particular animal we were seeking. In the NFD, he was there to see whatever there was to see.

Although the heat at Borgoria was intense, I didn't gripe too much about it. I had been dreaming about this safari for an entire year, and I would not have even considered turning back. I told myself, "This is Ah-frica. This is what you wanted." It was also what I knew best and loved most about being in Africa. My life in Karen hadn't been all I wanted it to be, so far anyway, but going on safari with Billy always exceeded my expectations.

For those first few days, especially at Lake Borgoria, camped under that long-awaited grove of yellow acacia trees, I was not the slightest bit worried. Lake Borgoria is in the Rift Valley, a fault line that runs the length of Kenya. The northern-most lake is Turkana and then, moving south, come Boringo and Borgoria and on down to Nakuru, Naivasha and Elmentaita. Lastly there is Lake Natron.

They all contain undrinkable, brackish water. A cruel joke of nature, in the middle of all that heat and drought, there were these vast bodies of water that remained undrinkable throughout the ages. Although not potable, they are all very beautiful. The plateaus of the Rift Valley surround Boringo, and Naivasha and Nakuru are graced with the presence of thousands of flamingos. There are sizzling, steam geysers on the shores of Borgoria that burst out of the ground. The water boils and bubbles as it sprays to the surface. It is witchcraft.

This early part of the safari was very familiar to me. I loved being in camp, being with Billy, and I loved sleeping in a tent. The days were filled with new and exciting adventures: hikes in the hills, drives around the lake in search of an elusive Kudu, and hours spent cooling our feet in a nearby spring while we made videotapes of the baboons. But I loved the nights even more; the way the air felt as evening approached, the changing light on the hills, the way daytime noises subsided and the sounds of the night took over. The temperature would drop twenty degrees and what had been almost too hot to bear became cool and balmy. The sun sets at exactly six thirty on the Equator, with a variation of less than ten minutes year-round, an event we always looked forward to. After a long afternoon walk, Billy and I would turn a corner and there, in a perfect setting, would be a few members of the crew, "the lads," with a table and chairs all set up to surprise me for "sundowners." We would have a drink, watch the sun set and listen to evening come.

Back in camp the campfire's flickering light made a terrain that had been familiar and secure during the day seem suddenly mysterious. I would sit in my tent, after my shower by the light of a gas lantern, and listen to the sounds of the camp as it got ready for dinner. I could hear the African voices of our crew in the distance and the doves calling from the Yellow Fever trees. Hyenas laughed, zebras barked, and something moved in the bushes near by. Yellow eyes appeared and disappeared. Nighttime was all sorcery and shadows.

It was mystical and a little scary. But I liked that. I liked being slightly frightened. I didn't even mind when Lordi, the cook, found several scorpions in camp. That was his name, Lord, or more correctly, Lord Hare, a fact that prompted many biblical jokes. (On that safari, we all put our trust in the Lord.) His African name was Mrithi, but he was very light-skinned, and, he told us, of noble birth.

I was not too upset when he found the scorpions. I considered it a good idea that we get used to them now, rather than later. That reasoning seems a bit strange to me now, but it made sense then. I had found many ways to allay whatever fears I might have. The principle trick was that I made up lovely little fictions for myself. I was even ready, should I be stung by a scorpion, to be strapped to the car generator and given a good jolt. I had been told by many people that this was the best thing to do for a scorpion sting.

Lordi, a small and graying fellow, was a wonderful storyteller and extraordinary mimic. He would launch into a story with only the slightest encouragement. In a flash, he was on his feet, acting out elaborate tales. My limited Swahili kept me from fully understanding all the finer points of his stories, but words were almost secondary. He did all the parts himself and very quickly, had us all falling about laughing. He would be the wife beating the husband on the head with a stick, then the battered husband; or an old man pounding on the door and hobbling around with his cane. Changing his voice and jumping about, dancing around in his shorts, his long chef's apron, and his wellingtons, he was a comical sight. As he told his tales, he would grin through several missing teeth, thoroughly pleased with himself. Often while Lordi was doing his stories one of the other "chaps" Wairangu or Lambat or John Samburu, would jump into the circle and take up a part. They would improvise until someone else was inspired and took over. It was great "bush" theatre.

The Lord was as inventive in the kitchen as he was on the boards. Considering that everything in camp from roasted peanuts to cheese soufflés, was cooked over an open fire, that was quite a feat. One night at Borgoria, Billy and I were served a plate of little fruit pies for dessert. On the top of each one, in letters fashioned from thin strips of dough, was written, very plainly, EPA. The P in the middle was larger, like a monogram. We pondered what this could mean for quite a while before sending Mweyo to fetch the Lord to enlighten us. Mweyo was a tall thin fellow who rarely spoke or smiled, but ran an efficient dining tent. He was another old timer and had spent many years on safari with Bill Sr. Lordi came tromping down from the kitchen tent looking mildly irritated at being dragged away from more pressing matters. He stood with his wooden ladle in hand and informed us that it stood for Apple Pie. Get it? EPA. Ap-Ple Pie. He trudged back up the hill mumbling to himself and shaking his head.

After several more days in Borgoria, checking out all the equipment and realigning our temperaments, our little band was ready to head north. Our crewmembers included two mechanics and one fellow from every tribe of the different areas we would be passing through. They were to be our translators. We had one Toyota Land Cruiser, a five-ton Bedford truck, (a make often used by the Kenyan Army, which made for some interesting encounters later on) and all our supplies. We were not planning on any major pit stops. Choosing what to bring and packing it all up had been a tactical feat for Billy. Along with all our personal items, we had all the anticipated spare parts for all the vehicles. A broken-down vehicle could be the end of the line. With no transport and no water, it would be only two days before every one of us were dead.

We had a sizable deep freeze that was filled with frozen food and cases of beer. There were boxes of dried foods, tool kits, and camping gear for the staff. We carried chewing tobacco and beads, gifts for the local chiefs. We had ample amounts of gin and whiskey. We had tents,camp chairs,toilet seats, mosquito nets, soap flakes, and a video camera. We carried two regular SLR cameras each and about six lenses apiece. We had a mountain of film. There was even a filter to treat any water that I might come into contact with. Although I would most likely get sick if exposed to the very different bacteria in the water, Bill's stomach was far more tolerant of the local fauna. We had audio cassette players and tapes that ranged from the "Sounds of Soweto" to Mozart, and our favorite, Paul Simon's "Graceland." We also carried, and this was the supreme touch, a bath tub. A green canvas affair that stretched over a collapsible metal frame, it looked very much like a coffin. It was a real luxury, and I had, rather in jest, requested it the year before.

"What else can I bring to the NFD to insure your total comfort, Memsaab?"

"Well, showers are nice, but a bathtub would be even better," I had teased. And there it was.

Should things not go as smoothly as planned, I could always be buried in it.

My job had been to pack for every single medical emergency or female problem I could think of. I don't think there was a potentially malfunctioning body part that I wasn't prepared to fix. I had piles of pills, endless sprays and jars of salves. I had ointments, spare syringes and yards of bandages. Anything could go wrong. Athletes foot to amoebic dysentery. Bug bites, snake bites, even human bites, you name it, I could fix it. And enough Tampax for six women, for six years. I didn't want to run out of that. There was nothing I had not anticipated, except the most obvious: dehydration.

After leaving Borgoria at dawn, we drove North towards Lake Baringo. Just short of the lake there is a side road off to the left that heads up over the Tugen Hills, and that is where we left the tourist world behind us. As we climbed ever higher over the western rim of the Rift Valley, the view back towards Boringo and Borgoria was breathtaking. We stood on the edge of the Hills and looked west towards the Laikipia Plateau forming the far side of the Rift. The water was shining in the early morning light, and as the sun's rays heated the air, mist rose from the lakes. Everything was shimmering:

the colors of the hills and the dry earth were deep blues and ochres dotted with the dusty green of the remaining thorn trees. The Plateau was an imposing precipice as the sun rose above it. You could see forever.

The road passing through Kabernet, President Moi's home town, was very well maintained, but rarely traveled by anyone other than the local people. As we headed farther afield, the roads became less of a feature as we became more of one. We caused quite a stir wherever we went. Due to the truck, we were often mistaken for the Army, or because we were mzungus, Billy and I were taken for missionaries. We stayed together in convoy with our truck for security's sake, and made quite a splash when we arrived in a tiny town. Many of these people had never seen a white person, let alone the sort of parade we presented.

There was a general plan to get to Lodwar in ten days time, and we were heading in that general direction, but the 'how' of that was a day-to-day event. We had decided never to take any road that was marked too clearly on the map. We were going to travel on roads that were not roads at all, but dirt tracks. Goat paths. We felt that staying off the roads gave a whole crap shoot ambiance to this adventure.

The days were long, driving from seven to four. It was always dusty and getting hotter every day. The further northwest we traveled, the more primitive it all became. Once we got to a town called Chemale, somewhere in the Kerio Valley, north of Tot and south of Lokor, there were suddenly feathers in hair and leather skirts. The Mzees had wooden plugs in their lower lips. The thermometer probably hit over one hundred every day and I was feeling the effects, but where we were and what we were seeing was so fantastic that I could ignore it. The land, as we drove along the foot of the Cherengani Hills had changed. Although the landscape was still fairly speckled with thorn trees and euphorbia and not totally arid, the native dwellings were becoming progressively more spartan. Where there had been tin rooves, now there was mud and grass. Many of the huts were built on raised platforms to avoid the invasion of snakes and scorpions.

Even if there was no one around when we stopped for the night, as soon as we began to set up, crowds of people would appear out of the bush. After an hour, there could be fifty people, sometimes up to a hundred, watching us. Curious, they would stand or sit on the ground and stare with the same facial expression seen on people watching only moderately engaging television programs. The smaller children would stand with their noses six inches from your face. I was stared at relentlessly. Not only was I the only female in this troop of eleven men, but I was the only blonde. I am sure I was an unusual sight, but I was not used to so much (unwanted) attention. To people who spent their lives tending goats in a completely remote area, our entourage must have seemed like a three ring circus. And after all, we were there to look at them, so it was probably only fair that they should be allowed to look back. But it took some of getting used to.

Our camp usually consisted of my tent, for what little privacy that provided, Bill's mosquito net (a far cooler, but decidedly more immodest arrangement,) a fly tent for dining, and a tent for the kitchen. If I was feeling particularly nervous at night, Billy would ask the crew to sleep in a circle around my tent. It was an odd feeling falling asleep with ten African men sleeping about three feet from my head. I would lie in my bed and listen to them talking softly to each other, in tongues I did not understand. I found it quite comforting. It was like being a small child and hearing your parents talking downstairs. You can't quite make out exactly what they are saying, but the sound is reassurance enough.

For the first week of the safari we wound our way northwest. We had crossed the Tugen Hills and were driving along the base of the Cherenganis. The towering bulk of the Elgeyo Marakwet was to our left as we crossed into the Turkana province. Some mornings Lambat would drive and Billy and I would ride on top of the Range Rover. We were cultivating our tans, feeling like children, and watching the incredible landscape go by.

Billy and I always had two crew members in the car with us for security. As Esecon was a Turkana, he had been riding with us since we passed into his tribe's province. Another benefit of having the crew with us was the entertainment value and Esecon was a great choice. Most Africans are natural storytellers and relish the chance to hold forth. Esecon was not only a teller of tales, he was a true magpie as well. I could not understand most of what he said, but listening to the cadence of it was entertainment enough. During his storytelling he would squeak and huff and bellow. He could express fear and surprise, disgust and delight, all with sound effects. The African Mel Blanc.

On the seventh day out, we were crossing the second parallel, about fifty kilometers from the Ugandan border, when we arrived at a small settlement in the Turkana Province called Kaputir. This little village is located along the Turkwel River where there was still some surface water to be found. Although it amounted to no more than a small pond, it was an unexpected blessing. At that time of year, most of the surface water in the Turkwel had already dried up. Then there was that little project that was going on up the gorge a few miles back.

The Kenya Government was building a hydroelectric plant in the mountains that separate Uganda and Kenya. This was a seriously misguided undertaking that would eventually dam up one of the only sources of water in this totally arid land. The government's justification for the plant, bringing electricity to the surrounding area, was an absurd notion. There was no one up there that wanted or needed electricity and, even if they had, no one had the facilities to put it to use. Even more to the point, every survey done on the viability of the project came to the same conclusion: "It ain't gonna fly." There would never be enough water in the dam to create sufficient pressure to generate any power. But, as with far too many such projects in Kenya, there had been an enormous amount of kickbacks in the awarding of the building contracts. But in 1988, the dam was under construction and this small patch of water at Kaputir still existed. It afforded the village people the chance to raise a few camels and goats. Kaputir was an extremely primitive spot, but the water made possible the barest semblance of a better life.

eight

Kaputir

We had taken an unusually long time that morning to cross the river further up and had attracted a great deal of attention. Billy was concerned that his truck might sink into the sandy bottom of the river and we had taken many trips back and forth with the much lighter Toyota to assure us of a safe crossing. Lambat, never camera shy, had performed pratfalls into the river for the benefit of my videotaping. With every trip across the river, he pitched himself from the top of the car and then floundered about in the water while I filmed it all. Despite the heat, which was extreme, everyone was enjoying themselves as we engineered the truck's safe passage. But we were hardly low profile.

We arrived in Kaputir around three and were escorted to a small clearing at the river's edge by the village elders. Upon landing in any village, the protocol was for Billy to sit down with the local chief and have a friendly chat. He was to reassure the mzees that we meant the people no harm, we were just passing through, and we were really very nice folks. If they didn't speak Swahili, one of our own crewmembers from that particular tribe would translate. A few warm beers and some chewing tobacco, (a substance that looked and smelled like camel dung and, when not in their mouths, rested behind their ears) usually greased the social skids. Once this "getting to know you" ritual had been completed, we were allowed to pitch our camp. So far, we had not had any trouble.

The little settlement of Kaputir was nothing more than a series of dung and grass huts strung out under the trees that flanked the river. There were bare breasted girls and Turkana warriors sauntering about, camels in the riverbed, and goats everywhere else.

Tall and lean with angular faces and prominent cheekbones, these men had wooden plugs the size of a champagne cork piercing their lower lips. Their hair was covered in bright blue mud forming a royal blue pillbox. Finished off with a few feathers, it formed a kind of crown. They wore heavy blankets rolled over at the waists and their skin was very black. Some of the women had large pieces of the common native cloth, called kangas, wound around them and secured under their arms. This formed a sort of strapless dress. But covering themselves did not seem to be overly important, as they would frequently take the fabric off to rearrange it, exposing their bodies completely. Some of the younger women were in leather skirts with their hair done in a braided version of a Mohawk. A strip of small, tightly twisted "braids" covered the center of their skulls from their foreheads down to the nape of their necks. The sides had been scraped clean with a sharpened piece of tin.

The Turkana have the reputation for being the fiercest fighters in Kenya, spending most of their lives battling their neighbors, the Pokot, over stolen cattle. As each tribe claims that the cattle were given to them by God, the battle is not only unsolvable but ongoing. These cattle raids can come at any moment and the men are always ready. They carried their spears and shields, (and more recently, rifles) with them wherever they went.

Their other notable adornment was a wrist knife. This looked like a circular razor blade that stuck out horizontally from the wearer's arm. The outside edge, the business end, was covered in a thin strip of removable goat hide. You could slice your own leg up with a wrong move, or someone else's face off with the right one. All the men of Kaputir had these knives on both wrists. They would play with the goat hide covers as they sauntered by my tent or sat and watched us doing whatever it is we were doing. If it was meant to remind us how fast that little sheath could come off and our veins opened up, it worked.

The women, often bare breasted and wearing huge neckpieces of beads and shells, screeched furiously at me every time they saw a camera. They all carried themselves so erect that you could never tell their ages from behind. No dowager's hump here, they walked with perfect posture, their shoulders barely moving, with easily swinging hips. This carriage was the result of years of transporting immense gourds of water on their heads for distances of up to fifteen kilometers. It often took six men, standing on each other's shoulders in a fifty foot deep pit, hauling water up with a bucket and a rope, hours to fill each gourd. The women dared not spill a drop.

Within half an hour after our arrival in Kaputir, the curious had started to gather. My tent was quickly surrounded by children and nursing mothers, all seated on the ground around my "verandah." They were watching me settle in. As I did some hand laundry and shook the dust out of everything else, my every move was carefully observed. At one point, a herd of goats appeared, determined to eat their way under my tent, but I very quickly put a stop to that. I had tried several times to shoot some photographs, but it caused such a fury that I had given up. Billy had better luck. The video camera had a telescoping viewfinder that allowed him to stand facing in one direction while surreptitiously shooting in another. Esecon would stand in front of Billy and wave jauntily, while Bill shot pictures of the people on his right. The results often had a strange horizon that tilted at odd angles, but it worked well enough.

It was hard not to shoot pictures of this stunning place. The land we had driven through as we approached Kaputir was far more barren than anything we could have imagined. Many parts of Kenya are so lush and green that we were not prepared for this sight: a landscape so shocking in its severity. There was only a sandy desert for miles in all directions, with nothing on it but tumbleweed to break the monotony. We had been driving through sand storms for days. None of us, except Esecon, could believe how desolate this landscape was. And yet, here at Kaputir, with the river affording the blessing of water and the blue shapes of the distant mountains of Uganda rising on the far horizon, the views were suddenly quite beautiful. There was even some greenery. There was also a tiny sliver of new moon. Barely clearing the distant mountain range, its light reflected in the river for just a moment before it quickly dropped out of sight. Then a million stars covered the extraordinary expanse of sky.

Billy and I were so intent upon having photographs of Kaputir that he decided to negotiate a deal with the village elders. Billy would buy two goats, have them slaughtered, and then host a party for all the villagers. The cooked goats were the final treat. Their side of the bargain was that they would allow us to photograph, with both video and SLR cameras, the ensuing dances and ceremonies. It took two full days to finalize these arrangements with groups of old men standing around the kitchen tent bickering over every detail. Billy finally told Esecon what it was that we wanted, and then left him to thrash out the finer points with the assistant chief, the head man on the other side of the bargaining table. Large quantities of tea were poured and even larger chunks of chewing tobacco handed out. Every detail was discussed and re-discussed. There was haggling over the number of goats and haggling over who was to dance and more haggling over when. All this back and forth was a form of entertainment and the negotiations were protracted. Once the final card—beer for the most prominent of the elders—had been put on the table, a deal was struck. The festivities were to begin at four that afternoon, when the sun's heat was beginning to lose at least some of its sting.

The intense heat we had been experiencing for the past week had left us all dehydrated and sick, but I was feeling the lowest. One always hears that if it's dry, the heat doesn't seem so bad. Not so. Jake and I had been on the Amazon River, hot, very humid, and buggy, and that was nothing like this. Every day, with every foot we descended, it grew hotter. It was well over one hundred and ten degrees at Kaputir and at that temperature, sweat evaporates faster than it can collect into droplets. You lose quarts of body fluid every day without realizing it and it is almost impossible to replace quickly enough. Water alone isn't going to help because you have upset your electrolyte balance. (That is where dehydration salts should have come in, a proper mixture of salt and sugar, or Gatorade, but we didn't know that then.) One ends up feeling nauseated, weak, headachy, dizzy, lethargic, and eternally thirsty.

When we reached Kaputir, Billy finally produced the canvas bathtub. As there was ample water, he ordered the tub filled and me to sit in it. After spending the hottest hours of the day lying in my tub reading a book, I felt momentarily cooler and a bit less ill. Momentarily.

Billy and I didn't know how badly dehydrated we were. We knew we needed a great deal of water and we thought we were drinking enough, at least we were doing what we thought was right, but we were always running at a deficit. And running to the loo. Another fact we later learned was that due to the low water table level in that part of the world, the water is so full of minerals that it is like drinking pure

Enos. That's a "liver salt." A laxative. These minerals cannot be filtered out, and no matter what we did to try to alleviate this problem and no matter how much water we drank, it just got worse. More than half of the crew was ill as well. Many times, we had to stop the convoy as one of the crew raced off into the distance "looking for a bush." If there was one. Everyone was suffering from what the Brits, in their eternal quest to make things sound nicer than they really are, call a 'runny tummy.'

I had willingly repaired that afternoon to what John Samburu called "Mama Safari's swimming." (John was a common name and so Samburu, this particular chap's tribe, had been added to distinguish him from the others.) After lying in my canvas tub for a few hours, I felt somewhat revived. The soothing effects were temporary, the temperature still hovered around one hundred, and I had not really addressed the real cause of the problem. But the impending ngoma was too exciting to miss, and so, when the people began to gather, I was out of my tub and dressed, stuffing my pockets with film and extra batteries.

As the kick off time approached, the sound of singing could be heard down by the kitchen tent. I had heard the Maasai singing at Governor's and some Samburu's at a staged event at one of the lodges, but this was the real McCoy. It was high pitched, seemed to consist of about five separate notes and strangely melodic. As with much African music there was a question and a response format. It reminded me of a child's nursery rhyme.

By four, Billy and I were at the site of the proposed dance, with Esecon and Lambat standing by to hold lenses and pocket exposed film. There were a few quiet minutes as the elders took their seats on their stools and opened their beers. The children gathered to watch. Then everything erupted. It began with the women, led by the witch doctor, dancing into the circle. They all held hands and moved forward with a slight jumping motion. Once fully into the clearing, they closed the circle and with arms around each other's waists, sang together. They then started a heel dropping motion. With backs arched and chins jutted out, they shrugged their shoulders forward causing their heads to bob and their necklaces and breasts to bounce up and down. The dust rose in ever thicker clouds as their feet beat the rhythm of the dance into the earth. We kept the cameras firing. Both SLRs were going all the time with the video camera often in Lambat's hands. We used close up lenses and wide angle lenses. We shot slides, we shot prints.

The men entered next. They too were singing a five-note song and jumping and clapping in time, but their presence changed the group dynamic. Esecon later explained to us that the dances performed were about war and victory and killing animals and courtship. Sometimes all the men sang and jumped in a competitive style, while at others they sang together following each other's movements. As all this was going on Billy and I stood on stools or lay on the ground to catch every angle. We moved around the dancing circle and shot through the dust and the moving bodies.

At six sharp the chief stood up and indicated that the end had come. The dancing stopped and everyone quickly disappeared back into the brush. It was time for the feast to begin. It had been so exhilarating that for those few hours we hadn't thought about the heat (and I thought about the heat every minute of every day). With the dam and the shifta and civilization in general encroaching upon the territories more every year, the culture of the Turkana people was slowly vanishing. Billy and I knew that this part of Kenya would soon become too dangerous for the likes of us to ever visit again. We felt priveledged to have seen what we had just seen.

The sun was setting as I walked back to my tent for a last dip in my tub. I could hear the sound of the men singing their final songs and there was the promise of slightly cooler temperatures. From my tent I could see our crew members out in the river gathering more water and talking to the local girls. To gather maji safi (*clean water*), a metal can was sunk several feet into the river bottom. This tapped into water that flowed below the surface and as it filtered up through the sand, it was purified to a remarkable degree. Evening came, as it always does on the Equator, in a heartbeat. Suddenly it was dark and silent except for the calling of the doves in the thorn trees overhead. Later that evening, that tiny slip of a moon rose over the distant mountains and, just as quickly, disappeared behind them again.

nine

Forcibly Detained

After leaving Kaputir, we spent one night in a dot on the map called Kateruk. The most outstanding feature of this spot was that it seemed to be home to millions of flies. Moisture seeking flies. After the heat, the other constant in the NFD was the flies. There were flies all over everyone, all day. I had been extremely irritated by them at first, but had finally found a way to stop slapping at my legs and fidgeting all the time. I made up one of my little fictions: I convinced myself that they would not really hurt me, they didn't actually bite, and, I continued, they really felt just like the drops of water that run down your legs after getting out of a swimming pool. It worked. It had to. You either come to some peace with the flies or lose your mind. And all that jumping around was wreaking havoc on the videotaping. The flies in Kateruk, however, were not like drops of water; they were seeking water. And any old place would do: your eyes, your mouth, your just washed underwear hung out to dry. Anything damp was quickly covered in flies.

The other high point of our stay in Kateruk was Esecon finding a scorpion. He came over to where Billy and I were sitting with the deadly insect crawling on his arm and proceeded to show us how he used to play with them as a child. He was laughing as he told us that he knew how to make it freeze. Esecon poked the scorpion with a stick, and as it raised its tail, ready to deliver a retaliatory sting, he spat at it. It froze mid-sting. Esecon calmly picked it up by its tail and flung it into the grass. Billy and I were left with our mouths hanging open. Luckily the sun had set and the flies had retreated for the night.

Our proposed destination the next day was Lodwar, but the Toyota developed fuel pump problems and we were delayed. The spot where we ended up was called Kalemenyang. Like many others, this little village was a collection of huts that had been built around some point of interest. In this case, as in Kaputir, it was the Turkwel River. But unlike Kaputir, there was no surface water. There were big thorn trees and the shade was certainly appreciated, but at Kalemenyang, the Turkwel had turned into a luggah, a dry riverbed. The only way to find water was to dig for it, and in Kalemenyang, that meant going thirty feet down.

Water was everyone's number one priority. Our truck had tanks that could carry enough water for the eleven of us for about a day and a half, but we could not take the risk of running short. Finding water was every day's main activity. Then there was digging for it, filtering it and, often enough, pouring it on my head. That was John Samburu's job. He carried around a container of water and every so often, at Billy's nod, he would come over and pour it over me. Although soaking in my tub was my greatest luxury, the paucity of water did not permit that to happen too often. Dousing my head was the next best thing. It helped me to cool down, but had the unwanted side effect of turning my hair into straw. I didn't really care, a wet head felt cooler than a dry one and I was grateful for any relief.

By the time we left Kaputir the heat, the dehydration and the effects of unfamiliar water on my digestive tract had finally taken me down. I no longer wanted to go anywhere or talk to anyone. I didn't care where we were or what we were doing. I couldn't even think about swatting at the flies. I just wanted to be left alone, to die in peace, buried in my green canvas tub.

I was barely able to hold my head up or speak coherently, and I have no idea if Billy knew how badly I felt. But I would have died in silence before I would have admitted out loud that I was miserable.

"This is what you wanted, Melinda. Is that not so? Ah-frica? The Safari Kubwa? A Grand Adventure?" I grumbled to myself as I headed for the "loo" for the tenth time that day. "You fancy yourself Karen Blixen. Or Margaret Mead. You are the Great White Huntress! No? Did those women fall apart with a few minor inconveniences? A runny tummy? I should say not." Well, then, neither would I.

Ever since my childhood, I had wanted to have one "Grand Adventure." At one point in my life, I had thought that spending a year abroad, in Rome or Paris perhaps, would have been exciting. But with the discovery of Africa, that idea had paled considerably. Every safari in Kenya surpassed the one before it and with each "personal best" my desire for the next thrill rose ever higher. And I couldn't get high enough. Until the NFD. Then there I was, the Great White Hunter and me, in the middle of the adventure of a lifetime. It was like being dropped into a movie. Granted, they didn't call "cut" at the end of each scene, and I was not helicoptered back to my air-conditioned Winnebago in time for dinner. But that made it more exciting. This was real and quite unbelievable. All the more so because it was me doing it.

No longer was I the asthmatic child I had been as a youngster, lying in oxygen tents or wheezing myself sick if I had to chase a ball ten feet. No longer was I being called a sissy by my three brothers. Me with the pale skin that burned too easily and a pudgy, unathletic body. Nor was I even the "delicate" ballerina I later became who, all through my teens and twenties, had to watch every step I took for fear of spraining a highly trained ankle. During those weeks in the NFD, I began to feel that finally, at age forty, I was strong and I was brave. I was finding qualities and strengths in myself that I had never known I possessed, qualities that I had always admired in women who have 'the guts' to do things like that. Discovering that I could be, even in part, the kind of woman I'd always wanted to be was more than just satisfying. I also knew that this was something my mother never could have done. Not that she wasn't physically strong enough or didn't have a great enough sense of adventure. She did. She just never allowed herself to live out her fantasies. She dreamed it, and she talked about it, but she never did it.

I did.

As we were setting up camp in Kalemenyang, we became aware of a general buzz in the air that made us uncomfortable. We had begun to develop a feel for the general atmosphere of the villages we stopped in, and this one felt less than completely friendly. Billy sent Esecon on a fact-finding mission. He was to wander about, talk to the people, and listen to what was being said. He reported back within the hour.

I had heard many stories about the speed with which news travels along the 'bush telegraph,' but this was my first real experience with it. It seemed that our arrival was expected. Even though our last campsite at Kateruk, a good six hour's drive away, had been for only one night, and although we had arrived, unannounced and totally unplanned, the residents of this village knew we were coming. And they were decidedly unhappy to see us. According to Esecon, the rumors about us were mbaya sana *(very bad).* Word had reached here that our mission was a medical one: we were there to cut off everyone's breasts and testicles and put them in our deep freeze. These amputated parts were then to be taken to Nairobi to be used for AIDS research.

Billy and I couldn't understand how they could come up with such an absurd idea, but we needed to calm the waters. Billy had his customary summit meeting with the chief. The deep freeze was a problem. The truck, ever so military in appearance, was another problem. But the real stumbling block was my presence. It was very hard for them to understand what I could be doing so far north? If not medical experimentation, then what? To say I was a tourist was unbelievable. American women did not go sightseeing on the banks of the Turkwel River.

Once again, Billy and Esecon sat in a small circle explaining our presence to the town elders. These mzees, wrinkled to an extreme degree, bone thin, and wrapped in only their shukas *(blankets),* sat perched on their three legged stools, talking to Billy and sipping the beer he had offered. They were there for what felt like an eternity. When they finally rose, they all shook hands and shuffled off into the darkness. As Billy walked away, he gave me the thumbs up. All seemed to be settled. Billy later took to calling us "The Goolie Patrol," using his British public school slang expression for testicle.

With that hurdle behind us, we moved in for a two-day stay to see what was going on in the village. As evening came and the heat subsided even a few degrees we walked down the river bed, the floor of which looked like petrified poker chips. There was an abandoned water hole where the children were playing. It had been deserted when the river water disappeared and another, deeper hole had been dug. There was a school nearby, as evidenced by their uniforms, and they were far less afraid of us than in other villages. They turned somersaults and performed handstands and allowed us to shoot whatever pictures we wanted.

The adults, however, were not so co-operative, shouting and waving their hands whenever the cameras emerged. All would have been lost, except that Lambat had mastered Billy's technique of surreptitious shooting. He carried the video camera down by his side, tilted up ever so slightly. No one could tell it was on, no one got upset, and the resulting footage was remarkably good. That skill and his distracting comedic behavior, made Lambat the perfect cameraman for this part of the world. Esecon would talk with his fellow tribesmen while Lambat ran the video camera. Billy and I stood by, empty handed, smiling and exuding politeness and good intentions.

The only other form of entertainment in Kalemenyang was the insects. Although there were fewer flies, something I was grateful for, there were enormous, white spiders, about the size of a man's outstretched hand. They came out at night, attracted to the light of our lanterns. We had to wear our boots at all times. With nothing on but kikois (pieces of native cloth), it was too hot for underwear, and our boots, it might have been kinky or even funny had it not been so hot, had I not been so sick, and had these spiders not been very poisonous. I told myself that were I to die of a spider bite in Kalemenyang, when I was lowered into the ground, in my green canvas coffin, I would be dried up and balding, but atleast I wouldn't be covered in flies. Big white ugly spiders, but no flies.

After two days in Kalemenyang, we set out again for Lodwar. As always, we tried to get an early start, making use of the relatively 'cool 'morning hours. By seven that morning, camp had been broken and we were packed up and ready to roll. It was a mere ninety-five degrees as we began to make our way across the riverbed. Crossing luggahs was always an unnerving event. Should the truck lose momentum, it would sink into the sand. We had sand grids, metal sheets that looked like slices of Swiss cheese strapped to the side of the truck. These would afford us some extra traction, but they were not foolproof. The 'Big Rains' had already started, and there were ominous clouds building up in the distant hills each day. We could not run the risk of getting stuck in a luggah.

The threat of a flash flood was very real. Without any rain where you were and with very little warning, the river could go into full flood in just a few minutes. The force of the water racing down from the hills many miles away formed a wave that could easily wash a ten-ton truck away. Walls of water twenty feet high were not uncommon. Billy held his breath with every luggah crossing. We always took it slowly; no spinning of wheels, no loss of forward momentum, and definitely no stopping. These crossings always provided anxious moments and this morning was no exception. Billy and I were leading in the Toyota, the Bedford was rolling along a few meters behind us, and all was going smoothly when, at about halfway across, more than ten armed and uniformed men came racing down from the opposite riverbank and demanded that we stop.

We wouldn't. We couldn't. We waved our arms and shouted that we were not about to even slow down. We had to get across that luggah. The men were in high temper, and our refusal to obey made them even angrier. As they ran along beside us, brandishing their rifles, they pounded on the sides of the truck. They howled at us in Turkana. We kept driving. Amid all the shouting in strange tongues and the cacophony of hands pounding on metal, Billy kept the Toyota rolling, watching in the rear view mirror to see that the truck was close behind. I could barely look at him. I held my breath.

Once we were across and stopped on the other bank, the men quickly surrounded both vehicles, dropped to one knee, and pointed their rifles at us.

"Oh, great, now we are going to be shot at," I said, expecting Billy to answer " Don't be so dramatic, Memsaab." He said nothing.

All the men were in camouflage gear, to my eye clearly military, and were holding relatively modern rifles. There was not a smiling face among them. They held their ground, rifles pointed at us, while Esecon started rapid fire negotiations and Billy slowly opened the car door. As he closed it behind him, I asked if it was time for me to start getting nervous.

"Not just yet, Memsaab."

William approached the chief, but I could see that he was getting nowhere. The African was shouting and gesticulating wildly and Billy was shouting back. He was clearly losing his temper.

Billy finally walked off with this fellow he had been arguing with and, as he disappeared around the corner of a mud hut, I felt my heart sink. All of our crew were out of the vehicles and scattered among the locals trying to figure out what was wrong and now Billy was out of sight. I felt that edge of panic. I was never too afraid as long as Billy was around, but when he was not with me, I could get jumpy. There was no one there but me and the fellows with their rifles aimed at my head, and the local people watching this drama unfold.

After what felt like ten years, Lambat came back and informed me that they were going to put us all in jail. It seemed that they still did not buy the "Mrs. Atwood: The Tourist" story. They were convinced that, if we were not looking for testicular specimens, then we must be spying for their unfriendly neighbors, the Pokot. The notion that I might be a spy seemed to me particularly silly. How could I have managed to spy for the Pokot from my apartment in New York City? But no one was interested in my opinion and, frankly, I had gone into shock with the mention of the word "jail."

I knew what "jail" would mean: the eleven guys would go to the men's jail and I would go to the women's jail. Alone. The prospect of being alone in jail with some jailer to "look after me" me was not a prospect I was looking forward to. This was not helping my stomach stay calm either. It was time, once again, to "find a bush," but there was no one around to run interference for me and I was too frightened to make a move out of the car on my own. The Lomotil I had been living on for days was wearing off and my options were rapidly narrowing.

Just before total panic set in, Billy returned. He climbed back into the car and informed me that they were not going to let us go until they got the DO (District Officer) from Turkwel to sort this all out. That was a relief, at least jail, and my certain defilement, had been temporarily postponed. I told Billy of my problem and he arranged to get my medicine bag out of the truck and for an escort to accompany me to the "loo." Then all we had to do was wait, in the car, in the heat, by the banks of the once mighty river, for the D.O. to arrive from Turkwel, a spot on the map a mere twenty miles away.

The DO showed up about an hour later, and we had yet another long conference. Billy had told me to speak only English, (as if I could speak at all), as would he. We must seize the linguistic advantage. We dragged out the map that showed our proposed safari route, trying, once again, to explain to the DO what I was doing up there. We talked about my being an American now living in Kenya. We told him about the other safaris I had been on, and why I wanted to see this part of the country. We recounted where we had been so far and where we were headed. Hopefully today. He nodded a great deal and finally announced that we were to follow him to his office in Turkwel. Once there, I was to produce my US passport. He wanted proof that I was an American citizen, and had actually made all those alleged trips to Kenya. Never mind that I had never been there long enough to effectively take up spying for the Pokot. Well, thank God I had my passport with me and I wasn't going to jail, at least not in Kalemenyang. I hoped, should we fail to get ourselves out of this mess, that the jails in Turkwel would be a bit nicer.

We stayed in Turkwel talking the DO's ear off for two full hours. He had an office in what looked like a World War II bomb shelter, all cinder blocks and peeling pea green paint. He was far more interested in all the international stamps in my passport, the tricky extra page fold out supplement, (and, I am sure, my very fetching passport photo), than in my suspect dealings with the Pokot.

Once he had made his very exhaustive investigation of my particulars, he started asking more questions about where we were going. Billy considered this a step too far and decided he had had enough of this nonsense. He began to turn the tables. He told the DO that he hoped it did not become public knowledge that we had been Forcibly Detained. When the man visibly jumped at those two words, Billy knew he had an opening. He quickly latched onto that phrase and began repeating it over again.

"An American citizen had been Forcibly Detained? By the Kenya Military? For no apparent reason? Forcibly Detained?" he repeated. "This is not good, bwana. This Forcible Detention." The more nervous he looked, the harder Bill drove it home.

"This could be mbaya sana for you if your superiors hear of this Unwarranted Forcible Detention Of An American Citizen. You might be the cause of an International Incident."

With that, the DO all but shoved my passport into my hands and pushed us out the door. We stopped just long enough to compliment him on his speedy conclusion of this unfortumate incident. This Forcible Detention. He was, quite clearly, the Henry Kissinger of Turkwel.

We tried to walk casually to the Toyota, but scrambled into the car, and with the truck racing to keep up with us, sped off. About two miles out of Turkwel, Billy suddenly stopped the car. We turned to look at each other and choking on the dust that was rolling in through the windows, we started to laugh. All the days tension was released. and we were holding our sides and howling.

ten

Bush Medicine

Upon returning to Karen, I learned that, in my absence, Graham had been at my house. I gathered from Mildred that he had been in Nairobi on some mission and had come out to Karen looking for me. I pumped her for details, but all I could get was, "Bwana Graham iko hapa." I hoped that he had been wildly jealous that I had been off on safari with young Winter, but I doubted it. I sent him a note via the milk run planes to the Mara informing him that I was back and had heard he had been up to town. Maybe this time my hinting around for an invitation would get a more forthcoming response.

Being away from your house for more than a day was a sure fired way to bring on staff upheavals, but problems seemed to occur no matter what you did. As soon as you got everyone sorted out and things running smoothly, someone would leave, or do something that required their dismissal. It was a never-ending rotation of personnel: retraining, upgrading, switching people around. Everyone was willing to do anything you asked and there was never a shortage of people to hire. There was always a brother, sister, aunt, child, husband or wife waiting in the wings. But each new person brought with them their own personality, history, needs and problems. And more relatives.

After Daniel had been sacked and Mildred promoted to cook, the vacant position of 'house girl' was quickly sought by Jotham's new wife, Celestine. Celestine was from the Luo tribe, a fact that pleased Bill Sr. He believed in having many different tribes working for you. It was a good policy to use the very pronounced tribal rivalries among the Africans to your own advantage. Naturally wary of one another, and apt to snitch, it kept your staff more honest. Jotham's wife got the job.

Celestine was a round faced, gap-toothed girl of about nineteen when she first appeared in my compound. When I saw her coming and going through the gates I asked Mildred who she was and was told that she was "Wife for Jotham." Jotham, like Mildred, was an Abaluya and he was a most willing fellow. Tall, amiable and loyal, he was not what you would call a go-getter, but rather wide grinning and slow moving. He did his job without causing any problems, but Bill Sr. reminded me that a married man is always a better employment risk than a bachelor. Fine with me.

Celestine came to Jotham as a complete package; she already had a daughter, Night. The Luos name their "totos" *(children),* after the time of day they are born. Night was a pretty little two year old, but she had the wretched habit of screaming hideously every time she laid eyes on me. Maybe I was one of the few mzungus she had ever seen, but something about my face frightened her. Mildred said it was my unkempt, curly blonde hair that did it.

Celestine had only been working for me for about four months when she announced that she was pregnant again and the baby was due in December. A few days later, she revised this story, telling me that she was due in August, and took her "maternity leave." As she already had one child, I could not figure out why this was all so confusing. But maybe, I hadn't understood her and this was a linguistic problem. I did think she looked too small in the tumbo *(stomach)* to be so close to term, but she should know, shouldn't she?

Every tenured staff member gets a paid maternity leave of two months, and when Celestine stopped working in my house, she was not malingering, she thought the baby's birth was imminent. It wasn't. Weeks went by and no baby arrived. Every so often, I would ask her when this toto was coming and she would look at me with a guileless face and say "Bado."

Bado, the most oft-spoken word in East Africa, means "not yet."

Staff members often give a nickname, based on some personality trait or physical characteristic, to people with whom they have a fair amount of contact. It's a cross between a compliment and an inside joke. Any woman with children automatically gets the title of 'Mama' and, if nothing more clever or personal can be devised, that is followed by the name of her first born child. I was, at least to my face, Mama Jake (which was pronounced Jack, as there is no long 'A' in Swahili). When thinking up a name for Celestine, I considered Mama Godot, but knew I would get more laughs out of bado. That is what I called her: Mama Bado.

By August not only had the baby not arrived, but no one seemed to know when it was actually due. This struck me as most peculiar. How can you not know? I finally asked Celestine if she knew when she got pregnant. She giggled and turned her face to the nearest wall. I asked Jotham the same question, but he didn't seem to know any more than she did. As the summer wore on, 'bado' was all I ever heard.

Jake had arrived in June to spend his summer holiday with me. Having Jake there always made a world of difference. I had someone to talk to and play with and share all that was going on. He and I always had great fun exploring our new 'homeland' and turning small forays into day long safaris. We had all the time in the world, God knows, and would often drive hours just to try out a new pizza place in Muthaiga.

Jake's relationship with the staff was very different from mine. Even sticking to the rules as laid out by Bill Sr., he could get away with far more familiarity than I could. One example of this was Mildred and Jake in the kitchen together. They were a study in culinary ineptitude. Mildred was just barely mastering the basics of cooking and Jake knew nothing at all. He could read a recipe written in English, but that was about the extent of his kitchen expertise. But that didn't slow them up. He was a teenager, after all, and knew everything and Mildred was eager to please and would join in whatever he came up with. Whenever Jake got a craving for Mexican food (and there were no Mexican restaurants in Nairobi at that time), he would corral Mildred into helping him cook up a few taco chips and some salsa.

Once in the kitchen, they would start chopping up kilos of tomatoes, onions and peppers, scattering flour all over the floor and dripping oil on everything. The dough for the chips would be rolled out and fried up. They followed the recipes, or at least they told me they had, but nothing much seemed to come of it all. Nothing you would want to eat anyway. Even though each attempt was tasted by me and summarily rejected, they forged ahead, undaunted. They tried another batch. More dough, more oil, more tomatoes, more very soggy chips. This could go on for hours until Mildred, up to her elbows in the twentieth batch of sticky dough balls would look at Jake and say, "Jack, you don't know." That was her final word. "Jack, you don't know." Mildred's son, Frederick, was Jake's age, and to her Jake was just a kijana *(a younster),* and he "don't know." Jake would feign outrage and tell Mildred how wounded he was that she was abandoning their ship. That would give them both a great laugh and they would give up on the taco chips. Until the next week.

One rainy Sunday in August Mildred came to me for money.

"Madame, mimi nataka shillingi mia moja."

"What do you want a hundred shillings for, Mildred?"

It had been a cold and damp July, and Mildred was going through a spell of ill health. She had been coughing for months, and none of the medicines I had given her seemed to help. As she was preparing to go to church that day, she asked me for an advance on her salary.

Although asking for "loans" and "advances" by ones staff is as common as sundown, it was unusual for Mildred.

"What will you do with this money, Mildred?"

"I want to see the Mzee."

Age is universally respected by the different tribes in Kenya and although mzee means old, it also means wise, respected, and venerable.

"And just nini *(what)*, is this Mzee going to do for you?"

"I will be better, Madame. It is good. Coughing comes too much, now. Too much coughing. He will help me."

"Well, that's mzuri sana *(very good)*. But what is it he is going to do?"

Mildred clung to her beliefs when it came to traditional African medicine. We had already gone through one period of bloodletting, when she was convinced that if she drained the blood from her legs she would be rid of whatever it was that was plaguing her. This was a new idea.

"He will cut me" she said, all trust and belief.

"What? Cut? Cut what?" I shuddered to even contemplate what was going to be "cut." Many body parts that were routinely cut off in Africa, were not even talked about where I came from.

"Wapi? (*Where?*) Just where is this guy going to cut you?"

"Just here. Kidogo tu." She pointed to her throat.

" WHAT? Mildred! What do you mean? He is going to cut your throat?"

I was making all the traditional hand signals that meant throat cutting to me: dragging my finger across my throat.

"Are you mchinga (*crazy?*) You are going to let someone cut your throat?"

"Oh no, Madame." She laughed as if that was just about the funniest thing she had heard all week. "Not like that."

"Well, like what?"

"He will cut. It will be good."

"Yes, I got that, but vipi *(how)*, Mildred? How will he cut?"

No answer. She just laughed. The conversation was over. If Mildred did not want to tell me something, no amount of coercion would induce her to come forth. She would clam up and, if I really pushed, she would become all but deaf. I gave her the one hundred shillings and spent a few moments in silent prayer for Mildred's throat.

That night, as dinner was being served, I inquired about Mildred's visit to the Mzee. When she spoke her voice was clearly strained. "What's the matter with your voice Mildred?"

"Nothing, Madame." she scratched out.

"What do you mean nothing? You sound awful. Mildred, ngoja, *(wait here.)* Mimi rudi sasa tu" *(I'll be right back.)*

Not all that sure I really wanted to look down her throat, I grabbed a flashlight

"Okay, Mildred, open your mouth. Say Ahhhhh."

I pointed the light down her throat and . . . Good Lord, her uvula was gone.

"God Almighty, Mildred, that thing hapana hapa *(is not here.)* What happened?"

"It is not bad, Madame. The Mzee . . . he cut ." Mildred was very calm about all this.

"Cut? How? What do you mean he cut?" I took a deep breath and tried to compose myself.

"How did he cut it? I mean . . . chiga na nini (*with what*) did he cut?"

"Na . . . (*with*) . . . " Big pause. Mildred was searching for the correct English words.

" Sijui . . . (*I don't know,*) Madame." Then she held up her first two fingers in a V and banged them together twice.

"Scissors?" I made the same motions. "Someone cut your uvula off with a scissors?"

"Ndio." (*Yes.*) Obviously. No shock. No surprise. Ndio.

There was not much to say after that. I gave Mildred some asprin, told her how often to take them and, if anything erupted in the night, to come and collect me and I would "sort it out." That seemed to calm the waters—mine, mostly. I was the only one who was upset. Mildred was extremely cool about the whole affair. She appeared to think that this was a perfectly natural thing to have done on the odd Sunday in August.

Mildred was convinced that cutting out her uvula would stop her coughing. "Coughing is finished now." I was not as convinced as she, but I hoped she was right. She was quite sure about it and made her statement, shooting from the hip. But Mildred never minced her words. I thought that an admirable characteristic, for the most part. There was one day that summer, however, when a bit of hedging would have been appreciated.

I had been trying to burn a little pre-cancerous spot off my forehead. I had been told by the dermatologist to put some ointment on it twice a day for three weeks. That would get rid of it. I had been doing just that and, as it became more bloody looking every day, I became more self-conscious about it. It was only the size of a pea, but I was convinced that I was beginning to scare people.

One night at dinner Jake, then a sassy sixteen, was teasing me about it.

"What's that big scab on your forehead, Mom? Oh, sorry. I didn't mean that. It's barely noticeable. Really. You can hardly see it. At least not from far away. Sort of like the two holes in your lip."

This was an old joke. I had two tiny scars on my upper lip, vestiges of the chicken pox. One day when Jake was about three years old, he remarked,

"Do you know how I know it is you coming to the school, Mommy?" His day care center was on the second floor and he was referring to looking out a window and seeing me park my car below and walk into the building.

"No, my darling. How do you know it is me?"

"By those holes in your lip. I see that and I know it is my Mommy."

From two bloody stories up?

We were having this conversation about my forehead when Mildred came into the room. I sought her help. I knew she wouldn't say anything too negative.

"Mildred, Jake says this thing on my head looks terrible. Sura mbaya sana. What do you think? It isn't that bad, is it?"

"Oh, no Madame. It is not bad. It is good."

"Asante, Mildred. You're my main man."

She then looked right at me and smiled her wonderful smile and said, "You know Madame, it is good, because when we do not know who you are, this is how we will know."

Jake started to choke.

"And when you are lost, that hole on your head is how we will find you." She continued to smile sweetly.

Jake fell off his chair laughing.

After a few weeks, not only did Mildred's cough came back, but she started to have other vague ailments as well. She would break out in rashes. "You know Madame, the eedgy comes," she'd tell me scratching at her itchy forearms. "The eedgy comes too much, Madame, too much eedgy." She had been going to the Karen Clinic, the local bastion of quick fixes and not-so-benign neglect, where they handed out either aspirin or malaria pills for every complaint. Mildred, we later figured out, was allergic to sulfa drugs. They gave her the "eedgy." If it wasn't the "eedgy" it was the cough that would not go away or a general weakness. Her joints ached or her wrists became swollen.

"It is hot, Madame. Too much hot." she would tell me, pointing to her joints.

She complained that she couldn't walk or that she didn't want to eat. She was sick increasingly often.

The first thought was AIDS. We had her tested at the Kenyatta National Hospital. Negative. Chest X-rays. Negative. Blood tests, a little anemic, but nothing serious. She listened to my advice, for the most part, and took the mzungu (*white man*), medicine I gave her. She had lost a great deal of weight and was unhappy about it. Africans do not think that thin is beautiful. I advised her to eat more fatty foods and went so far as to buy her some Joe Weider's Body Builders Quick Weight Gain Powder at the health food store.

Then she seemed to pick up. She was stronger, I could see her working in her garden during her hours off, and she put on a few pounds. She told me that it was obvious that she was feeling better by her color. Couldn't I see how less black she was? I could not, but I took her word for it.

"I will be better, Madame. It is good now. I will be better."

I wanted to believe that and so I did.

Graham left Kenya in July. Before I met him he had quarreled with his employer and had threatened to leave if certain things at the balloon launch site were not changed. As nothing had happened, he felt he could not back down. Even with me as an added inducement to staying, he decided to go. We were, by then, spending many hours both on the roads and in the air traveling back and forth between the Mara and Karen. Although the distance we had to contend with was irritating, it put a very romantic spin on it all.

There were no phones in the Mara, and if I wanted to communicate with Graham I had to write him a letter, drive down to Wilson Airport, and put it on one of the Airkenya flights going down to Governor's that day. I always tried to put it into the hands of one of the pilots that knew us both, but that wasn't always possible. I never knew, until he either responded in the same manner or arrived at my door, whether my note had reached him or not. Sometimes my letters ended up in the wrong camp, and only if discovered by another one of the balloon pilots would they get delivered, by vehicle, some time later. "Later" could mean a day or a month. Many never got there at all and left me sitting in Karen wondering. Sometimes they got there an hour after I handed them to the pilot. Anticipation was a good part of the fun, but never knowing was a larger part of the frustration. How I felt about my love affair with Graham was very much how I felt about my love affair with Africa. Both were romantic, thrilling, and difficult—all at the same time. But, so far, neither was ever dull.

When Graham left Kenya that July, he told me that he had things to attend to in the UK. All my inquiring as to just what those 'things' were did not get me much more of an answer. I did press him about whether he was going to be seeing his wife, and just what form that "seeing" would take. The idea of him slipping back into his marital bed was very distasteful. It would have been one thing had I gone into this relationship knowing that he returned to his wife's bed for conjugal visits every so often. If I had accepted such an arrangement from the outset, then I would have had to live with it. But that was not what I had understood. Graham had always assured me that he and his wife were separated, and that after many years of living in different countries, they were no longer "together" in a marital sense. I had no reason to disbelieve him, but more to the point, I wanted to believe him.

He told me that he would definitely be coming back to Africa, but when I asked when that would be, all he would say was that it could be two weeks or two months. I remember thinking that it was odd that he took almost all of his things with him, including every audio-cassette he owned and a large ship's model he had made. Watching him pack up gave me a funny feeling in the pit of my stomach, but I chose to hang onto the things that I wanted to believe and pushed any nagging doubts out of my mind. He left the day before my birthday and before leaving, presented me with an armful of my favorite color roses and a little gold ring. I cried a good deal the day he left, but I told myself that he loved me. He would be back.

With all this high romance going on and my life in Kenya becoming easier and more enjoyable, I had all but made up my mind to stay. For one more year? I changed my lease arrangement with His Excellency to one that was renewable on a three-month basis. The battle contesting my mother's Will had finally been settled and I was beginning to think about getting a house of my own, and to bringing some of my own things over to furnish it.

Shortly after my mother died, her house in South Carolina was sold, but due to this law suit, her every possession, and there were a great many of those, had been put into storage. When I asked her lawyers what was to become of all that, now that her Will had finally been probated, they informed me that if I wanted any of her furniture, I had better come and get it before everything was auctioned off. Her Will also provided funds for Jake's tuition. That made my finances a great deal easier and it would allow me to stay on in Kenya for another year.

The other big event of that July was discovering that Katherine, Mildred's thirteen-year old niece, her brother Ernest's daughter, was pregnant. Unplanned pregnancies are not big news in Kenya, but what made this one notable was that Katherine, who was painfully shy, did not have a boyfriend calling on her. She was living with Mildred at my house and I knew that she had only had her first period that summer. She was not about to tell anyone who the father was. There was some discussion that it might have been Mildred's son, Frederick, as he was visiting Mildred during the period in March that we suspected this had occurred. Neither Mildred nor I could believe that. Katherine's father was sent for. I was told that, if necessary, he would beat the truth out of her.

One afternoon, while visiting the Winters for my daily tea-time chat, Bill Sr. announced that his cook, Illiab, had told him that there was incest at my house. It seemed that every one in town knew of Katherine's predicament and everyone, with the exception of me, thought that Daniel was the father. He had been around until about mid-March, but Katherine was his niece, I repeated that to Bill Sr.

He had been told that Katherine was Daniel's daughter. I raced home to speak with Mildred.

By the time I had heard about Katherine and Daniel, so had Mildred. She told me that Ernest had shown up with the chief and they had made Katherine confess. They found out that not only was Daniel the father, but that he had raped her. He had poured vodka (mine, no doubt) into a Fanta, gotten her drunk and then raped her. Mildred also told me that had the father been Frederick, a minor, and Katherine's cousin, he would have been banished from the family forever. As it was Daniel, and no blood relation, the family could do no more than to have him thrown into jail. Katherine would be sent back to her home in Kitale, and the new baby would be sold. Katherine, a fallen woman at age fourteen, would be married off to whoever would have her. The sooner, the better. The punishment was less suited to the crime than to the criminal. In this very male oriented society, females took the greater fall.

Katherine was sent away to a home for unwed mothers. All my pleading with Mildred to get Katherine an abortion had been in vain, they are not legal in Kenya. (This is when she told me about the ice cubes and herbs.) Several months later, however, Katherine miscarried. She had probably gotten her hands on some kali dawa (*strong medicine)* supplied by someone more knowledgeable and experienced in these matters, and had caused herself to abort. Mildred was pleased about this.

"You know Madame, this is good thing. Katherine will not find baby now. Baby is kwisha *(finished)."*

I agreed with her that it probably was for the best, that baby was unwanted.

Mildred corrected me.

"It is not good because Katherine did not want, Madame. It is a good because baby had spots. "

"Spots? What do you mean spots?"

"Ndio. Spots." She patted herself all over and said it again ndoa ndoa, (*spots.*)

"You mean like a leopard has spots? How can a baby have spots, Mildred?"

"The baby it was mbaya sana. It had too much spots."

And that was all she would tell me.

eleven

Carpets in Kiambu

As 1988 was coming to an end, I began to seriously entertain the idea of staying on in Kenya. Were I to do that, what would it take to make my life there better? One thing I knew I wanted was a house of my own with my things in it. With my mother's Will finally probated, it stood as she had written it, this was possible. I also wanted Graham to come back. But I knew that just having a man around would not solve my problems. Not only had men never solved anything before, but I didn't want my reason for staying in Africa to be because I was hankering to be Mrs. Somebody. What I really needed was something to do, a job. Loneliness had been a constant for me in Kenya, and I had tried to get used to it, but having nothing to occupy the hours, or my mind, was becoming intolerable. I also hoped that having a job would show the local folk that I was not just a "two year wonder," another American on an extended safari in Kenya. I wanted people to know that I was going to stay. I wanted to be a part of the community.

Finding work in a country like Kenya is not a simple task. With the enormous unemployment problems, the government is not all that anxious to hand out work permits to American ladies. Unless, of course, some of their American financial good fortune is going to benefit Kenya. If one is in a position to bring hard currency, in my case American dollars, into the country, doors do swing open and the government can become almost solicitous. If one is also in a position to offer employment to a fair number of people, one will find that the skids are greased just that much quicker. With the money my mother had left me freed up, I was in a position to do both of these things. That is what I did: I bought a little business: Kufuma Carpets.

Kufuma, "to weave" in Swahili, was a small enterprise that made woolen carpets, and I had known of it's existence for years. Although at one time it was a single company, owned and run by Joy Mayer, an Australian woman, it had since been divided into two separate entities. One part resided at Lewa Downs, my friends, the Craigs', ranch, up near Nanyuki. I had visited there many times, seen their operation and had even purchased a small carpet. The other half had landed in Kiambu, a suburb on the other side of Nairobi. The carpets were very popular among the tourists as well as the ex-patriot community and they had always had are reputation for quality.

Just before Christmas of 1988, I heard from Billy, in one of his quick swings through Karen, that the Kiambu section was soon to be for sale. Another American expatriate, married to a safari colleague of Billy's, owned that half. The asking price was relatively small. It was going on the market because the owners little girl, suffering from multiple forms of epilepsy, was about to start school and the time spent running Kufuma was now needed to care for this child's special educational needs.

I had a knack for needlework, and had even done some weaving when Jake was a baby. Armed with that slim resume, I considered myself totally suited to taking on this business. My eagerness to have something to do filled in any gaps in the rational consideration process.

Bill Sr. and I sat for hours and discussed every aspect of this proposed venture. Bill, of course, dispelled endless advice on every aspect of what I was to do. He did, I was relieved to hear, concede that it was a good idea, but he didn't stop there. He already knew how much I should pay for it, how I should run it, what my market was going to be, what I should charge for each carpet, how I was going to arrange my days, what company vehicle I should purchase, how and when I could expand, what products would be suitable for that expansion, and how I would deal with all the predictable labor problems. He also made it very clear to me, as he did in most instances, that I was incapable of doing this alone. I was an American, and therefore, on top of being just plain ignorant, certainly too liberal in my attitude towards the Africans and far too inexperienced in doing business in Kenya. Or probably anywhere else for that matter. But, he was quick to add, I didn't have to worry, because he would be right there to help me.

Listening to him made my head spin, as it often did, but I did find the idea of running a business in Africa all by myself a bit daunting. I was willing to listen to his advice. Initially I wasn't quite as convinced as he that I couldn't possibly cope on my own, but the more he listed all the things that I needed to think about or do, the more overwhelming it all seemed. This situation was very reminiscent of that first, very shaky day in Africa some eighteen months before. And it occurred all too frequently in my dealings with the Big Bwana.

We got in touch with the owner and made plans to go out to Kiambu the next week to look things over. There was, however, some miscommunication, she forgot what day January First was, and no one was there when we arrived. All we could do was walk around and peer in the windows. I was building up quite a head of steam over all this and being shut out just further whetted my appetite. The more I thought about it, the more I wanted to do it. When the owner finally showed up some days later, I was pawing the ground. I took a cursory glance at the books and signed on the line.

With that settled, and my stay in Kenya definitely extended, I wanted to find a house. Bill Sr. had mentioned to me many times that were I ever serious about staying in Kenya, he would sell me his house. He was forever going on about leaving Kenya, either plotting his escape to South Africa or other unlikely spots such as Crete. Sometimes he was going with Barbara. Sometimes not. But no matter what his mood, the work he did or planned to do on his property in Karen never stopped. He planted trees, he added rooms, he built bigger storage spaces for all Billy's safari gear. This did not seem to be the behavior of someone who was about to sell his house. But, he assured me, he would sell it to me when I was ready.

I was ready. And on my way to the States to settle accounts with my mother's lawyers. I would take out a loan to buy the house, collect the things I wanted shipped over, and be back in February. I would have my new little business and a beautiful new house and a greatly improved life in Kenya.

I never did buy the Winter's house, although I very much wanted to. If you ask me what happened when I returned from the States, I would tell one story. If you asked Bill Sr., or even better, Barbara, they would tell you another. Suffice it to say that the end of "the deal" was acrimonious and painful enough to sever my relationship with Bill Sr. for the next three years. Barbara didn't speak to me until many years after that and Billy was caught in the middle. He and I did manage to remain friends, but it was difficult for him. Now, all these years later, all has been forgiven. We do not, to this day, agree about whom did what or who said what or what actually happened, but we have chosen to forgive and forget. We kissed and made up a shortly before I left Africa and that is all that matters.]

The only point, relative to this story, is that when the deal fell through and my relationship with Bill Sr. was suddenly gone, I found myself alone again. And probably more alone than I had ever been in Africa. The Winters had been my life line ever since I arrived there. Without them I was, or I felt at the time, utterly stranded. I had come to totally rely on Bill Sr. I looked to him for advice and friendship. He had fostered my dependence, but I had certainly allowed it to happen. When this problem with the house occurred, it was as if I had been expelled, once again, from my own family. I had been thrown out. And beyond the hurt that I felt, there was fear. I had just bought a new business, I had told President Moi's people I was leaving his house, I had a container full of my mother's furniture on it's way over to Kenya, specifically chosen for that particular house. And it had all gone wrong. I had no idea what I was going to do. But cry.

For about a week. And then, somewhere in the second week, I stopped crying and I got angry. Angry is better than sad, it gives you more energy and it gives you more power. And I was mad.

"So, you think I can't do this without you?" I shouted at Bill Sr. in my head, night after sleepless night. "That I am lost without you to guide me? You think I can't cope on my own? I am just a stupid, helpless, American woman who can't figure out what side of the road to bloody drive on. You think I can't do anything without you. Yeah, well, watch this." My anger at Bill turned to defiance and defiance gave me courage. Once brave, I felt strong again.

I got back on the horse.

Of course, there is the argument that I didn't have one helluva lot of options. The clock was ticking and I had no choice but to deal with what was before me. (I prefer the image of myself as brave and strong.)

Having no place to put Kufuma was a fairly serious problem. I had planned on putting it in the storage units that Bill had just built, but that was clearly out. I didn't have the time to sit around and rethink this, nor could I get out of it. The papers had gone through and like it or not, I now owned a little carpet-making business in Africa. This realization gave me a slight fit of nerves, but once again, having no way out cut short the time I could spend worrying about it. The minute I took legal possession of Kufuma, I was on duty. I went from the life of long lunches and not too much to do all day, to being shot out of a cannon.

I was supposed to spend the month of February with the previous owner (and Bill Sr. of course) learning the rudiments of carpet making. She didn't seem to have much interest in all that and after giving me about two afternoons of her time, she left on a safari to the coast. I was pointed in the right direction, told "Here you go kid, have fun," and cut loose. I knew nothing about making carpets, nothing about running a business, and least of all about doing either of the above in Africa. But I was, for some unknown reason, full of hope and high spirits. Battling my own demons and putting on a show of bravery in the face of what I was sure would have been Bill Sr.'s doubts gave me confidence. It was way out of proportion to what I knew how to do, but I felt unstoppable. I believed that I could do it and I charged ahead.

Kiambu was about as far to the northeast of Nairobi as Karen was to the southwest and in those early days I drove out there every day to attend to whatever it was I needed to attend to. Kiambu was primarily a tea-and coffee-growing area but the lack of development in the surrounding area made it feel more rural than Karen. Kufuma shared space with a coffee grower in a large warehouse, called a "go-down." (I have no idea why they were called 'go-downs' unless it used to be that one had to "go down" to get to them.) It was set in the middle of a tea plantation. Kufuma was called a factory. Given the size and scope of the enterprise it would have been called a "workshop" in the States, or maybe even a "studio," but in Kenya, Kufuma was a factory.

The first thing I wanted to do was to get acquainted with the people who now worked for me. The previous owner had introduced me to everyone, pointing out the various strengths and weaknesses in their work, but I couldn't remember anything she had told me. There were about fifteen weavers and ten spinners. Everyone, except Ruth, an

Akamba, was from the Kikuyu tribe. Spinning had traditionally been a uniquely male occupation, but two women had crept into the Kufuma ranks. The weavers, all women, ranged in age from eighteen years old, invariably carrying a toto or two, to the real old mamas, the Mzees. (I later found out that these ancient specimens were about my age.) The more senior members had been working for Kufuma for over twelve years. Along with all the babies slung on their mother's backs, there was also a small group of three year olds running around the coffee bean drying racks. I very quickly slapped the smallest ones into rubber pants in an effort to put a stop to the little puddles I was forever stepping in and the older children gained a soccer ball and a tire swing hung from the rafters of the building. Those new toys, along with the yarn dolls I had learned to make in grade school, made me a big hit with the children, while the adults found my diapering efforts hilarious.

Aside from playing arts and crafts with the children, most of my time was spent trying to figure it out what I was doing. I had no experience with such trivial matters as "keeping books" and the social skills I needed to work with the Africans in this situation was something I had never even thought about. Of course I had planned on Bill Sr. being there to lead me through all of this, but left on my own it was a very different arrangement. The fact that the whole thing didn't totally self-destruct within a few weeks was due solely to my employees knowing exactly what they were about. They kept on doing what they had been doing for years, and allowed me to come up to speed as quickly as I could without wreaking too much havoc on everything.

What I lacked in experience I made up for in enthusiasm. I have always had an inordinate amount of energy, and I was pouring all of it into getting Kufuma back up on its feet. I was so excited about finally having something productive to think about and do that I could hardly wait to get out of bed in the morning. Doing something that was actually interesting had my long-dormant creative juices working overtime. The more I did, the more confidence I gained, and the further I was willing to stick my neck out the next time. I drove up to the factory every day revved up and ready to put everything I had into this new enterprise. I usually arrived in Kiambu bearing small candies and bottles of cough medicine for the children (they all had colds that spring), and boxes of tissues—part of my futile effort to discourage the mothers from wiping those little runny noses on their clothing.

I had been told many times by Bill Sr. that I should never trust anyone who worked for me, but I had been fortunate in my house staff, and so I ignored that piece of advice. Thinking that I was right and Bill was wrong was especially satisfying at that particular point in time, and it encouraged me to strike even more of what he had said from the record.

Up to this point my experience with the Africans that I employed, and Mildred was indeed the leader of that pack, had been quite positive. There had been the trouble with Daniel, but he had been the exception to the rule and something else I could lay at Bill's feet. I had no real reason, other than Bill's dire prognostications, to doubt anyone. I approached the Kufuma people with the best intentions. I was going to do all I could for the factory and, by extention, the workers, and I expected them to do so as well. In many ways, it was quite maternal. Along with being their employer, I was also taking these people under my motherly wing.

My friends in the USA have told me many times that they found the European's attitude towards the Africans patronizing on a good day and bigoted on a bad. I felt the same way when I first visited Kenya. What I eventually came to understand is that, Kenya is not the United States. Bill Sr. kept trying to tell me that, but as simple as it sounds to say, "Things are different there, culturally different," the extent of the statement is hard to grasp until you are dealing with it daily. It pervades everything from the brand of soap powder you buy to the relationships between the races. There are long held attitudes and feelings that are not going to change just because one American arrives and announces "There is inequality at play, here." The different races behave towards each other in ways that Americans find disturbing. But it is the way things have been for a long time, is built into the fabric of life, and is probably the way it will be for some time to come.

One example of this relationship is that Africans often look to their European employers as a mother figure. I was called not only Mama Jake, but also "Mother." I was told by many of the Kufuma people on numerous occasions that I was their "mother" and that they looked to me to take care of them. This situation became far more apparent when I had forty people looking to me for help and support than when there had been only the four of my house staff. Having been raised in very comfortably in the USA, it wasn't that big a leap from lending a hand to the homeless or sending money to the Red Cross to feeling I could help my employees. When I took over at Kufuma, I wanted to create a good product and sell carpets, I wanted Kufuma to be profitable (it was in a financial hole when I bought it.) But I very quickly got caught up in helping the people who worked there. It was probably more important to me than making tons of money. I didn't need tons of money, but I needed to feel useful.

I could make things happen that these people could not. I led a life of privilege, especially in Africa, and they had almost nothing. They struggled for food and shelter, clothing was barely a consideration and getting their children educated, even rudimentarily, was something most would never be able to accomplish. (Everyone had to pay school fees in Kenya. The sums were miniscule by American standards, one hundred dollars a year, but that's a great deal if you only make forty dollars a month.) Most monthly wages immediately went to pay off debts: to the butcher, the land lord, the man at the duka. This left almost nothing to pay the school fees that had to be handed over up front, for the many children everyone had. I could, at the very least, provide these people with a decent job, decent wages, and, considering there were, at that time, twenty five of them, whatever other small help that was possible.

The one young woman at Kufuma who stood out from the very beginning was Mary Wambui. She stepped forward one day when I was trying to make myself understood and announced that she spoke English. She would help me. The next time I looked for an answer, there she was again. She was calm and steady, and very bright. She was one of the weavers, and not much more than twenty five, but as her English was quite good, she had fallen into the role of Kufuma's salesperson. Whenever we had a visitor to the factory, few and far between in those early months, Mary would take care of them. She showed them around and helped them to either pick something out or to place an order. If someone wanted to order a carpet, the cost was figured by the square centimeter. Mary would listen to the customer's specifications and then quote the correct price. She could even add in percentages when we were finally able to raise our prices. She did all the calculations in her head.

My next task was to drum up more business. Not knowing what to do, I did what anyone who has watched enough Judy Garland movies would do: I put on 'a show.' I hired a big, decidedly ugly room at the Sarit Center, a "mall" near Nairobi, and chose a date several months in advance when we would exhibit and sell our carpets. I knew by then that no one knew where Kufuma had disappeared to after Joy Mayers divided it up, and I planned on handing out maps to the factory. I asked Mary Wambui if we could have one hundred carpets ready by the designated time. After some quick calculations, she pronounced it possible and the starting gun went off.

A Kufuma carpet was a labor-intensive product. The wool came straight from the sheep to be carded by hand. Carding is a process where the raw wool is combed between two wire bristled brushes. This lines up the fibers of the wool and makes it easier to feed them into the spinning wheel. It is filthy work and takes a fair amount of muscle. While the fibers are being combed, all the leftover pieces of sheep dung that haven't already been sorted out fall into the carder's lap. The raw and greasy wool is then spun into a two ply strand on a foot pumped spinning wheel and then wound into two-kilo hanks. Only the colors that came from the sheep were used. What never ceased to amaze me was that out of a three hundred kilo bale that looked and smelled as if it were more dung than wool, the Kufuma spinners could pull out up to eight different shades. These would range from ivory, as white as it ever got, to an almost black brown, with greys, browns, oatmeals and beiges falling in between. I could never tell, looking at the wool in its raw state, what it would look like when cleaned up, but the spinners could. They could also blend colors or repeat a certain shade over again if necessary. They produced beautiful, soft colors consistently.

The spun woolen hanks were washed with cakes of basic kitchen soap in a cement pit and then put in the sun to dry. Finally in the hands of the weavers, the wool was knotted into thick pile carpets or woven into a flat weave style. As each carpet was made individually, the size could be determined as the warp was being put on the loom. Our only size restriction was that our largest carpet was 12x15 feet.

The looms were Ethiopian in design, there is no history of weaving in Kenya, and they resembled an upright letter "A." There was no shuttle, no treadles, and the work was all done by hand. The warp, the backbone of any weaving, was fashioned from the thick double-ply wool making Kufuma carpets extremely thick and durable. They were practically indestructible. The designs, at that point anyway, were mostly geometric or borrowed from the traditional patterns used in the kiondos, the baskets the Kikuyu tribes people wove. It all added up to a product that was rugged, vaguely ethnic looking, and yet rather luxurious, in a pioneer country kind of way. I was about to add some new designs and hoped these would make our product a bit more sophisticated.

My shared office space in Kiambu, one room under a corrugated tin roof, was shared with a fellow named Fred Kunguru. He was a tall, angular Kikuyu who had previously been hired to put silk screened designs on tee shirts. Fred was fluent in English, had a high cackle of a laugh, and a great imagination. He was also talented, willing to try almost anything, and he put long hours into his work. His dream was to have his own art studio and to be able to support and educate the eight children he had scattered around Kenya. He often dressed in a beret, a smock covered with splattered paints and a long colorful scarf around his neck. He looked like an African Pepe Le Pew. I saw him everyday and he became a solid fixture in my life in Kiambu. He was also a great source of encouragement to me. As I tried new designs or dragged everyone through my new ways of doing things, Fred always told me that what I was doing with Kufuma was quality work, and that quality work would always sell. Just hang in there.

twelve

A Settler's Cottage

While all this activity was going on up in Kiambu I had begun my search for another house in Karen. The first thing I did was to scan the messages pinned on the door down at the dukas. I had found Kipele that way, and a lawn mower, maybe I would find a house. I also put the word out that I was looking. Karen is a very tightly knit little community, and the better houses always went by word of mouth. Which is precisely why no one had ever heard of the one I found. But I didn't know that then and when I saw the ad for this particular house in the Nairobi Standard, I called Mr. Mwai, the real estate agent, and ventured out to see it.

Located less than two kilometers from the Karen dukas, I was just through the gates and barely halfway up the driveway when I knew I had found exactly what I was looking for. If I had drawn it on paper, it couldn't have been more perfect. It was quaint and slightly dilapidated and I could see Denys Finch-Hatton sitting on the back veranda. Low and long and made of white stone, it had a roof that was tiled in cedar shingles and sagged noticeably in several places. It barely supported a center chimney. It did not escape my notice that this house was a smaller, and considerably less tidy version of the Winter's house. There was a massive fig tree in the middle of the driveway and several jacarandas in the front yard spreading purple blossoms all over the lawn. Before the car was even parked I was humming the theme from *Out of Africa* and thinking that maybe I had found a suitable replacement.

Mr. Mwai led me around the grounds. As we walked through the upper part of the property, about two and a half acres of cultivated, although overgrown, gardens, I was delighted to see that all the best Kenyan flora were represented. There was a bottlebrush tree, a profusion of day lilies, and many African agapanthi. The scent coming off of the many yesterday, today, and tomorrow bushes was heady. In the back, there was an open expanse of lawn surrounded by more flowering trees. There was a nandi flame and several more jacarandas and two enormous podocarpi. The area was littered with small outbuildings, but they were primarily off to the side. Mwai informed me that one had been a shelter for goats and one was a storage shed. There were also several dog-houses with some very thin-looking animals chained to it.

As we walked down the flagstone path leading to the hedge that separated the two sections of the compound, Mr. Mwai pointed out all the more desirable features. He seemed to feel that the large patch of sukuma weeki, a spinach type green, was a big selling point. The name means "push the week along," it's the local version of Tuna Helper. The bottom two and a half acres were growing wild with tall grasses. There was, of course, a fair amount of maize, another staple of the local diet, but what caught my eye were the stables and the side access road that led back out to the main road. These sheds had previously housed the owners cows, (no Kenyan can be happy, nor feel prosperous, regardless of how much money he has in the bank, without owning at least half a dozen cows.) I could put Kufuma there. The access road would allow the wageni to visit the factory without having to come through my house. The wheels in my brain shifted into a higher gear.

It wouldn't break my heart to give up my daily trek back and forth from Kiambu, a forty minutes drive from the factory to Karen. I was forever getting stuck in the Nairobi rush hour traffic or the mud in Kiambu. Whenever it rained the drive through the coffee fields would wash away. I had already spent many afternoons digging my car out of the mud. I also felt that Karen would be more accessible to Nairobi and yet not too far from Muthaiga. Muthaiga housed most of the diplomatic people and was right next to Kiambu, but Karen was the more popular shopping venue. It had the Horseman, in those days the only restaurant in which a lady would care to lunch, and a few other shops as well. I thought those very ladies would add to Kufuma's drop in business, and we might be able to encourage the tourists to come by after their requisite visit to the Karen Blixen Museum. There was also the small matter that Kiambu had almost no phone service. There was a phone in the Kufuma "office," it just never worked. Karen was incrementally better in that department. I was mulling over all of these factors as Mwai and I headed back up towards the house.

As we walked up the path, Mwai pointed out one more feature that, unbeknownst to him, practically sealed the deal. This property had a borehole, it's own well. I never gave water a second thought when I lived in the States, but not having enough is a serious problem in Kenya. When the rains fail, as they do every few years, the crops are ruined and animals, both domestic and wild, die by the thousands. If the reservoirs are low, the town councils can take it upon themselves to cut off the flow of water to any given town without prior notice. Karen seemed to be on everyone's hit list. When the city cut off "the mains" the whole town could go without water for weeks. What little there was had to be meted out carefully, and the solutions to these shortages were many and varied. Some of my friends took to bathing in rounds. One tub full of water would have to serve the whole family: first dip went to the Mama, followed by the children in descending age order, and what was left was used to flush the toilets. Papa was sent to the club for a shower.

If you had your own borehole, however, the supply would be almost endless. Every so often the water table below the ground would drop too low and the pump would shut down, but that would never last more than a day. I wasn't too thrilled with leaving toilets unflushed, I was not quite the bush woman some others were, but to go without water at Kufuma meant unhappy workers. No water meant no washed wool, and no washed wool meant no weaving done. And that meant no money earned for those "dry" days. The fact that there was a borehole on this new property was a major factor in my deciding to buy it.

Having ambled back up to the house, I asked to see the inside. Mr. Mwai looked at me as if I had a screw loose and quickly informed me that the owner would not permit it. I couldn't understand that. When people in New York are looking at real estate they are at liberty to open your medicine cabinets and poke around in your refrigerator. Not so in Kenya. There were two reasons for this: one I understood rather quickly and the other I didn't figure out until four years later.

Several days later I returned with an architect for another look around. This time, the reason for denying me access to the house was glaringly obvious: the interior was a disaster. It was, quite literally, falling apart. The tiles were crumbling off the bathroom walls and the holes in the roof of the master bedroom were big enough to drop a large dog through. The very low ceilings were stained in ever-expanding brown circles by the many years of constant leaks. The press-board was peeling into shreds. The smell of mildew had my sinuses in full revolt. The kitchen hadn't had a coat of paint since it was first built, probably fifty years, and the hallways resembled a rabbit warren. The whole place was dark and damp and depressing.

I looked about, pretending to be non-committal, but was secretly delighted. I had renovated several apartments in the States and I knew this would work. And the challenge was irresistible. I already loved the land, thought the location to be ideal, was sure the stables would be perfect for Kufuma, knew the borehole would save me many problems, and now had the added fun of a full scale renovation. Driving back to Moi's house that afternoon I was in better spirits than I had been in since I had been back from New York. My desire to jump in and tackle things that should probably be left well enough alone was back in full force. I took that to be a good sign.

The other reason for not viewing the interior of the house was something I didn't understand until I was leaving Kenya. I was shocked at that time, to find that none of the imported tiles I had so lovingly put in my kitchen nor the brass bathroom fixtures and fancy door knobs for which I had risked a jail term smuggling through Kenya Customs, added one shilling to the selling price of my house. The value of property in Kenya is based solely on the answers to the following questions: What is the acreage? What type of soil is there? Is there water? And can the land be subdivided? The low value placed on the actual dwelling stems from the old Kenyan ways of doing things. Temporary houses, or more likely mud huts, were not what gave a property its value. Fertile land which could be used to grow crops, raise cattle and divide up among your offspring, did.

I knew none of that then, and I am sure it wouldn't have mattered if I had. I was convinced that this little "settler's cottage" was going to be the house of my dreams. I did take one piece of advice and brought out an architect, an Asian gentleman named Bhagwant Grewel, to give me a more local opinion on the feasibility of the renovation. He neglected to tell me that almost no one in Kenya does large scale renovations. It is much easier and cheaper to just build from scratch. But that wouldn't have mattered either. I was stuck on this idea and I was going ahead with it.

Where was Graham during all this? He was in England selling his flat, or he was in Spain importing a gyro-copter, or he was in Switzerland flying balloons over the Alps making commercials for a candy company. He called every so often, but those calls always ended up with me howling at him in protest of his long absence. He had many excuses for why he hadn't returned. As much as I complained, he always managed to talk me out of burning his picture and forever eliminating his name from my vocabulary. I missed him and I wanted him to come back to Africa. He said he missed me too and would be there as soon as he could. Just not quite yet. I particularly didn't like that he was in Spain, but chose to believe him when he said that he and his wife were never there at the same time. Love is, indeed, blind.

In May, however, we managed to make plans to see each other. I was going up to London for a week of R and R. That was about all the time I dared be away at that point. Graham said he would meet me there and we would go off to the country for a few days. I was anxious to see him again and tell him all about my projects in Kenya. My life had changed dramatically since he left and I was happy to let him know that I hadn't shriveled up and died because he left town. I wanted him to come back, but I didn't need him to.

Graham and I spent several days driving around England and Wales. We stayed in old inns and funny B & Bs. We walked down twisted little lanes and drank beer in postcard pubs. One afternoon we had a picnic of champagne and fish and chips in the middle of a field under a threatening sky. The rain came and drenched us both, but we continued to sit there and take pictures of each other in the rain. It was spring and the land was green and the trees were in full bloom. It was a most romantic time. I flew back to Kenya with Graham's sworn promise to follow as soon as he could. I was mollified, again choosing to believe everything he said. I returned to Karen ready to throw myself back into Kufuma, forgiving Graham his every sin and putting all my doubts about his honesty and very suspect fidelity behind me.

thirteen

Sleights of Hand

I walked into the factory one day and realized that I didn't like the majority of our carpets. I looked at stacks of them rolled up in a corner and noticed that they were all dark in color and unimaginative in design. We needed something new. And we needed them in time for the upcoming show.

After an enthusiastic attempt to come up with new designs, or at least thinking about it a great deal, I ran into a slight snag: I didn't know how. Facing a blank piece of graph paper for several nights didn't get me too far and so I asked Mary Wambui for help. She sat down and showed me how to do it. All Kufuma designs were put onto graph paper with each square representing, vertically, a single knot, covering, horizontally, two warp threads. It took me awhile to get this straight, but Mary was her steady and thorough self and baby-sat me through the teaching process.

I played around with various motifs, but finally settled on some primitive animal designs. Borrowing the basic ideas from what few books I had, or could be purchased in Nairobi bookstores, I altered them to fit a carpet. Whereas I found my animal designs whimsical and amusing, the Kufuma people found them incomprehensible. I had taken it for granted than anyone who was born and raised in Kenya would certainly know what a rhinoceros looked like, but most of these people had never seen a rhino or a hippopotamus. Wild animals didn't roam around in Kiambu, at least not in 1988, and these folks didn't spend a lot of their time hanging out with the tourists in game parks. When I further confused things by altering the shape of the actual animal, adding a fanciful tail or tongue, it became unrecognizable. I had to explain to everyone what the different animals were and why I had altered them. That led to further discussions as to why I thought it was funny and what is, after all, humor. Mary Wambui was the only one there who seemed to be laughing with and not at me.

The other problem that popped up as soon as the actual weaving began was that my new designs were much too intricate. I had worked on a Swedish loom, and I had some expertise in needlepoint, but both those types of weaving bore little or no resemblance to what was done at Kufuma. Needlepoint designs are rendered on graph paper, but that is where the similarity ends. But to me, a square was a square and I made my animal designs like a needlepoint canvas. Although they were too complicated, no one wanted to tell the new owner that. Rather than insult me or, more likely, stop production, the senior weavers set about finding a way to make it happen. I should have noticed that it took weeks to finish what, based on it's size, should have been a relatively quick carpet, but I really had no idea. I just applauded the results when each one was completed. The other by product of all that frantic weaving was that everyone's salary kept going up. Kufuma weavers were paid for how many square inches they wove each week, the spinners were paid by the kilo, and my new designs took up a lot of time and a lot of wool. As we approached the show in June, everyone was in high spirits.

In the following years we did many more designs, all of which were far less difficult. There were hotel logos and people's signatures, there was even a photograph of a warthog, and they all sold quite well. But those first design attempts were my favorites. Should you ever happen to be in Keekorock Lodge in the Maasai Mara, look at the dining room walls. Those are our animal carpets hanging there!

Jake arrived back in Kenya just in time for the exhibition on June sixteenth. He designed the new maps on the computer he had brought with him, and then lent me a hand carting all the necessary gear down to Sarit Center. We had decided to put a live demonstration in the middle of the room. We set up two looms, resting back to back, and several spinners with wheels and carding combs and all the attendant mess. It was a bit on the rough and ready side, but it was attention getting. Even if we didn't sell many carpets, we could at least hand out our maps.

The so-called exhibition hall, on the second floor of the Sarit Center, was a vast, florescent lit, decidedly homely space. But then again the entire Sarit Center was decidedly homely. It was, at that time, Nairobi's only "Mall," but funds had run short and it had never been finished properly. It looked as if it were still under construction. What lights there were, flickered constantly and ramps had been installed, as well as staircases, because there had been no money left for elevators. I think the exhibition hall was just a utilization of whatever space was left over on the second floor. Fearing that even with our one hundred carpets spread all over the walls and floor, we would still look lost, I did what I could to cut the space down with some moveable partitions. We took up as much of the floor as possible with the spinning and weaving exhibition. By the time we opened our doors, I was satisfied with our presentation. Mary Wambui was there to help me sell the carpets and take as many orders as we could.

The show lasted four days and was surprisingly successful. We sold a great number of carpets, took even more orders, and handed out hundreds of maps. It was, however, painful to stand around for eight hours a day answering the same questions over again. By Sunday afternoon, when we headed back out to Kiambu, I had no idea what I had said to whom or how many times. Although I can't say that I ever enjoyed those exhibitions, the first one certainly helped me learn the ropes. For four days, I had been asked every question, idiotic or otherwise, that anyone could possibly come up with about carpets. Of course, following Mary Wambui around with a tape recorder would have been all I needed to do, but this had been my crash course. Most of what I did not know on Thursday, I had learned by Sunday.

For the next month, there was a steady stream of wageni pouring into the factory. They all arrived with Jake's map clutched in their hands, and business took a decided turn for the better. I had hotels calling me up to place large orders for safari camps and lodges. Our stock carpets practically walked out the door. By July, we had so many orders that we had to double our monthly order of wool. Jake was spending his daylight hours on the computer, putting all the carpet designs on electronic graph paper. He had been using a computer since he was nine years old and knew exactly what he was doing. I was a total neophyte and found the whole process frustrating and intimidating and threatened, hourly, to throw the monitor out the second story window. Jake more than earned his keep that summer.

By the end of July, my son and I were driving around delivering the completed orders and collecting large wads of cash in return. I had never been handed cash for something I had created before, certainly not large bundles of it, and Jake and I were very pleased with ourselves. One of the significant positives about doing business in a place like Kenya is that you don't have to be a financial wizard, or have eternally deep pockets to make a success of things. A little effort and moderate ingenuity go a long way. It also helps that the amount of money expended, as "start up cost" is small compared to what that same kind of enterprise would cost in the States. As business climbed and our bank account began to edge into the black, everyone was happy. That's when I announced that we were going to move the whole operation to Karen.

The process of actually buying the house was well under way. Bhagwant had agreed with me that my little shack was indeed a diamond in the rough. (Of course, he would have been one big fool not to take on this extensive renovation.) While he was preparing the preliminary drawings of the work to be done, I was trying to get the owner, Mr. Boniface Mathenge, to agree to a selling price. He would not pay the slightest attention to me. Neither Mr. Mwai nor Mr. Mathenge would talk to me about money. The problem was that I was a woman and they were African men and they simply would not talk to a woman about such a weighty and traditionally "male" matter as a property transaction. They understood that it was my money, they knew that there was no "Mr. Atwood" back in the United States from whom they needed to get the real Okay. They just couldn't bring their chauvinist selves to talk to me about it.

After several frustrating and, to my liberated American mind, insulting attempts to address this issue, I asked my British, well spoken, three-piece-suited friend David Duff for help. Bill Sr. had introduced me to David in my early days in Kenya. Despite his extremely proper demeanor, he was enormous fun. The three of us had spent some merry afternoons out in the bush on improptu picnics and lingering over long lunches. We once killed an entire evening, and several bottles of wine, making up bawdy limericks about young William's quasi-famous American safari clients.

David had become a good friend of mine and was now going to

stand in as my paterfamilias. When he walked into Mwai's office and announced in his best Oxford educated voice and manner that he was "Mrs. Atwood's financial advisor," the wheels finally began to turn. I sat on one side of the room, all but invisible, while the three men negotiated the sale price of my house. David and I had worked out various hand signals, and as he made these prearranged signs to me, I would in turn smooth my skirt or clean my sunglasses in response. The deal was finally settled.

The next hurdle to cross was yet another side to doing business in Kenya that I knew nothing about: "Bringing Money Into the Country." When I started living in Kenya I didn't set out to become a petty criminal, but after learning the ropes and taking the advice of folks who lived there, I guess, by USA standards anyway, I became one. The first thing I had to do was to get over any residual scruples I might have had. This was not the United States, I was running a business, and this was how the game was played. "When in Rome . . . " These financial sleights of hand initially made me nervous, but I came to enjoy the entire cloak and dagger act. For awhile, anyway.

The currency in Kenya is the shilling but, unlike American dollars or British pounds, it is not "hard currency." Regardless of the fact that it is utterly worthless outside of Kenya, it is illegal to take any shillings out of the country. As they are worthless, I never understood why anyone would care, but that is the rule. The flip side of that is that you can usually bring money in. You may not, however, stash this in your mattress, nor may you use it to purchase anything you choose. Any foreign currency brought into Kenya must be converted into shillings through the Central Bank of Kenya. Immediately.

Another rule at that time (most of the restrictions on foreign currency no longer exist) was that Kenyan citizens were not allowed to have foreign bank accounts. Of course, this made it impossible to educate your children overseas or even take a holiday outside of Kenya. This would have made for a desperate situation for any Kenyan citizen except that no one obeyed the rule. No one would be so foolish as to announce that they had a foreign bank account, but everyone had them.

Although you were supposed to exchange your imported money at the Central Bank of Kenya, it was far more profitable to do so on the black market. I had heard of black markets, but had never involved myself in such back alley endeavors. But the difference in the exchange rates on and off the black market could be significant, especially if you are talking about relatively large sums of money. Ten cents on the dollar adds up if your are playing around with thousands of dollars.

It goes something like this: say you were buying a car from a private person in Nairobi. If for some reason he wanted to be paid in shillings and you already had that kind of cash in your Kenyan bank account, you could write the seller a check, or hand him cash, and that was that. If, however, they wanted some of that money to end up in their account overseas, the negotiation got a little trickier. You first had to decide what the value of the shilling was in the USA or the UK. Then you translated your shilling price into the other currency and did the transaction, by wire transfer, out of the country. Your unnamed account into their unnamed account. Other than a few covert phone calls to your bankers in New York, it wasn't too difficult.

The real fun began when you were paying for something in shillings but bringing the money into Kenya from an overseas account and going through the black market. First, you had to find someone who wanted hard currency in his account overseas. That wasn't too hard, almost everyone wanted hard currency. Then you had to get that person to give you the shillings at a much greater rate than the Central Bank would have and at a rate that was not going to make their doing this deal useless. You shopped around, asked some circumspect questions, and it could usually be done. Until you had a steady source though, the dodgy part was to find someone who would give you a good rate and whom you could trust. Because as common as all this hanky panky was, it was illegal. You probably wouldn't end up in jail for black marketing money, but you could be deported.

Oddly enough, Boniface Mathenge did not have an overseas account. He wanted his shillings paid to him in Kenya. That was fine with me, but I still had to bring my dollars in and exchange them, somehow, somewhere, with someone. I did manage to locate a chap who became my steady exchanger for quite a few years, and in the months before I actually purchased my house, I wrote more than a few checks to people in England that I had never heard of. I, in turn, would go to my "man's" office in Nairobi to receive plastic bags full of cash. Bag after bag, over a period of many months, was deposited into a "client account" at my attorney's office. My attorney only reluctantly accepted my little bags of cash. Adopting the look of someone who smelled something rotten, he gingerly lifted each elicit parcel from his desk, handed it to his secretary, and made it very clear to me that he didn't want to know anything about the whole dangerous business.

Then there was the Stamp Duty to contend with. The Kenya government demanded six percent of the sale price of any real estate for Stamp Duty. Given all the wheeling and dealing that went on with the transferring of money, it was only one's word what the actual sale price was. As everyone fudged the papers when reporting the final figures, collecting the correct amount of Stamp Duty was a rare event indeed. I was used to lawyers and official documents and Uncle Sam knowing just about everything one did or had or spent or inherited. Only gangsters lied to the American Government and they went to jail if they were caught. Not so in Kenya.

Stamp Duty was paid when the property actually changed hands. The "correct" amount was put into escrow by the buyers attorney with an additional 3% held on deposit, just in case you had been less than honest, which was true of almost everyone. It then was up to an official agency to come out and inspect the property to make sure it was only worth the pittance you reportedly paid for it. The official inspectors often took up to four years to get around to this task. Not only did they hold your money for all those years, but it was highly possible that by then you had added a swimming pool and tennis courts. I was wisely advised to photograph the entire place before I tore down a single wall. I would need to prove that it really was the disaster it was when I bought it.

I did state the correct figure on all papers and I did not fudge on the Stamp Duty. I was willing to, but my very strict mzungu lawyer said that should I be caught, the problems I would encounter would not be worth the shillings involved. Mentioning deportation always went a long way towards keeping me somewhat on the straight and narrow.

On July seventh the walls of the new house at 141 Dagoretti Road started coming down. Jake and I arrived on the scene that day to see more than one hundred men at work. There was no electrical equipment in evidence, but the manpower was impressive. There were men hauling stones and more chiseling them into the correct shape. There were people digging foundations, others ripping out the old plumbing and at least ten men pulling down all the ceilings. My shambamen, Steven and Francis, were chopping dead branches from all the trees to allow more sunlight to reach the house, and moving bushes from one place to the next. All the planting around the house would be buried under the huge amount of rubble that was shortly to accumulate and we tried to save the larger plants. There were also outbuildings and, it seemed, puppies to be removed.

Mr. Boniface Mathenge had left a litter of three-week-old puppies, along with their starving mother, for me to dispose of. Most of the local folks kept dogs for guard purposes rather than as cherished family pets. I didn't have too much trouble with the idea of taking them all to the KSPCA, but I knew I would be in a good deal of trouble if Jake decided to rescue them. My son is an Animal Lover, the type that emits a huge "Awwwhhh" if the word "kitten" is even brought up in conversation. He feels compelled to speak to and pet every dog he passes on the street. Ever since he was a baby he has wanted to take home any furry thing he laid his eyes upon. The first words Jake ever spoke were "Mom, can I keep it?"

So, before he even brought the subject up I told him that we were not going to keep any of those puppies. We already had a new German Shepherd pup, Zeke, as well as Kipele, and we did not need any more. Jake would just have to understand that we couldn't rescue every homeless animal that came along.

I called Josephine, the wife of Boniface Mathenge, and asked her to please come back to the house and remove the dogs. She said she would. When we went by the new house the next day my staff verified that she had done so. But about an hour later, when I was talking to Stephen Karanja, out of the corner of my eye I caught a glimpse of some dusty looking creature as it dashed behind a tree.

"Karanja, what was that?"

"What, Madame?" He had a very badly concealed smile.

"That thing that just ran by? Over there?"

"I do not know, Madame."

"Oh, yes you do. What was it?" I was sure he was collaborating with Jake.

"Oh, that. That is the puppy."

"What puppy?"

"The one Mathenge left."

We caught the small escapee, a ratty looking little thing, and took him home to feed him. At only three weeks old, he should still have been nursing, but his Mother had been gone for two days; I couldn't let him starve. But, again, I stressed to Jake that we were not keeping this dog. As I was making this speech the puppy was licking pablum off my fingers and wagging his flea-bitten tail at Zeke.

I called Josephine the next day and asked her to please come and collect the one puppy that was left. She said she would, and then informed me that all the rest had been put to sleep. She would do the same for this one. Saying nothing, back the puppy went to 141 Dagoretti Road the next morning. I was now feeling quite guilty, but I did believe that we were doing the right thing. When we went over the next day, the puppy was still there; it had escaped one more time. This time it was under the staff house growling and snapping at everyone. Mildred applauded this behavior, telling me that this was a very good sign.

"You know Madame, this is good. This puppy he will be kali sana *(very fierce)*. He will be guarding the house kapissa *(completely)*. It is good he is kali."

We considered naming him Prince but settled on Rat.

Rat was a cross between a German Shepherd, a Labrador Retriever, and a Hyena. He was extraordinarily sweet with us, we liked to think that he knew we had rescued him, but he was ferocious with anyone he didn't know. Regardless of your skin color, if Rat didn't know you he would back you up against your car and pin you there until he was called off. He was not deterred by either rocks thrown at him or food offered as a bribe. He was also a very hardy specimen and never got sick or needed the babying that many other breeds, like Kipele, imported into Kenya, required. He actually grew up to be a decent looking dog, considering his very spurious bloodline, and he had the most soulful eyes you ever saw. He was, of all the dogs we had in Africa, my personal favorite.

The plan for the new Kufuma factory was to convert the current stables adding another, larger section. I needed to house about ten small looms of varying widths, and three much taller ones. We also needed space to display the carpets, house all the stock and provide a separate place for the spinners. Their work was much more chafu *(dirty)*, and they needed to be separated from the newer, cleaner carpets. Although Bhagwant designed me a beautiful new building, I chose to do something much simpler. I wanted to keep as low a profile as possible.

In the strictest sense, the zoning laws of Karen did not permit businesses to exist on residential property. My mzungu lawyer told me that I would never get my operators permit for such an endeavor. But, after my year and a half of living in the President's house and my many dealings with his "people," I had made a few friends in high places. The zoning permit roadblock disappeared with a few phone calls. At the time it struck me as rather subversive, but after even a few months of running Kufuma, I had found that "the law" in Kenya is a many splendored thing. Nothing is ever done by the books. The rules that I had been brought up with did not exist and those laws that were given at least lip service were often based on old tribal customs. Kenya is also a land of keeping your head down and drawing as little attention to yourself as possible. If no one asks, don't volunteer any information. Should you get caught with your hand in someone's cookie jar, a few hundred shillings in the right pocket usually rendered tongues mute and memories short. This was a revelation to me and all those high jinx struck me as most entertaining. For awhile.

fourteen

Cooking Pots and Babies

I had been promised that the factory would be finished by early August and I made plans to move Kufuma from Kiambu to Karen at the end of that month. Given the choice of whether they wanted to come along or not, only one weaver chose to stay behind. It seemed to me rather odd that these folks were so willing to just pack up and leave their families behind and follow me to Karen. But employment was, for all these people, their primary concern. And jobs were scarce. If having a good job or any job for that matter, meant working hundreds of miles away from home, so be it. It was the norm for men to work away from their homes for almost eleven months of the year. For the women of Kufuma, moving to Karen simply meant that they took what children they could with them, usually the ones under three, and left any others with their extended families. It was also a filial duty to send as much money as possible back home to help with the support of elderly family members and any remaining children.

Jake and I made the decision to move all the Kufuma employees ourselves. This was partly in search of another adventure, but also because it didn't occur to us to do it any other way. It took me a long time to break the habit of trying to save money on "expensive" manpower.

Before we could move a soul, we had to secure housing for everyone. I asked Mildred what I should do. Nothing, she informed me, my staff had to do it. Once it was known that a mzungu was behind the transactions, the rent would automatically double. So each one of my house staff started scouting around Karen to find suitable housing for the arriving Kufuma folks. "Suitable" meant that in each nyumba (*one room house*) there was to be "cement down na magi" *(a cement, not mud, floor and running water nearby)*. Stima (*electricity*) was not on the "must have" list. It was too expensive a luxury. The rent they were willing to pay was between one hundred and one hundred and fifty shillings a month, at that time about six dollars. We also wanted them housed as close to the new factory as possible. It was far better for them to walk to work than to take a matatu, (*small bus*), that cost an additional fifteen shillings a day.

Any given village, including those around Karen, could be made up of six nyumbas, or ten nyumbas, or even hundreds. There would generally be one pit latrine for every ten or so nyumbas and, if lucky, a water spigot nearby. By the time we were ready to move the Kufuma people, Mildred, Celestine, Jotham and Stephen had secured thirty such nyumbas. Each one had a month's rent on deposit and a small padlock on the door. That was to discourage either squatters or dishonest landlords. I was footing the bill.

Although there were some high ranking government officials and a handful of wealthy African lawyers residing there, Karen was predominantly a European town. There was definitely not, what I would have called, low-income housing. If someone worked in your home and you wanted to provide living space for them on your property, that was one thing. But most workers lived in separate villages. These were usually nothing more than shantytowns, row after row of shacks built of stones with corrugated tin rooves. They were often a sea of dirty children, mangy dogs and open sewers, and, in the rainy season, endless mud. The Kufuma people may have considered these places utterly unsuitable, but they never expressed that to me.

I have been asked if my relative wealth was ever embarrassing to me, as far as the Africans were concerned, and in the very early months of Kufuma, it was. I certainly had enough guilt about it to do many of the things I did, in terms of financial aid, that I should not have done. Almost anyone who can afford the plane ticket to get to Kenya is already, by African standards, a rich man. Furthermore, the white man in Kenya is the upper class. This fact may not be universally liked, but it is more or less accepted. (It also has the very odd effect of clumping all white people together into one social class. This effectively eliminates almost all of the social lines in the sand that are commonly drawn in the USA or England. Classes based on job prestige, ethnic background, wealth or even educational status are nonexistent in Kenya. Your skin color is your class.)

I did not live any better than most anyone else of my "tribe" in Karen. I made a concerted effort to keep any financial excesses to a minimum. I drove a station wagon, not a Mercedes, or even a far more prestigious Range Rover. I never wore any jewelry or dressed in anything other than tee shirts and jeans. I ran my little business to support myself, my house was relatively small, by Karen standards, and my staff members were kept to the minimum. I did not want people in Kenya, and by that I mean any people, to have any idea what my background was. It wasn't that I was hiding it, it's simply that I had left my life in America behind me. I was living in Kenya and I was trying to do things as they were done there. Learning how to really live in a country like Kenya was a slow process with many hard won lessons along the way. Moving everyone from Kiambu was just one of them.

For "moving week" we had my station wagon and a rented pickup truck for Jake to drive. We had divided the people into groups of five and had posted a list in the Kiambu factory, listing when each person was to join his group. They were to be ready to pile their belongings into the truck and themselves into my car for the fortyminute trip to Karen. Along with loading up all the looms and the carpets and the wool, spun and raw, Jake and I figured that the whole process would take us six days.

I had given everyone at Kufuma two hundred shillings for moving allowance, (an obvious indication of my guilt for uprooting them) with which they were to buy any new mattresses, blankets or such that they might need. By moving day, however, most of the money had disappeared and no one seemed too anxious to tell me where it had gone. I was a bit irked when I learned of this, but when many of these folks, landing in Karen without these barest of necessities, simply turned to me and held out their hand for more, I was down right irritated. It seemed to be expected that I would just replace the missing funds. There were no explanations, no apologies, just outstretched hands.

I could not, and would not, do that. It's one thing when you have one person to bail out of a jam for the second time that week, but it's another when there are twenty five of them. I did feel sorry for their situation and even partially responsible for some of their hardships. But everyone had understood what the money was for and I did not feel it was now my responsibility to replace whatever was missing just because someone had been improvident. It was possible for me financially, given the small amount in question, but it would not be a good precedent to be starting. I could hear, loud and clear, Bill Sr.'s voice in my ear telling me what trouble I was going to have if I didn't "play by the rules" as it pertained to African employees. I began to wonder if those weren't words of wisdom, or at least experience, that I should not have been so quick to disregard.

Along with all the personal problems that arose each day, we had vehicular ones as well. The engine of the rented pickup truck blew up after the third day, leaving Jake stranded on the road for the entire afternoon trying to talk the Kenya police out of arresting him for blocking traffic. I was left with one grumpy teenager and my car to finish the job. With five people and all their babies crammed inside and all the cooking pots, mattresses, chairs and clothing strapped to the roof, the progress was slow, and, by the end of each day, my sense of humor gone. By Saturday, we still had many more people left to transport. We resorted to renting an open backed, five-ton truck. All the remaining folks piled themselves and all their gear into that and, in one fell swoop, made it to my house in Karen. All I had to do was ferry each one to his new home, hope they would accept it, unload all their possessions, listen to all the problems they had neglected to tell me about until that very moment, argue about handing out more money, and get back to my own home by dark. A few either refused to stay in the homes we had rented or had nothing to sleep on when they got there. By the end of the each day, I had several more weavers sleeping in my staff quarters, either on the floor or bunking two to a bed. Mildred came to my rescue and took in those who were in the direst of straights. By Saturday night, Jake and I had collapsed, in a Kenyan state of shell shock.

Eleanor and Melinda in Zaire

Harry at Lake Kivu in Zaire

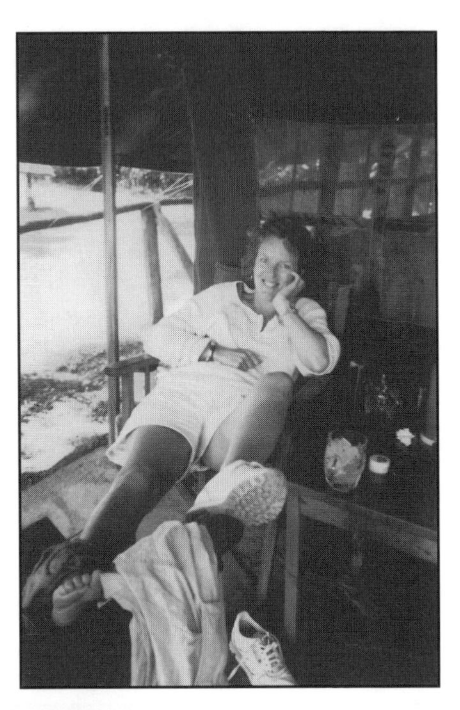

Melinda with a sprained ankle

Celestine with Jack

The finished living room

Melinda's office

Master bedroom, finished

The house from the back

The house from the side

Corey and Melinda at Samburu

Kufuma/Kushona Tu folks with starter squares

Ruth and baby Christine

Stephen Karanja, Elemina, Melinda and all the children who lived at 141

Jotham, Night, Wilson with Kipele, Celestine with Fannis and Dorcas

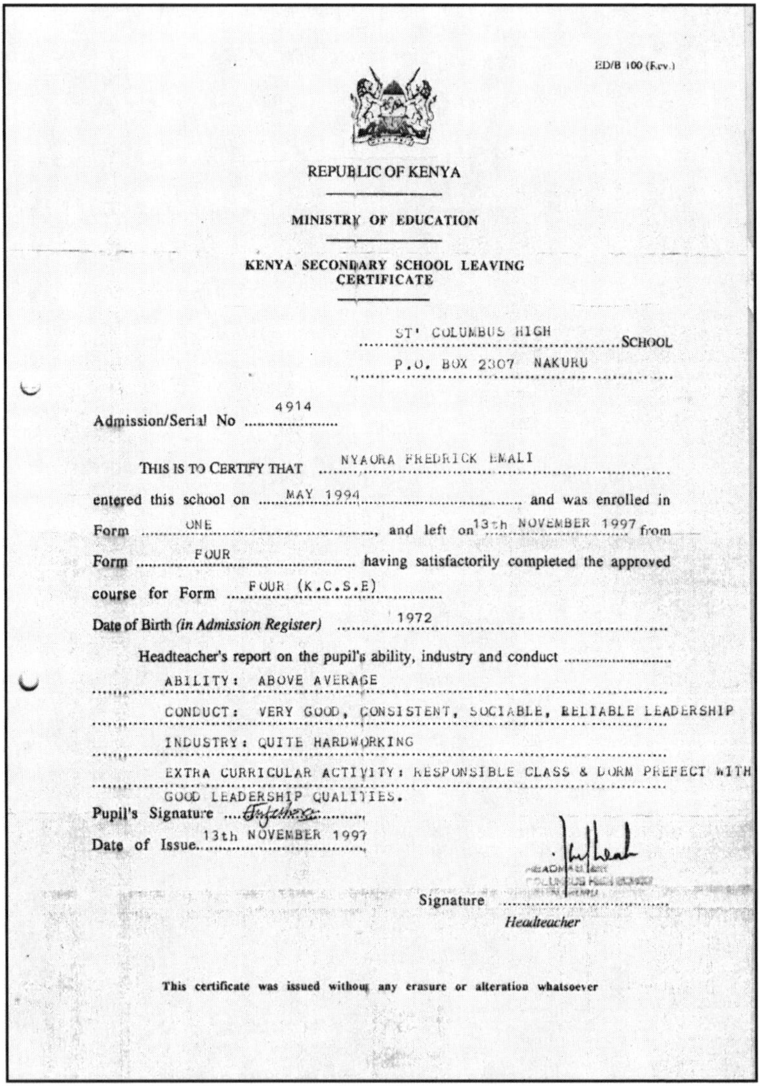

ED/B 100 (Rev.)

REPUBLIC OF KENYA

MINISTRY OF EDUCATION

KENYA SECONDARY SCHOOL LEAVING CERTIFICATE

ST' COLUMBUS HIGH SCHOOL

P.O. BOX 2307 NAKURU

Admission/Serial No 4914

THIS IS TO CERTIFY THAT NYAORA FREDRICK EMALI

entered this school on MAY 1994 and was enrolled in Form ONE, and left on 13th NOVEMBER 1997 from Form FOUR having satisfactorily completed the approved course for Form FOUR (K.C.S.E)

Date of Birth *(in Admission Register)* 1972

Headteacher's report on the pupil's ability, industry and conduct

ABILITY: ABOVE AVERAGE

CONDUCT: VERY GOOD, CONSISTENT, SOCIABLE, RELIABLE LEADERSHIP

INDUSTRY: QUITE HARDWORKING

EXTRA CURRICULAR ACTIVITY: RESPONSIBLE CLASS & DORM PREFECT WITH GOOD LEADERSHIP QUALITIES.

Pupil's Signature

Date of Issue 13th NOVEMBER 1997

Signature

Headteacher

This certificate was issued without any erasure or alteration whatsoever

Frederick's Secondary School Certificate

fifteen

Lucy

The new factory was not finished when scheduled and the winter rains poured through the half-finished roof. It can be surprisingly cold in Karen in August and the damp, muddy floors of a full construction site made the chill at Kufuma more dismal still. Only a few looms could be set up, slowing our production to a crawl. This did nothing for our sales, and it made for some very long faces as well. I spent every day either howling at my contractor to get the damn roof finished or trying to sort out all the non-work related problems of my employees.

There were shauries *(problems)* with new landlords and shauries with thieving new neighbors. There were money shortages and an endless line of sick children. The rains were heavy and the villages were awash in mud. People were unhappy about the walk to work and unhappier still about the higher prices in Karen of all their basic commodities. Whereas two weeks before there had been singing in the factory and I had been everyone's savior, now I was the villain. I was greeted each morning with silent, hostile glances and constant complaints. I was doing the best I could to get it all sorted out and each person's problems attended to, but most of the time I was only playing catch-up.

I was then informed by a friend that another reason everyone was so glum was that I had not "christened" the new factory. The Kikuyus believed that until a proper consecration took place, good fortune would never smile on Kufuma again.

I sought out Mary Wambui's advice on this and she explained to me what was required. Two mbuzis (*goats)*, had to be slaughtered, and their blood strewn around behind the factory. The entrails and assorted other parts had to be cooked and eaten and an ngoma (*party*), had to be thrown. Mary added that a contribution of several cases of soda pop or beer by the new owner, (the obvious cause of all this misery) would be well received. It might help her popularity index as well. I don't know if I was more fascinated than repulsed by this information, but I was willing to go through with it if it made everyone happy again.

James Kiaruri, my Kufuma headman, accompanied me to pick out the goats, one black, one white, and I picked the day for the party. Sadly, the last Friday of August would not see Jake still in town as he had to get back to school, but the end of the month meant payday. With money in workers pockets, I could shut the factory down for a few days. The date was announced and the two goats duly tethered behind the factory. I made a point of avoiding too much contact with these animals, I didn't want to get too fond of them, and focused instead on the preparations for the party. As the chosen day approached and the roof of the factory was finally nearing completion, things were finally looking brighter. But on the Wednesday night before all this was to take place, the fates intervened again.

It was past midnight when my ringing telephone awoke me.

"Hello, Madame. This is Martha."

I could tell by the static on the line that Martha, one of my weavers, was calling from a pay phone. This was not going to be good news.

"What is it, Martha?

"There was a fire."

" A fire? Where?"

"Here, at Dagoretti." Dagoretti was the little village where most of the Kufuma people lived.

"Was anyone hurt?"

"Lucy. Lucy was in the fire." Lucy was one of my employees.

Even if Martha's English had been good enough to describe it to me, she did not know how badly Lucy had been burned. All she could tell me was that Lucy's landlord had found her and taken her to a local hospital. She did not know which one. There was no way to reach him at that hour, he probably didn't have a phone anyway. I said I would come to Dagoretti first thing in the morning and we would find out what had happened.

At eight o'clock the next morning I gathered up Martha, a few others, and the landlord, Mr. Mwangi, and went to find Lucy. Mwangi had taken her to the little Kikuyu hospital several kilometers down the road from Dagoretti. It is a "private" hospital for Africans, meaning it was government subsidized, but run by the Presbyterian Council of East Africa.

On the way to the hospital, Mwangi told me what had happened the night before. It was quite late when he smelled smoke and by the time he got to Lucy's room, the fire had already ripped through it. He had found Lucy lying on the floor in a puddle of mafuta, a cheap kerosene that fuels the primitive stoves sold at every roadside kiosk. These small stoves were nothing more than a refashioned tin can that gets twisted into a smaller shape and a wick stuck into a hole in the top. The combination of bad design and poorly mixed chemicals made explosions of this nature a common occurrence. When Mwangi arrived, he found Lucy was badly burned, but she had not cried out. Her three year-old daughter, Muthoni, was unharmed and was being looked after by one of the other Kufuma people.

As hospitals go in Kenya, "Kikuyu" was a fairly good one, but my first impression, upon walking through the doors of the ward that morning, was shock. I tried to stay calm and made a concerted effort to look authoritative and in control. I wanted to bolt for my car. I had learned in all the years spent in hospitals with my mother that if you look as if you know what you are doing, people assume you do. In Kenya, where a large number of the doctors in this type of a hospital are mzungu, from either the States or Europe, it was easy to pass myself off as one. Once I assumed an authoritative demeanor, I had easy access to wherever I wanted to go.

The women's ward where Lucy had been sent, the Mount Kenya ward, was a sight I had only seen in documentary films. There were women of all ages and in every manner of dress spilling out of the beds and onto the floors. Some were in rags, some were naked, and others were in their full, beaded, tribal regalia. Most stared at me while others looked vacantly into space. Some seemed to be just wandering around the ward. Every bed was full and almost every one had a nursing infant in it as well. The sheets that did not begin to cover the black rubber mattress liners were decidedly gray. There were dozens of other women, non-patients, hovering about feeding ugali, a kind of unsalted, cold cream of wheat, sukuma weeki, and Fanta to their sick relatives. Nurses are not responsible for feeding the patients. It is up to their families to do that. There was ugali and spilled soda pop all over the floors.

Lucy was lying in the nearest bed of the first row as we came into the ward. At first glance it appeared that she was in some kind of an iron lung, but it turned out to be a large, cage like structure lying over her midsection. This was to keep the sheets from sticking to her burned skin. She was awake and immediately started to talk to me. She quickly pulled the sheets off the cage and showed me her burns.

"Mbaya, Mama. Mbaya sana." (*It is bad, Mama, very bad.)*

As the sheets flew back, I was hit by the smell of burnt flesh that rose on the rush of air from underneath. I looked down at her naked body lying there and all I could manage to say was "Ndio. Mbaya sana. Mbaya kapissa." (Yes, *It is bad. It is completely bad.)*

I had seen my share of horrible sights in hospitals, but I had never seen a serious burn. I was trying not to look too shocked as I told her that we would get her fixed up. I would help her. She was lying on her back and I could see that the burn seemed to come from the back and move around her chest. It was a macabre embrace from behind. Her breasts were all burnt as were the underside of her arms. The insides of her thighs were raw. All the skin was gone, and what was left was white and bloody. Whole sections of her body seemed to be nothing more than large, open wounds. And this was not the most badly affected side. I couldn't understand how she was conscious at all, let alone lucid and talking. I paid as much attention to all the burns that I could, it seemed very important to her that I see all of them, and then told her I needed to talk to her doctor.

He was a Canadian and I was grateful that he was English speaking. He asked me who I was and what my connection with Lucy was and then told me it was one of the worst burn cases he had ever encountered. She had burns over fifty percent of her body, and they were very deep. She would, most likely, not survive.

"You can never tell with burns," he said, "but as her crotch and rectum are so badly affected, the chances of infection are overwhelming. She must have been squatting when the mafuta spread across the floor and shot up under her. If this were the States there might be a chance to save her, but I really doubt that it is possible here."

He would do whatever he could.

He went on to tell me that the first big hurdle was the next forty eight hours. Kidney failure is common after such a violent assault on the body. The next test being the three weeks after that. And, if she managed to live through that, she would be looking at many more months in the hospital with hundreds of skin grafts.

"She is in for the worst year of her life. You do know that they will have to soak her in salt water and scrape off the decaying scabs. It's very painful. And then what kind of a life will a woman, as badly scarred as she will be, have in a country like this?"

It would be, he concluded, the greater mercy if she died.

As her employer, I was responsible for Lucy until her family arrived. It was up to me to decide what to do for the next few days and I decided to leave her at "Kikuyu." It was a small hospital, but from all I had heard about Kenyatta, the National Hospital in Nairobi, the better choice. Here at least I had made my mzungu presence known and I hoped Lucy would get some attention. I knew that being a mzungu in Kenya still afforded one preferential treatment and I was certainly not above using that fact if it could help. This seemed to be the best chance she had.

Later that morning her mother arrived from Kiambu, more than an hour's matatu ride away. I tried to tell her, via Martha's translations, that we would do everything we could, and then drove her to where she would be staying. She worked as a coffee picker in Kiambu and the matatu ride from there had most likely used up her entire week's earnings. I gave her some money.

All the Kufuma people were noticeably upset about what had happened to Lucy and the next days at the factory were depressing ones. Several of them visited her in the hospital and daily prayer meetings were held in the back yard at lunchtime. The interest factor ran high. With only the births, weddings and deaths of those around them for the high points in their lives. one of their members being in this kind of condition had a certain bizarre excitement to it. It was all very dramatic and gave everyone something new to talk about.

Lucy survived the first week and by the next weekend, her parents wanted to move her to Kenyatta Hospital. They thought, wrongly I felt, that the larger, government run hospital would offer better services. They wanted her moved as soon as possible. No amount of my great mzungu wisdom, nor financial backing at "Kikuyu," was going to persuade them otherwise. Despite my lobbying to keep her where she was, they went ahead with their plan to move her.

After waiting for two hours at "Kikuyu" for the resident ambulance to arrive to get Lucy moved, I grew impatient and called for another one from a neighboring hospital. Lucy was wheeled from her ward and loaded onto a different stretcher to make the journey to Nairobi. It was torturous to even watch. When we finally arrived at Kenyatta National Hospital we had to move her again onto another stretcher. The scabs were all coming off on the sheets as we tried to shift her. She was burning up with fever. The nurses gave her, at my insistence, a shot of some drug, but I don't think it even touched the pain she was in. The scene was nightmarish and it was unfolding in the middle of the surreal clamor of an emergency ward.

The Emergency Ward at Jomo Kenyatta National Hospital was a sight I was not prepared for. There were bleeding bodies everywhere, victims of stab wounds, barroom brawls, domestic violence and the car accidents that are such a frequent occurrence in Kenya. Some people were bandaged in haphazard fashion; others just sat on the floor in pools of their own blood. There were hundreds more people sitting on wooden benches waiting to be seen, sometimes for days. Children, badly dehydrated from the effects of untreated diarrhea, endemic in all of Africa, wailed piteously in their mother's laps. Nursing mothers leaned against pregnant women already in labor. Malaria victims babbled to themselves and passed in and out of consciousness. And always, always, the presence of the additional two people who were there to "help," for every one person there to be treated. Every so often a "sister,"(nurse) would stick her head out of the loosely curtained examining rooms and shout at the overly curious to move away. That would cause a slight backward motion of the small crowd, until her head disappeared and the crowd surged forward again and the watching resumed. A steady stream of ambulances arrived bringing more badly wounded. Orderlies were pushing wheelchairs and stretchers through the already over crowded halls. It was hot, airless, and frightening.

Along with Lucy's mother, several of the Kufuma people had come with me that morning and, once we had arrived, we too sat and waited. For hours. After all the paperwork had finally been completed, they would not take Lucy to the burn unit until they had given her a permanent IV. As there was no small IV tubing available, it was necessary to cut ever-larger holes in her ankle until they got the only available size into a vein. I stood at her head and talked to her. I could not watch what was going on at her feet. I was afraid I might faint. The burns had all gone septic and the smell was dizzying. Only when we had to transfer her, yet again, from the stretcher to her assigned bed in the ward, did the pain become too much for her. I was holding the IV bottle while the nurses, the Kufuma people and her mother rolled her over onto her stomach. Only then did she cry out.

It was late that afternoon when we finally left. I had to guarantee the hospital that I would pay for all the medicine and salves Lucy would need. This is another service that is not made available at the government hospital. There was, very often, no medicine to be had, even if one could pay for it. In this case, it just required my signature. Lucy's mother was to stay there, sleeping on the floor, to make sure that her daughter was fed.

Things continued to be quiet and sad at the factory, and everyone kept up their prayer vigils hanging onto their belief that Lucy would pull through. Many Africans are extremely fatalistic. If they believe that they are going to die, they will simply lie down and die. But as long as they refuse to accept that, there was some hope. Everyone prayed for Lucy daily, clinging to the belief that Mungai (*God)* would see her through.

The following Thursday night I was waiting for Mildred to call me to dinner when I received a phone call from Lucy's sister. She told me that Lucy was "mbaya sana" and asked me to help.

I called Kenyatta and asked the nurse on duty about Lucy's condition. I was informed that they couldn't tell me anything over the phone. I insisted to know how Lucy was.

"If that girl is going to die tonight," I said through gritted teeth, "I want to know about it. Sasa tu (*Right now)."*

She finally admitted that Lucy would not, in all probability, make it through the night. I hung up the phone, went downstairs, and told Mildred to forget about dinner. We were going to the hospital. Mildred would not allow me go out alone and both she and Femina, Celestine's maternity leave replacement, piled into the car with me. I did not know what I could do for Lucy, but I felt that, at the very least, we could see that she did not die alone. It had been very important to my mother that I was with her when she died and I have chosen to believe that even people in comas somehow know we are there.

We drove out to Dagoretti to gather Martha and Ruth, the one non-Kikuyu and oldest member of Kufuma, and headed to the hospital. There was no moon that night and the darkness made everything seem more foreboding. I was always nervous driving around Nairobi at night, but I hoped, as I was on an errand of mercy, that Mungai would watch over me too.

We got to Kenyatta around nine. It was way past visiting hours, and I put on my "mzungu doctor" air. Striding through the halls, with four bibis trotting along behind me, no one questioned what I was doing.

The burn unit was peopled almost entirely with scalded children, who were playing ball in the hallways. They all seemed to have one arm, their faces, and half their trunks burnt. This was the result of reaching up for something that was boiling on a stove higher than their heads and bringing it down upon themselves. The burnt skin was all white. Most were badly disfigured by the ensuing scar tissue, but still hobbling about the ward, chasing a ball.

We found Lucy in a room by herself and she did not appear to be conscious. She had an oxygen mask on her face, was covered in sweat, and panting heavily. I went in and put my hand on her forehead and spoke to her, in my halting Swahili,

"Wewe iko hapa sasa Lucy. Rafiki yako iko hapa." (*We are here now Lucy. Your friends are here.)*

I then went out and asked Martha to come and talk to Lucy. I was quite sure Lucy would hear her. Martha was frightened and skeptical, but she followed me. Her hands were shaking as she started praying over her friend. I was walking out of the room to afford them some privacy, when the sound of Martha's high-pitched keening stopped me. It sounded like a cry of pain and I turned around to see if she was all right. I stood for several moments watching the two of them, Martha standing next to the bed, eyes closed and head tilted back, with her hand trembling just above Lucy's forehead. I looked down at the bed and in the very next moment, Lucy stopped breathing. I stood there and stared at her very still form. I had seen that stillness before. It is unmistakable. Not ten minutes after we had arrived, Lucy was dead.

I called the nurse in and said I was certain that Lucy had stopped breathing. The nurse informed me that she would not confirm or deny this fact until a doctor came and made an official pronouncement. We were told to wait, me, the now weeping Kufuma women, Mildred and Femina and the burnt children playing ball. As a doctor had not shown up in an hour, I told the nurse that we could wait no longer. The nurse finally said, as we were "family," they would confirm to us that Lucy had, indeed, died. We all nodded at this pronouncement and left the hospital in silence. No one had spoken a word when we arrived at my car. As I reached for the door I heard Mildred's voice coming out of the darkness, "She was waiting for you, Madame."

Before we left the ward, I had asked how Lucy's mother would find out about her daughter's death. The nurse informed me that when the old lady arrived the next morning and saw the empty bed, she would just figure it out. If asked, the hospital would confirm it. I couldn't imagine that being the way that I found out that my child had died. I felt very uncomfortable going home to my dinner knowing that Lucy's mother would face that empty bed tomorrow. I decided that we should drive out to Kiambu and tell the family ourselves.

And so we went; Ruth, Martha, Femina and faithful and true Mildred. Although I was taller and physically much stronger than she, I always felt safer when Mildred was around. I had the car and I had the flashlight and I was a mzungu in this Third World country, but Mildred was always solid and capable. She had a depth of spirit that I had only seen in Africans and we communicated in ways that only women do. She looked out for me and I for her. I was especially grateful to have her along as we headed out into that moonless African night.

We drove out to Kiambu and up into the coffee plantations. Having lived in Kenya for a few years, I was no longer nervous about a good many things, but that night I was scared. Driving around Nairobi at night was dangerous enough and we were headed into a very rural area where stopping a car and robbing its passengers was a common occurrence. The very least I had to worry about was a flat tire. But we pushed on. Martha was directing me as we turned off the main road and drove deeper into the coffee fields. It was extremely dark and the path was deeply rutted. The coffee trees formed a solid wall of black leaves brushing against the sides of my car as we drove into what felt like a place of no return. I was progressively more afraid as the minutes went by. I am not a praying woman, and it probably had to do with all the events of that evening, but as we went deeper into the dark I kept hearing in my head, "Yea, though I walk through the valley of the shadow of death."

After what seemed like an eternity, we came upon a clearing and a little collection of nyumbas. Leaving the headlights on high beam and Femina standing guard, we went in search of Lucy's family. Martha was leading with me right behind pointing my big Maglight onto the path before us. We very quickly came upon Lucy's mother walking in our direction. She said Jambo and quite calmly shook everyone's hand, going through all the usual greeting formalities. Silently she led us to the grouping of huts that her family inhabited and preceded us into each one separately. Everyone present greeted us. There were low burning fires, smoky interiors, and half-naked children. Each family member shook my hand and said Jambo, but despite my being ready for it, no one said, "My God, what has happened?! What are you doing here?" The unlikely sight of a white woman arriving in their little village at eleven o'clock, with headlights glaring into the moonless night, followed by a retinue of four unknown African women, had to cause someone to wonder what was going on. But not a word was said, nor were any questions asked. We proceeded into the main hut, greeted everyone there, and calmly sat down. Martha started to speak.

They all listened very patiently, waiting for Martha to complete her story. She was speaking in Kikuyu dialect and I didn't understand the exact words, but I knew when she spoke the word 'died.' Everyone gasped and some started to cry. Lucy's father was weeping when he left the room, but he returned in about five minutes. We were then led in a little prayer and after several more minutes of silence one of the uncles looked up at me and said, "You can go now." Accompanied by Lucy's mother, we three visitors walked back to the car, now surrounded by dozens of children. We shook hands with her and said pole, once again, and then we just drove away, disappearing into the night just as we had come.

The next days at Kufuma were even more somber than the ones prior to Lucy's death. To add to all the problems the move from Kiambu had caused, we now had a death in the ranks. I knew that everyone felt that the decision to move the factory had not been a good one. Everything had gone from prosperous and forward moving in Kiambu to downhill and deadly in Karen. The death watch over Lucy had put a further delay on the "christening" of the factory. It now had to be stalled even longer, until after the funeral. Nothing was going well and I was to blame.

I was advised by several of my friends not to attend the funeral. (It was one of those Colonial rules about non-fraternization that I was forever breaking.) I had been invited by Lucy's parents and encouraged by Mary Wambui to attend, and I felt it was fitting that I do so. Although Mildred was an Abaluya, and different tribes do not, as a rule, attend each other's funerals, she came along too. She was also less emotionally involved than all the Kufuma people, and she could act as my guide and advisor, making sure that I didn't make any cultural gaffes. I looked to her that day to steer me in the correct direction.

The first stop that morning was at a church in Kiambu. It was a small wooden structure sitting in a clearing on the side of the road. Wambui had given me directions on how to get there and I drove out with a few of my own house staff. Nyamburra and Stephen Karanja were Kikuyus and friendly with the people at Kufuma, and they came along with Mildred and Femina. I should have expected it, but as we drove up to the church, I was surprised to see that I was the only mzungu in sight. I greeted Lucy's parents and shook hands with everyone that came up to me. Many spoke only the usual Jambos and poles and then moved on, but several people launched into lengthy speeches in Kikuyu. As I didn't understand what they were saying I could only smile and say Ndio and Asante in reply. I assumed that since they were smiling at me and pumping my hand that what they had to say was positive

I don't know what was said at the church service, for it too was in Kikuyu, but the singing was haunting. Nyamburra, seated on the other side of me, told me that all the songs were traditional Kikuyu burial songs. Most were sung in a question and response style and were lilting and melodic. The church was filled to capacity with everyone dressed in their best clothes. Lucy's coffin was up in front by the altar, but there were few other adornments.

After the service, we piled back into my car, this time with four more Kufuma workers seated on the tailgate, and followed the pickup truck bearing the coffin into the coffee fields. We were bound for Lucy's parent's house, where I had been that dark night two weeks ago. I was surprised to find that it was only a short drive to get there, no more than ten minutes from the main road, and the walk from the car to the house was only a few hundred yards. It had seemed so far away and frightening before. We all hiked up the hill together and arrived at the burial scene.

There was a huge mound of freshly dug earth behind the house and in the clearing near the front door sat the coffin. It was made of simple wood, and was set on several stools. There were no flowers atop her coffin, just her school photograph. Most people were seated on the ground, but there were a few chairs on the periphery and I was offered one in the shade. I sat with James and most of Lucy's family. Mildred was across the grass watching me.

As the proceedings went along, I noticed that every few minutes someone would go over to the coffin and spray it with an aerosol can. I turned to James and asked him what they were doing. He whispered back to me, "We don't want Lucy to smell." It was a can of air freshener, and she had been dead almost a week. There was no embalming in Kenya.

The next part of the service involved friends and members of Lucy's family standing by the coffin and saying a few words about her. I had been to a few African ceremonies before this. There had been farewells to balloon crew employees and celebrations of various staff accomplishments. I knew that the telling and retelling of every detail of the life of the person in question was the norm. No one ever seemed to tire of hearing the same facts told over again. But that day it was all in Kikuyu and I was left to imagine what was being said. When her father spoke and I heard "Atwood" and "Kufuma" uttered every so often I did realize what the general topic was, but I did't know what was actually being said about me. When the government representative, the local council member, got up to make his speech, however, he spoke in Swahili. That I could understand.

His name was Karanja, (the Smith of the Kikuyus,) and he was dressed in a coat and tie. Because of his position in the community, the little congregation paid great attention to his every word as he launched into yet another retelling of Lucy's death. He started at the very beginning, from moving Kufuma from Kiambu to Karen right up to the night of the fire a month before. He told of all her suffering in "Kikuyu" hospital and the move to Kenyatta in Nairobi. He didn't leave out a single detail right up to that last night at the hospital when she had died with Martha and me in attendance. He had the "audience" in rapt attention.

I was seated on his left, but thought I was hidden in the shade of the tree. I was surprised when he turned to face me directly. He changed his tone and spoke a few words in English, informing me that this next part was going to be about me. Then, still facing me, he continued. He listed all that I had done for Lucy, from giving her a job to paying her hospital bills. Everything that had occurred over the past month was recounted in a tone of glowing admiration. I was thoroughly embarrassed by all this and by the time he finished I had my face all but buried in my lap.

He wound up his speech with a final asante sana for my visit to Kiambu and for coming up to see the family to tell them that their daughter had died. To me this had been just a basic courtesy to anyone who would be suffering the loss of a child, but in that situation, and in that country, it seemed to be cause for mention. Applause broke out among the mourners and I was already blushing when he motioned me to stand. I stood up and smiled, trying to catch Mildred's eye.

"Can this be the right thing to do?" I thought.

When I finally saw her she was smiling at me and clapping as vigorously as the person next to her.

Before the casket was to be lowered into the ground a professional photographer emerged and started to take pictures. Mildred kept nodding me on and so I stood with all the Kufuma people behind the coffin and had our picture taken. I was surprised and very uncomfortable, but it also appeared to be the thing to do.

The casket was then lowered into the ground, the dirt piled on top, and more songs were sung. Everyone had been given a bouquet of fresh flowers and as we made our way over to the gravesite, Mildred told me that we were all to file past the fresh grave and stick the flowers upright into the earth, as if they had grown there. I was standing with the Kufuma people waiting for the flower ceremony to begin when the people in front of me started murmuring to each other and moving aside. A path opened up in front of me. I stepped aside, assuming that there was someone behind me who needed to pass by, but when I turned around, I saw no one. Then I felt a hand on my back and heard Mildred whispering "It is for you Madame. You must go now." It seemed that I was to place the first flowers.

With Mildred pressing me from behind I proceeded to the grave and stuck my flowers into the dirt. I then stood with Lucy's parents and shook a hundred hands as all the mourners filed past. As I was gathering my house staff together and about to leave, the councilman came up to me and thanked me, once again, for all I had done. I was not too eloquent at that moment and all I could manage to say was that I had only tried to help. What I really wanted to do was to get out of there before this new halo that had been placed on top of my head got any heavier.

On October seventh the christening of the new factory finally took place. I was glad to have it done with, not only for the good fortune that was now in store, but also to get rid of the two goats. They had been on the property for over a month and they were beginning to blend into the scenery. Visitors to the factory were forever commenting on them asking me if they were to be shorn and the wool used in the carpets. What could I say? "No, actually, they are here for a sacrificial ceremony. We are going to chop them up next week and throw their guts all over the back yard." The goats also managed to escape their tether at least once every day and always seemed to end up fertilizing the grass in the front of my new house. I feared that if this went on much longer I would either throw them off my property or think up names for them and adopt them as mascots.

But the day of the party finally arrived and I was willing to allow the sacrifice to proceed as planned. I did tell James that I wanted nothing to do with that part of the ceremony. I didn't want to hear any goat death screams, I did not want to know how the blood was collected, I was not interested in observing how the gore was sprinkled over the grass, and I didn't eat meat. Someone else could have my portion. What I would do was supply the beer and the Fanta and the many loaves of bread that Wambui had suggested. And a cassette player. They had the tapes they wanted to dance to and I would supply the very expensive, imported batteries.

I also planned on shooting several roles of film of the festivities so that we would have a picture album of the proceedings. I knew that this ngoma would be cause for every single child of every single worker to visit the factory. There would be upwards of thirty there that day and I had arranged to have T-shirts made up for all of them. The T-shirts were bright red with "I am a Kufuma Kid" printed on them. The multi-talented Fred Kunguru had silk screened several dozen of these for me with a Bush Baby, a small marsupial that resembles a Koala bear, sitting behind his new design for our logo. The red made for good color contrast in the pictures and the album was most successful. Everyone was delighted with the pictures of themselves, and it made for a cheerful record of that long awaited day. It didn't last too long. When I went to look at it a few months later I found that almost all the pictures had been "pinched." It wasn't too difficult to tell who had nicked what, everyone just took his or her own photo, but the result was that there were many empty pages and only the most unflattering or otherwise undesirable pictures were left.

Those, and the two photographs that had been sent to me by Lucy's parents of all of us standing over the coffin. I thought that everyone felt that those particular photographs belonged to me.

More likely though is the superstition surrounding them. I had written in the front, that the album was dedicated to Lucy. I think that the Kufuma people felt that stealing those particular photos would tempt all the evil spirits that had plagued us back in September to return. With the roof finished, production back to normal and the factory finally christened, things were once again going well. No one would dare risk bringing all that bad luck down upon us again.

sixteen

Celestine's Toto

By the middle of September, the factory was nearly finished, but it was now clear that the house was not going to be ready on time. I had stupidly believed the contractor's promises and had, accordingly, given my notice to the President. Having said that I would leave by the end of September, I felt compelled to do so. Rather then get into more shouting matches with Bhagwant, or put myself through the misery of living in all that plaster dust, I decided to live elsewhere for a few months. In a notice pinned to the door of the Karen dukas, I found just what I was looking for: a small cottage, just around the corner from the new house. It was available for short term let. I drove over to meet the owner, Mr. Tett, took one look around, and agreed on a three-month renewable lease.

The cottage was a small thatched roof affair with a tiny, enclosed yard. It had one bedroom and was only partially furnished, but one bedroom was enough for me and I was more than happy to bring over some of my own furniture. It was also just a mile from the new house and atmospheric enough to fuel my still strong fantasies about living in Ah-frica. At the end of September, I left President Moi's house for the cottage and moved Mildred et al to the new house. Their quarters had been repainted and freshened up and were ready for them.

Back in the spring, when my container was being loaded in Savannah, someone had forgotten to include a couch and the whole thing had been held up at the docks. That turned into a small blessing when the deal with the Winter's house fell apart and I had no place to put everything should it arrive. It wasn't until the end of July '89 that it finally set sail from Georgia. It was due to arrive in Kenya in early October. Around the time I moved over to Tett's place, I was vaguely expecting it to show up in Mombassa, and was certainly surprised when I got a call from the clearing agent saying it would be pulling into my driveway in two hours. All my worldly goods had not been lost on the high seas, halleluia, but I had no idea where I was going to put everything. I raced over to Dagoretti Road and commandeered Stephen and Wilson into taking all the construction paraphernalia out of the garage. We were still unloading cement bags when the container arrived.

The flat bed truck containing two boxcars, each twenty feet long, could barely get up the driveway. The maneuvering it took to get up to the house without crashing straight through my newly planted gardens drew the attention of all the Kufuma people down at the factory. I had hoped to keep a lower profile when my things from the States were unloaded, but with this enormous truck smashing through the trees, it was not to be. Counting all the construction chaps and the Kufuma people, I had an audience of about one hundred people watching as all my possessions were unloaded onto the driveway.

As each piece appeared, I inspected it for damage. The container had been packed in the States, but it had been unpacked and re-packed in Nairobi at a Customs stop. It was well known that these Kenyan Customs officials did not wear kid gloves. Several tables had legs knocked off and a much-loved antique tall-case clock of my mother's had obviously been dropped. The sight of the top of it, smashed into many pieces, had me in tears right away. Then, with the opening of a box from her apartment in New York City, I could actually smell my mother herself. Professional movers had packed her apartment before I could do any sorting of things and they had packed everything in sight. As I rummaged through the boxes, trying to see what should be stored where, I found packages of crackers, boxes of pasta and a handful of small notes that had once been pinned to the refrigerator. As I pried open each one, finding things that I hadn't seen in four years, the sight of my dead mother's handwriting or the smell of her perfume from a box of her clothing nearly knocked me over. At one point a music box that had belonged to my grandmother was opened and started to play. That stopped me dead in my tracks.

When I had gone to South Carolina to select some pieces of furniture, everything had been strewn all over a warehouse. Seeing my mother's furniture in a decidedly garage sale atmosphere had been difficult to take, but seeing her things sitting in my driveway in Kenya was even stranger. It felt as if I were being tossed around in a time warp with large pieces of my childhood swimming up in front of me. The juxtaposition of my two lives was surreal. Having such a large audience didn't help the situation. All the Kufuma people stood there for hours watching this enormous amount of furniture and boxes being unloaded as I stood wiping tears away at the sight of almost every item.

Once the unloading had been completed, the truck started backing down the drive. It managed to demolish the few bushes it had managed to miss on its way in. Then Wilson, Stephen, and I began storing everything in the garage. We spent the better part of that afternoon packing everything away leaving the clock for last. I had heard that there was a clock wizard in Karen, reputed to be able to fix anything. I was going to take my clock to him for repairs as soon as I could. As the garage doors had been pulled off their hinges some days before, our only form of security was to nail large planks of wood across the opening.

With most of my life, and now most of my "things," finally in Africa, I probably should have had a greater sense of being half way across the stream, but I never thought of my life over there in terms of a fixed period of time. As far as I was concerned, I was there to live. I rarely thought about what was yet to come. I never thought about going "home." This was my home.

One afternoon towards the end of October, as I was making my daily survey of the progress on the new house, Jotham came to me, looking stricken. He was rubbing his hands together and shaking his head. "Baby is coming now." He was referring to Mama Bado's now almost mythical baby and was seeking my permission to take time off to go to the hospital. I had noticed that Celestine had gotten very large in the tumbo, but she still told me "bado" every time I inquired as to her prenatal progress.

Jotham and Celestine bundled up all the necessary gear and headed off down the road to the bus stop. They were back three hours later. Pamwani hospital was on the other side of Nairobi, and that was at least a forty-minute car ride away. When I heard of their return, I went down to the staff quarters to see what had happened. There they sat, in their nyumba, Celestine swollen and giggling, Jotham shaking his head, and Night screaming at the sight of me.

"What happened, Jotham? Didn't the baby come?"

" Hapana. No. Bado, Madame. Bado."

"Well what did the doctor say?"

"He said 'Bado'."

The next day Jotham came to me again, wringing his hands, asking to take Celestine to the hospital. Once again the two of them headed off down the road only to return several hours later. Again I asked what seemed to be the problem and they just smiled and told me "Bado." By the third day I was no longer going to get too excited about this.

Bado, indeed.

The following night, sitting at my little cottage, I was not even thinking about further requests to go to the hospital. I was, instead, dealing with the most common household hassle in Karen: no electricity. The power had failed night before, but I was convinced that the *stima*, (electricity) would be back on shortly, and had been rather upbeat about the whole thing. I set lighted candles in all the rooms, made myself a drink and sat down to enjoy the approaching twilight. Sunset is always a magical time in Kenya as the light changes from blue to red and the sounds of the day become the sounds of the night. Witnessing sundown was a ritual I thoroughly enjoyed. When the power did not come on after an hour, I decided to fire up the *jiko*, the African version of a charcoal grill. It took me quite a while to get the fire started, but I was in one of my "on safari" moods and was reasonably patient. Once lit, about nine o'clock that night, I popped myself some popcorn and settled in to read by candlelight. After awhile, cursing Graham for not being there, to take advantage of all that candlelight, I went to bed.

The power came on the next afternoon. There had been a major blowout in Nairobi, but it had been fixed. Or so I was told. On this next night, not wanting Mildred out walking alone after dark, I had sent her back early to the new house. The chicken and rice she had started were simmering on the stove and all was looking quite hopeful. I was writing Jake a letter, feeling reasonably mellow, and looking forward to watching a new videotape I had brought back from London. Very exciting stuff.

It was six forty five when everything went black. Mildred was gone, I was hungry and not in the mood for more popcorn. I decided not to wait for the power to be restored, but to drive down to The Horseman to get some take away. The phone lines were not down, that night, and I called ahead to order my Chinese a la Ah-frica dinner. As I headed for the fence that separated my little yard from the main compound, I heard them coming: The Dogs! Mr. Tett, my landlord, a once-upon-a-time Brit with an indecipherable accent, had a pack of killer dogs that hated everyone in general and me in particular. They went into full attack mode the minute they heard my cottage door open. I had never been afraid of dogs before, but I was convinced that these were mad, probably rabid, and truly terrifying. Tett had told me that they periodically chewed each other's ears off or attacked anyone crazy enough to get out of his car without the benefit of a firearm. He said that he really should get rid of the worst of the lot, old Pete, as he was becoming "a bit of a nuisance."

Every time I left my cottage, regardless of the time of day, I had to run the canine gauntlet. With this pack of wolves snapping at my legs, I locked the gates of my little compound, and bolted for my car. As the dogs always chased me down the long drive, (why I didn't run the damn things over I will never know,) I had to do battle with them again when I reached the main gates.

This was an even bigger hazard for there was no guard at the gates. Everyone in Karen had a guard at their front gate, but Tett was too cheap to hire one. I had to get out of my car to open the gates, get back in the car to drive through them, get back out again to close them behind me, and back into the car again to continue. Not only was this hazardous as far as the dogs were concerned, but dangerous for another reason. All that jumping in and out of your car at night sets up a perfect opportunity for some mcora (*scoundrel*), to pop out of the bushes and demand to see the color of your money. It took one helluva lot to inspire me to go through this ritual more than once a day.

I finally collected my food at The Horseman, hearing the usual "Yes, Mrs. Atwoods" and "Asante sanas." The waiters at Rolf's knew almost everyone by name, and I was especially liked as I still tipped like an American. I headed home, faced the dogs, got through the gates and, at last arrived back at my little cottage. I had just relit the candles, poured myself a glass of wine, and started to eat my dinner when the phone rang.

"Hello?"

"Hello, Madame, I am Mildred."

"Yes, Mildred, I recognized your voice. What is it?" I hesitated to ask. Your staff never calls you up to have a little chat.

"Baby is coming. Celestine is finding baby."

"Sasa? Now?"

"Sasa tu. (*Just now.*) Baby is coming.You come in your car quickly to us here, Madame. Baby is coming."

Mildred did not get unnecessarily excited about too many things, but she sounded serious. I felt it imperative to ask her what hint she had that would lead her to believe this birth was actually happening. After the events of the past three days I was not about to forgo this hard-won repast just to go charging off into the attack-dog-filled night for yet another one of Celestines "Bados".

"Maji. Celestine has found water now."

"Water? What water? "

"Maji." Mildred restated what to her was the obvious.

"Oh, THAT water!" Good Lord.

"Okay. Mildred. Ngoja (*Wait).* Stay put. Mimi na cuja (*I am coming).*"

She told me that she was at the Karen roundabout, and stuffing a spring roll into my mouth, I headed back out through the snapping jaws, the endless gates, and down to Karen. My entire staff was clustered under the street lamp, looking as glum as a bunch of condemned men. Along with Celestine and Mildred, there was gathered Francis, Stephen, Nyamburra, and the expectant father. Jotham was beside himself. He was rolling his eyes, wringing his hands, and shaking. Celestine, lying on the side of the road, was wailing at the top of her lungs. I was trying to make some sense out of what Jotham was telling me, get the more essential ones loaded into the car, and the rest sent back to the house, and find out where this hospital was.

"Where are we going, Jotham?" I asked, as we lifted Celestine into the back of my station wagon.

" Sijui. Madame."

(Second only to 'bado' as the most oft used word in Swahili, sijui means' I don't know')

"What do you mean? "

"I don't know where hospital is."

I was afraid that was what he meant.

"How could you not know where it is? You have been going there for over a year and you don't know where the bloody place is?"

I was losing my sense of humor and Celestine was making so much noise that I could barely hear him anyway.

Sticking my head into the back of the car I said, "Celestine? Can you hear me?" I put my hands on her belly to see how tight it felt. That was about all I could recall of being in labor myself. I vaguely remembered that there had been enormous interest in how 'tight' my belly felt.

"Celestine?"

"Yes, Madame."

"Are you all right?"

"Yes, Madame."

"Are you sure?"

"Yes, Madame."

"Well, then, try to be quiet, Mama. You are okay. Do you hear me? You are okay. We will take you to the hospital. Jotham is here, we are all here, you are going to be okay." I was trying to be soothing and authoritative at the same time. I don't think it was all that successful.

"Jotham?"

"Yes, Madame."

"How did you get to the hospital this afternoon?"

He stopped and thought about this for a moment. I waited. He looked up at me and smiled.

" I knew what bus to take."

That took the last bit of whatever gumption was left in Jotham and Celestine sounded as if she were having her leg chewed off by a hyena. I started the car and headed down the road. To anywhere. Movement gave us all a false sense of purpose.

I turned to Mildred, good old levelheaded Mildred.

"Where am I going Mildred?" She told me that she knew where the hospital was.

"I know, Madame. I know the road."

"Good. What road is it on, Mildred?"

"The main road, Madame."

"Where?"

"In Nairobi, Madame." Mildred was calm and confident.

"What main road?"

"In Nairobi."

"Yes, but which main road in Nairobi? There are mingi, *(many.)*"

"The main road at back."

"Back of what?" I was not so calm.

"Nairobi, Madame."

Swell.

I took a deep breath and reconsidered my situation.

"Well I don't know where that is or how to get there."

"Pole, Madame"

"I know Mildred. I am sure you are sorry and sure you know where we are going, but I don't."

Still racing down the road at eighty KPH, going God knows where, I finally said,

"Okay, forget Pamwani. We are going to Nairobi Hospital."

Mzungu land. But what were my choices?

We arrived at Nairobi Hospital after a very noisy half-hour. Celestine was still carrying on as we assisted her into the emergency room. They call it "Casualty" in Kenya. Jotham was wringing his hands and Femina, who had managed to come along as well, stood by exuding concern. I didn't think we needed all of them to assist in this baby's birth, but they were all very supportive of each other in a crisis and liked to see what was happening. Mildred was her usual calm self. Standing there in her headscarf and US Air Force parka, (a gift from her brother, Wilson) she was a pillar of strength. She helped us get through the admission process and put Celestine into her bed. The midwife examined the patient and said the baby was fine and was indeed, coming. Breathing a sigh of relief, we settled in to wait for "Baby to come out."

I asked Jotham if he wanted to be present at the birth. He did not think so. He said he would faint. I had just launched into my speech about the psychological benefits of men being present when their children were born, when I saw Mildred was shaking her head at me.

"You know, Madame, this is not good. Africa man, he don't know. He is not good. Jotham, he will fall down. He is not helping to find baby. It is good Jotham, he stay out."

I had learned that there were some things that I shouldn't argue about with Mildred. If she said it was so, it was so.

After about an hour of some good contractions things slowed down. I recalled that this was common enough and I was not alarmed. We waited. And we waited. And we waited. We tried pacing the floor, Mildred, Celestine, and I, hoping to get some more contractions going. Up and down the maternity wing floor we trooped, a merry threesome, but no luck. By midnight the nurse told me that it would be several more hours and advised me to go home and get some sleep. When I said I was leaving, Jotham and Celestine looked at me with such horror that I didn't have the heart to go. I told them I would be nearby and went out to my car to try to sleep. The troops, with their infinite patience in these matters, were hovering about in the waiting room. We were all going to see this through. We had come this far, what's a few more hours?

I finally gave up on sleeping in the car at about three, and went back to see what was happening. Surprise, surprise, bado, and it didn't look like much was going to happen until morning. The nurse told me that the baby had not "come down" yet. I didn't understand what she meant. When I had Jake, he "came down" at about seven months into the pregnancy. She assured me that that was only with European women. African babies did not drop into the birth canal until the last minute. Although I thought that an extraordinary piece of information, and made a mental note to look into this later, I was too tired to pursue the matter right then.

They were also telling me that this was going to cost me more than a few shillings. Eight hundred shillings (forty dollars), a day for the room, fifteen thousand shillings (seven hundred and fifty dollars) for a doctor, twenty one thousand shillings (one thousand dollars) for an operating room if they performed a Cesarean section. Not a lot compared to American hospitals, but I was beginning to doubt my wisdom in bringing Celestine to Nairobi Hospital in the first place. But it was a little late for that.

The problem with my footing the bill was not that it would cause me irreparable financial hardship; the problem was playing favorites. If I paid for Celestine to be in this hospital for as simple and utterly commonplace a procedure as having a baby, then I would be obligated to do the same for anyone else who worked for me and wanted to give birth in a private hospital. You had to be very careful not to do anything for one staff member that you weren't prepared to do for all of them. Jealousies and real friction arose all too easily. Tribal rivalries are omnipresent and favoritism by the employer just made a touchy situation worse. It would have been best if I had had the good sense to stay out of their childbearing problems.

I finally gave up the vigil at the hospital and departed. I dropped the support team off at the new house, minus Jotham, and struggled back through the gates and the dogs to my cottage. I fell into my bed at about four. The power was still out.

When the phone rang at seven the next morning, I considered knocking it off the hook and claiming phone failure. Phone lines being down was another utterly commonplace occurrence in Karen, and I knew I could get away with it. I picked it up. It was the nurse at the hospital and I could vaguely hear her telling me that things had not progressed as we had hoped. They did indeed need to do a Caesarian Section. As I was paying the bills, they needed my permission.

"Okay. You've got it. Goodbye."

She continued. Wouldn't I rather send Celestine to Pamwani Hospital, where she was headed in the first place? That would be so much better for all concerned. They knew her there and had all her prenatal records. Wouldn't that be the better plan? I had no idea what was better, but I told her to stand by. I would get back to the hospital as soon as I could.

I found Jotham sitting on Celestine's bed and both of them in tears. They were distraught, but Jotham's terrified face told an even sadder tale. The whole thing confused him no end and now scared him to death. Celestine was not helping the situation any by announcing every two minutes that she was dying. She was exhausted, I knew that, they both were, but she was losing control. Jotham sat there on the side of her bed wiping the tears from his eyes.

The midwife from the previous night, Njoki Githinju, entered the room and in response to my questions told us that she had done all her training at Pamwani. She listed all the virtues of the place and what we could expect. When she added that she was prepared to come with us, the decision was made; we were going. Feeling much less guilty and munching on some of the toast from Celestine's breakfast tray, I headed toward my car. The ambulance, carrying Jotham, Celestine, and Njoki took off ahead of me, racing to the other side of Nairobi. Driven by some madman of a driver, the journey to Pamwani was a real safari rally drive. We smashed over the potholes that so distinguish the roads in Kenya, but miracle of miracles, we arrived without shattering a universal joint or even puncturing a tire.

We passed through the admission process quite easily as we had Njoki in tow and my usual hospital demeanor going. They wheeled Celestine into an admitting room to "prep" her.

The room where I waited was also being used for admitting girls who were already in labor. There was a constant stream of them. I must have seen at least twenty processed in the hour I waited there. Outside, in the hall, there were fifty more exhausted looking new mothers, sitting on the floor, each holding a newborn baby. A "sister" was walking down the line, passing out slices of bread. Breakfast. I asked what they were doing, sitting on the cold floor like that, and was told that they had all given birth the night before and were waiting for bed space. This is a hospital where they put them two to a bed. But check out time was not until later and they had to wait. Pamwani is one of the largest maternity hospitals in sub-Saharan Africa, churning out over two hundred babies a day. All you have to pay is the equivalent of about eight US dollars for the entire prenatal care program, the delivery, and the postnatal visit. Of course for many Africans in Kenya, that is an unaffordable sum, but for many more it obviously worked.

We finally got Celestine up to the operating room. She was frightened and exhausted, to say nothing of being in the last stage of labor. She had started to panic.

"I am dying, Madame! I am dying! Don't leave me, Madame. Mimi na kufa. I am dying!" she wailed as she clutched and tore at my sweater.

"No, you are not dying, Celestine. You are having a baby. You are okay. You are OKAY! The doctor is coming. You are Okay. It will be all right. Bas, *(enough.*) You know I won't leave you."

No one actually knew when the doctor would show up. He had been seen, somewhere in the vicinity, but it obviously did not strike him as too urgent that he perform this little service. By the time he finally arrived, I was getting my female hackles up, but none of the nurses said a word.

I was not sure if Celestine understood exactly what a Caesarian section was, but she later told me that she knew that they were going to "cut" her.

An orderly finally came and wheeled her away and within minutes, we heard the baby cry. Hallelujah. We had made it. I was teary and proud and very happy that it was over. Celestine had survived and the baby was fine. It was a girl. I felt like an aunt.

I found Jotham sitting downstairs on a long row of bottom-worn benches, staring at the floor. As my white ankles came into his field of vision, he raised his gaze to look at me. His face was a study in questioning terror. She's dead, right? No, "Baby has come out," and everyone was fine. He didn't even smile. He just nodded and dropped his head back into his hands. I tried again.

"Sawa sawa, Bwana. Habari mzuri sana. Toto yaku iko hapa sasa." *(Everything is OK, Bwana. The news is very good. Your baby is here now.)*

I asked him if he would like to come and see his new daughter? He nodded. He had been sitting there for hours convinced that Celestine had entered into some kind of mysterious netherworld and that she had indeed died. He was now, with my news, somewhere between relief and exhaustion. He got to his feet and followed me up the stairs into this murky region of women, blood, birth and magic. And... a daughter.

She was to be named after Jotham's grandmother, Fannis. I thought that a rather catchy name, Fannis. Fannis Kufuma Opondo. (I thought it should have been Fannis Melinda Opondo, but Kufuma did have a more African ring to it. And 'merinda' means skirt in Swahili. There is that little problem, with 'L's and 'R's and Kufuma was probably better.) Fannis. That was her Christian name. Her Luo name was Anyango, which of course, meant morning.

[I was very curious to know how many names there were in the Luo language. I knew there was Day and Night? What about morning in the rain? Celestine told me that there are about ten names. The hours of the day are grouped into sections: morning, noon, afternoon, night. There is also Raining in the morning and Sunny at the different times of day. There are also a few more specialized names: Okecho is a child born during a famine. There is a name for a child that is born on the verandah, and one that comes after twins is named Okello. There is even a name for a child born after a beer party, but I no longer recall what it was.]

Fannis resembled Jotham, except for her white hands. Not just the palms but, her whole hand was white. And I mean white like my hands are white. Mildred straightened me out on this point,

"You know, Madame, Fannis she is going to be the black one. "

"But of course," I thought, "How silly of me."

But then again, what other color was there? In the years that followed I found that the Africans often categorized each other by these variations on the theme of black. One child was 'red' and one was 'brown' and yet another was "the black one." I was also to learn that to be too dark was considered, by some, to be less attractive. It was a tribal distinction.

After Jotham stared into the bassinet and nodded that he had recorded this event, they took mother and baby off to the post-op ward to recover. This was a blessing; Celestine would not have to share a bed.

I said goodbye to Njoki who had stayed with us throughout this ordeal, gave her some money, as was customary, and drove the new Papa home. He was asleep on his feet. I told him when the visiting hours were and left him at the new house to boast and pound his chest with the other staff. I knew he would tell this tale over and over again. And why not? He could wring some serious mileage out of this. I went home to my little cottage, through the gates, and the dogs and fell, face down, into my bed.

I was over at the new house the next day when I spotted Steven Karanja.

"Karanja, did you hear habari mzuri *(the good news)*, of Mama Bado?"

"Oh yes, Madame. We have all heard the news and are thanking God for him."

There is no gender pronoun in Swahili and he and she, him and her, are often switched when speaking English.

"Him? What do you mean 'him'?"

"Yes, Madame. The baby boy for Jotham."

"Boy? Who told you the new baby was a boy?"

"Jotham. He told us Celestine she had a boy."

"Oh, Lord. Karanja, you had better send Jotham to talk to me."

When Celestine was ready to come home, I went to Pamwani with Jotham to collect her. I was still being quite helpful in this matter, but what I really wanted to do was to carry the baby to the car. I am a softy when it comes to babies, but I also felt that Fannis was somewhat my toto too. The proud parents liked this idea as it meant I had special feelings for Fannis and I would help to take care of her. I would probably have to send her to Yale one day, but for now, as I had also labored for her, Fannis was yango, *(mine.)* We turned more than a few heads as the three of us paraded out of the maternity ward: Jotham leading the way, me carrying the black and white baby, and Celestine trailing behind, giggling.

On the drive home, we all had the great fun of recounting the whole long saga to each other. We talked about who did what and how scared we all had been. There was much press given to how brave Jotham had been. He liked that part. I did my most dramatic imitation of Celestine clutching at my clothes and declaring "I am dying Madame, I am dying." There was high hilarity in the back seat as I repeated my performance over again.

As we drove up to the house, they both thanked me for all my help and said that God would now look out for me too. I said I was happy to help them. I am never sure about collecting good deed stamps to cash in with God, but I let that one slide.

A few days later Mildred, from whom all folklore flowed, told me that Celestine's family would show up any day now and take Fannis away. Jotham had not paid the full bride price and so he did not 'own' this toto. He would also be thoroughly castigated for the C-section. It was clearly his fault. He was from another tribe, and she had not been "cut" when she had Night, now had she? It was going to cost him one goat and hundreds more shillings to appease her family. Illiab's job was to sit down and negotiate a reasonably good deal with Celestine's 'Dad', or Jotham was in big trouble. Forever. He could be looking at a lifetime of chai *(bribery,)* and endless harassment from his in-laws. No wonder he was in tears that birthing night at the mere mention of an operation. This was blackmail, pure and simple.

There were big negotiations in my back yard, but no one made off with Fannis and by the time I left Kenya Jotham had yet to come up with the goat. I did, however, try to make it very clear to Celestine that the next time, should she be so careless as to get pregnant, she would be on her own. She assured me that she wanted no more totos.

"I do not want, Madame."

"Well, then do not have, Celestine."

"But what if Jotham he wants a boy?"

Two years later I noticed that Celestine was, once again, pregnant. She had a fit of giggling when I pointed out that her attempts at birth control had obviously failed. She had been having injections at the local clinic, but something had gone wrong. "It was a meestake." This time, however, the birth process was considerably easier. It all happened in a matter of hours, on the actual day that she thought it would.

To make sure that this child was as welcomed into my house as Fannis had been and that he was guaranteed a place in New Haven with his older sister, Celestine and Jotham named him Jake.

seventeen

At The Foot of the Ngong Hills . . .

I returned from a trip to New York in October, hauling a huge amount of goodies for the new house. There were many things, like doorknobs, fabric, tiles, lighting fixtures and sometimes nails, that you could not get in Kenya. I had tried to pack everything into my suitcases so that I didn't attract more than the usual amount of attention, but one large box of doorknobs didn't make it. I was pretty adept at getting through Customs without being hit, but that day I was sure I would be stopped.

When choosing a Customs line to go through I purposely stood behind an Asian family. The African Customs officers routinely singled out the Asians for extra scrutiny. I imagine it was a matter of one upmanship. I knew that the Customs man would make the Asian unpack every single item in his luggage. Having done so, he would be sated and probably wave me by. All was going smoothly when he spotted the cardboard box.

"What is that Madame?"

"What? The box?"

"Yes, what is in that box?"

"Oh, that. That's just doorknobs."

He looked at me quizzically. "Door knobs?"

"Yes, you know," and I made the twisting hand signal for turning a doorknob. "Door knobs."

"Oh, you mean locks,"

"That's right," recalling that 'locks' was the correct term in Kenya, "Locks."

"But, Madame, you have too many locks. It must cost you much money."

I said nothing.

"You have to pay duty on so many locks."

I had a wad of shillings in my pocket, at the ready. "Yes, mzee, I have to pay duty."

He paused for a split second, thrown by this rare burst of honesty. "OK. You wait for me outside."

"Outside?" I wanted to be sure I had heard him correctly.

"Yes. You go out and I will come." He pointed to the main exit of the customs hall.

He wanted me to wait outside the building and to pay the duty charges there. I knew, and he knew, and he probably knew that I knew, that Customs charges were not collected outside of the arrivals building on the pavement. He was going to pocket the cash.

"Sawa sawa mzee *(OK).* I will meet you there."

I wheeled my pile of goods out the door, glancing back at the long line of people waiting to pass his inspection. I had a good twenty minutes before this illegal rendezvous could possibly take place.

I asked a woman, an American tourist, standing by the outer curb if she would watch my things while I bolted for the lot where I had left my car. Diving into the front seat, I whooped when the engine turned over on the first try. I raced back to where the woman and all my gear were waiting, and threw it all into the back of the car. Thanking her quickly, I hit the accelerator and snickered all the way to Karen.

The now promised occupancy date on my house was November. Again, I asked Bhagwant not to give me false hope. I could stay in the cottage and I could go on a safari with Jake for the Christmas holidays if it was not going to be ready. But if Jake was going to be with me in Karen, the house had to be finished. I was assured, countless times, that there was absolutely no problem. It would be ready in mid November. At the very latest. There was no doubt that I would be moved in, with time to spare.

Graham had been gone almost sixteen months by this time and I was beginning to wonder if he would ever come back. After our romantic idyll in May, he had promised he would return to Africa as soon as he could, but as the months dragged on, I had serious doubts. He had endless excuses about all the pressing matters he had to attend to in Spain, but they rang hollow to me. None of my groaning in protest seemed to light too big a fire under him either. By December, however, he started to talk about taking a specific job in the Mara. There were some actual negotiations afoot. Infuriatingly vague, he could not be pinned down any further. He called every so often from his now seemingly permanent home in Spain, and told me he was always working to get back, he just couldn't say exactly when. I wanted the whole matter out of my mind, but I waited. I fumed and I howled and I complained, but I waited.

What made erasing his name from recent memory all the more difficult was the vast number of rumors that were forever reaching my ears. Kenya is a small place, especially as far as the European community is concerned, and the gossip level runs high. With little else to do or talk about, everyone is anxious to hear, to say nothing of pass on, every dirty tidbit.

Even factoring that in, I still had never encountered as many rumors about one man as there were afloat about Graham Elson. People were forever coming up to me, "well meaning" friends, or women I had met, and telling me that they "just hated to tell me this, but . . . "

There were endless stories about Graham and his wife, ranging from the far fetched—that she had children by another marriage—to the more probable, that they were far more "married" than he wanted me to know. I was always hearing that their long distant arrangement just made their times together that much sweeter. I was told that they were running a Bed and Breakfast in Spain, and one rumor had it that they were planning to spend their Christmas vacation that year flying around Africa. I was told that he had only gone back to Spain because she had called in the cards, demanding that he return. I could not imagine anyone demanding anything of Graham, but maybe she held a better hand than I.

There were persistent rumors about one particular stewardess. She was, I heard many times, pining away for the man. Last seen during one of her many visits to Kenya, she had been weeping over the Elson's Christmas card that had been sent to one of the other balloon pilots. Those tales even went so far as to say this stewardess and Graham had a child, a boy, who was stashed somewhere in Hawaii. I even heard rumors about myself. They had some other woman doing what I had actually done, but they were close to correct. I tried to ignore or dismiss all that I heard, but the sheer volume made it difficult. All I needed was to overhear from the adjoining table at lunch, "Do you know what I heard the other day about this pilot who used to be in the Mara?" and my stomach would knot up.

Each one of these stories sent me into fits of anger and doubt, and each one was duly brought up for Graham to answer to on the impossible international phone lines. He would deny whatever had been alleged and then launch into a tirade about how idiotic and small minded the people over there were to be wasting their time "talking such rubbish." How could I believe someone who obviously just wanted to get my goat? Furthermore, how could I believe these stories when I could see that even the rumors about me, or his having children, were untrue? I didn't know what to believe. I knew that when I called him and his wife answered the phone neither he nor she seemed the slightest bit fazed by the situation. He told me that she knew all about me and this was just part of their very British marital arrangement. And I certainly preferred his version to all the other ones I was hearing. But I also knew that the presence of smoke is almost always an indication of the attendant presence of fire. In this case there was, floating all over East Africa, one helluva lot of smoke.

Jake was due to arrive in Kenya on December seventeeth and as that day drew closer, my once even keel came right out of the water. The house was nowhere near finished. Everyday I went over there and every day I became more frantic. There were large sections of the roof that were not finished and the cement bases for the wooden floors had not even been poured. The kitchen cabinets were not installed and the windows had no glass in them. The area that had been done for Jake, a wing off the kitchen that contained a bedroom, a sitting room, and a bath, his "flat," was the only part that was actually habitable. It looked wonderful, but it wasn't big enough for both of us to live in. Nor did it finish the rest of the house. Bhagwant kept promising me that it would be done by the sixteenth of December and I kept telling him that I found that hard to believe. It was, to me, physically impossible.

When I drove into the driveway on the morning of the fourteenth, there must have been two hundred men at my house, working frantically. They were splashing paint around and nailing down floorboards.

The molding in the bedroom was going up and the tiles in the bathrooms were being put into place. Sort of. Lights were being installed and the roof was almost finished. I had never seen so many men working on one house in my life, and they started at dawn and went until sundown. For the next two days. It was an incredible last-ditch effort, and almost successful. But I had moved out of Tett's place, Jake was in an airplane on his way to Kenya and I had to move in. This was the deadline. On the sixteenth of December, I opened the garage doors and started to move the bulk of my furniture into this barely ready house.

When I pointed out that all that frantic fixing up had made for some very sloppy workmanship, Bhagwant assured me that after the holidays he would fix it. I would move out of the main house and into Jake's flat and he would redo whatever needed redoing. I found that rather incredible, but the whole process of building this house had been quite fantastic, why not this too? Besides, I reassured myself, I was withholding ten percent of the agreed-upon price for six months after the completion of the work. This was standard practice in Kenya and it was designed specifically to protect the client from just what I was facing. It never occurred to me that the ten percent was built into the price. No one expected to collect it.

I stayed up the entire night of the sixteenth getting the house ready for Jake's arrival. I wanted him to walk in and be totally thrilled. I hung curtains and pictures. I put away all the china and made up all the beds. My staff had been let go around midnight, after spending the day unpacking boxes and moving furniture, but I wouldn't quit until it was done. By the time I went to collect Jake at the airport at six the next morning, I had not slept in twenty four hours. I was falling down I was so exhausted, but the new house looked wonderful. Jake was very impressed, especially with his flat. He had the very good sense to tell me how everything surpassed his expectations.

He was especially thrilled to see some of his grandmother's furniture again. They had adored one another, and he had nothing but fond memories her. Looking at all the things that had been in her various homes was a joyous stroll down memory lane. I wasn't quite so thrilled. I felt as if far too many ghosts were floating around my new house. Every time I turned a corner, I was startled. I had not seen many of the things that were now hanging on my walls, sitting on my tables or standing in my living room for over four years. And everything was fraught with memories. There were even old photo albums I had not seen in decades. Pictures from my mother's childhood, as well as mine, gave my memories a rush. Those were the good memories, but there were far too many sad ones.

I had spent many miserable nights wandering around my mother's house at four in the morning. I had been waiting for her to get better, kmowing she was only getting sicker and finally, in those last four days, waiting for her to die. The memories of her death and the very painful three years that had preceded it were now everywhere I turned. There were smells and sights that made me jump when caught off guard. That whole Christmas was flooded with feelings I had chosen to suppress and memories of almost every year of my life. I was alternately sad, confused, and angry.

After our first Christmas on Dagoretti Road, Jake went back to school and I moved into his "flat." All the furniture that had been set up in the house only three weeks before was now put back into the garage and the doors nailed shut again. The re-fixing of the main house was going to take place and there was a considerable amount to do. The wooden beams that had been put into my bedrroom ceiling, cut from uncured wood, had already warped. The polyurethane on all the wood floors was smeared and streaked from being walked on before it was dry. All the kitchen tiles needed to be re-grouted. Most of the doors didn't close properly and many of the lights didn't work. The hot water heaters didn't turn on when they were supposed to and if they did, they cut off before they got truly hot. There were holes in the roof through which you could see the sky.

The rain in Africa can be frightening in it's intensity, and it was now pouring through the holes in the roof and into my light fixtures. It not only soaked all my curtains and carpets, but gave me pause to consider my immanent death by electrocution as well. Many nights, waking to the sound of the rain pounding on the roof, I bolted out of bed, just to spend the next hours pulling up rugs and laying towels all over the house in an attempt to hold back the rivers that were coursing through the hallways. When the towels reached their water saturation capacity, they had to be wrung out and put back down. I did not go back to bed until the rain stopped and, on many nights, it didn't. All this was obviously the result of doing too much too quickly. To say the work was 'sloppy' would be charitable.

The two and a half months I spent living in Jake's wing could only be described as miserable. The rain was incredible that year and everything was cold, damp, dark, muddy, and extremely inconvenient. Mildred was on her leave and Celestine was only in the early stages of learning how to cook. Not that it mattered, all the appliances had been removed, and I didn't have a proper kitchen anyway. But I could have used Mildred's cool head and calming manner. I always felt looked after when she was around and her absence just added to the darkness of the days. My cooking for that time was done with a local electric kettle and the toaster oven from my mother's apartment in New York City (with a voltage converter of course). The evening hours, and those begin at six thirty in Kenya, were especially long that season. My lingering impression of those months is one of mud and wet and cold. There were far too many mediocre spring rolls and an overwhelming loneliness. All of which was alleviated by too much Scotch and endless shouting matches with my contractor.

For everything I was promised, there was the exact same number of things that didn't happen. I was told, straight to my face, that the roof, the tiles, the power, the wiring, and the heaters would be taken care of in a day or two. And then it would simply not happen. Every day I was told that it would get done in the next few days. And then it didn't. When confronted with my howling protestations, the contractor would just look me in the face tell me the same lie yet another time. After weeks of this, the situation got extremely heated and the level of my hostility escalated precipitously. When I wasn't cold, wet, bored, and lonely, I was frothing at the mouth.

At the end of January, after an eighteen-month absence, I got a phone call from Graham.

"I am coming back to Kenya."

"Yeah, right."

He insisted that he would call me from Heathrow within the next few days.

Then all of a sudden, there we were in Nairobi, face to face. It felt nervous and unreal and yet Graham fit so well into the very air of Kenya that it also seemed absolutely natural. It was as if no time had passed at all and we were right back to where we had been a year and a half before. Except that I wasn't really the same.

When Graham had left Kenya, on that July fourth, I was still fumbling around over at the President's house with not much of a life at all. I hadn't even decided to stay in Kenya. Since then I had lost my best friends, designed and built (almost anyway) my house and taken on twenty five employees at Kufuma. It was an entirely different existence. As we walked around my back yard, with my pointing out all that had been done on the house and showing him the factory, he allowed that he was rather impressed.

"I didn't know you were so clever."

"You thought I was just another pretty face?"

I wonder that I didn't faint in astonishment. Or video tape the whole exchange. I think it was the only compliment the man ever paid me. His British reticence took some extreme forms.

Graham stayed with me for a few days and we got "reacquainted." He would tell me very little about what he had been doing, why it took so long to get back or what his plans now were. Was he going to stay in Kenya? For a month? A year? And, the biggest question of all, "What about Pamela?" He was evasive and vague about everything I asked him, but to questions about his wife, he simply got angry. He would not talk about her or their relationship. I thought I had the right to know. He did not. If I pressed it too far, he shouted me down. There was an anger lurking right below the surface in Graham and I did not want to tap too far into.

But I was glad that he was back, still clinging to the idea that this would make things better. I would not be so lonely now. I could go down to the Mara on the weekends and he could come up to Karen every now and then and we would have, for Kenya anyway, a normal relationship.

eighteen

Mildred

Just after Christmas, before it was time for Mildred's annual leave, she told me that she needed to go back to her home in Kitale. Immediately. When I asked her why, she recounted a dream she had recently had about her father. It was an omen. Apparently he had not been buried properly, either not in the right place or not with enough honors. This particular discussion took real nuance of language and I never did get all the details straight. She felt that this on going illness of hers had something to do to with his incomplete burial. It had been her responsibility, as his child, to see that he was buried properly. She felt that she was being punished from the grave.

"Mildred, do you really believe that?"

"Oh, yes Madame. You know Madame, we did not bury him in right way. He is calling me now. I heard him in my dream. I will die soon. I have to go to home."

"But I thought you were a Christian and didn't believe all this stuff?"

"I myself do not believe, Madame. But he is calling."

She took her leave a few days later, and when she did not return when expected, I feared something must be seriously wrong. I knew Mildred wouldn't leave without a word to me and her continued absence had me worried. And I was lost without her. Mildred ran the house and she took care of me. More than my simple affection, she had my trust, and now she had, as they say in Kenya, gone missing.

When she had not returned by February, it was time to find out what had happened to her. I summoned her brother Wilson, who now worked for me as a car mechanic and general fundi, and asked him to go to Kitale to find her. He returned within the week and reported back to me. It wasn't good news. Mildred was in a hospital, in a coma. She was lying like a plank—he imitated her posture—and he could get no response from her.

"She is dying now." Wilson told me.

"But Wilson, what is the matter with her? "

"Nothing is the matter, Madame."

"Well, something has to be the matter. Why would she be lying like that?"

"Even me, myself, I do not know Madame."

"Well, what do the doctors say?"

"They say nothing is the matter." He paused and considered the effect his next statement might have on me. "She has, nini, the spell."

"What?"

"She has a spell on her."

I had read about this ability to simply lie down and die if someone thought they had been bewitched, but I had never seen it happen. I thought it was old Kenyan folklore. But there was Wilson, a quite reasonable fellow, telling me that this was the case.

"Daniel Ojijo has put spell on Mildred, Madame. She will die now," he continued. It had been awhile since I had heard Daniel's name. There he was, rearing his unwelcome head.

"Wilson, you can't be serious. I thought all of you were Christians and didn't believe this stuff."

"Even me I do not believe. But it is true. He took her things and he put a curse on her."

Much of the Christianity brought to Africa by the missionaries was but a superficial veneer spread thinly over far more ingrained and basic beliefs. It was all fine and good to quote the Bible and name your children Matthew, Ruth or Naomi, but when push came to shove, they almost always reverted to the religious traditions that had been handed down for generations.

"But, Wilson, how can this be?"

"It is true, Madame."

"Good Lord. Well, Wilson, what are we going to do?"

He paused.

"Get a witch doctor, Madame."

"A what?"

"A witch doctor. He will take the spell off Mildred and she will be better. It is good."

I had a better idea.

"Wilson, why don't we just tell Mildred that Ojijo has been located and that I met with him and made him take the spell off. Tell her that I was very kali (*fierce*) with him and threatened to call the police if he didn't do it. Just tell her that it was removed and that it's okay now. She'll believe it and she will get better. Right?"

He laughed out loud.

"No, Madame. She will not believe."

Francis, Mildred's friend, (she always told me they were not lovers. "I am not keeping nicely with him, Madame,") was one of my shamba men. He was an ex-school teacher, and whether they were "keeping nicely" or not he was close to Mildred and very fond of her. As he joined Wilson and me that morning in the driveway there were tears rolling down his face. Francis agreed that the only thing to do was get the witch doctor. Once again I questioned his belief in this hocus pocus, but his answer was just to weep and shake his head.

I gave Wilson some money and told him to do whatever he needed to do. I also gave him a small, framed picture of Jake and myself, saying that it was my counter magic. Jake and I would not allow her to die. We had strong powers too. Francis told me that Mildred put great store in what she considered my vast knowledge of medicine. Although it seemed a bit of a stretch to mix witchcraft in with my supposed medical knowledge, who was I to say what people can or cannot do if they believe something. And it was no more far fetched than my mother putting her life in the hands of macrobiotic gurus and eating seaweed and brown rice in an attempt to cure her cancer. Wilson nodded solemnly and put the picture in his pocket.

As Wilson was packing, the other house staff members and all the people from Kufuma came to listen to his long story, to weep together and express their sympathies. Pole. Pole sana. They were always extremely sympathetic and supportive of each other in the face of life's tragedies. The pace of life is slower there to start with, and when illness or tragedy surface, there is always time to listen to someone else's shauris, and to say pole. Pole sana.

Wilson left for Kitale and the vigil began. I had asked him to telephone me the minute anything happened, but days went by, then weeks, without a call. I couldn't understand what was wrong. He was as reliable and steady as his sister. It didn't seem possible that he would just take my money and run off. Celestine said that if I wanted to go to the faith healer in the next village she would be glad to take me. This woman, Mary Akatsa, was a clairvoyant and could tell me if Mildred was going to live or die. I did not go. I didn't want to know.

Finally the call came. Wilson reported that the witch doctor had done his magic and that Mildred had emerged from the coma. She was out of the hospital and was going to be coming back to Karen soon. I believed him, and I was certain that they both believed that it was the witch doctor who had restored Mildred to life. It was March when Mildred was finally well enough to travel back to Karen. Ernest, the other brother, was dispatched to help Wilson bring her home.

When I first saw Mildred she was sitting in the staff quarters, too weak to stand, rail thin and ashen. But she was alive. I sat down next to her and gave her a hug. That was really trespassing on the colonial rules about getting physical with one of my staff, but I didn't care. I told Mildred that I was now in charge of her care and feeding, and that she was going to eat what I considered a proper diet, not just maize meal and cabbage. I would supply her with meat, vegetables, potatoes, fruit, and vitamins.

She looked at me and smiled her wonderful smile and just said. "Yes, Madame."

Of course none of my other staff would complain about her favored status. There was a communal cooking pot and everyone would start to put on a bit of weight.

I feared, however, that she was far more ill, traditionally speaking, than we knew. If we didn't see great improvement soon, I would break another cardinal rule of life in the tropics, and my own rule as well, and take her to Nairobi Hospital for testing.

The "Heal Mildred" campaign began in earnest. I bought all kinds of things to make soups, as she couldn't hold down much else, and fruits of every variety. I had cases of little cartons of juices on hand and she was instructed to drink one an hour. She was seriously dehydrated. Apparently the whole time she was in the hospital in Kitale, she was just left on her own with no I.V drip, no glucose solution. She had trouble swallowing, but she was brave and kept trying. I tried to get down to the staff quarters twice a day to check on things, but some days it was difficult for me to face her. My biggest worry of course, was that she had cancer. As much as I rationally understood that I was dragging up all my old terrors about my mother's death, watching Mildred waste away gave me nightmares. It was often with considerable dread that I headed down the path to her nyumba each day. I braced myself for what I would find. I feared that one day I would walk in and she would be dead.

But she wasn't dead, just very weak, and resigned to her fate. Once again, I was bumping up against the this propensity to just accept life as it is dealt them. Urging Mildred to fight back, I started my lecture series on "Trying to Get Better." I told her that she had to TRY. She had to get up and walk. Even if she didn't want to, she had to make herself do it. If she just lay there, she would get weaker. It wasn't easy discussing the atrophication of muscle tissue, but I tried to get her to understand. I was also trying to save my Mother's life all over again. I felt, just as I had when my mother was dying, that if I could just infuse Mildred with enough of my strength and energy, she could make it. Unlike my mother, though, Mildred believed me and took my words to heart.

I made up different routes for her to walk each day. Once around the staff quarters, twice around the garden, once down to the Kufuma factory and back. She could not walk without help for quite awhile, but as the weeks wore on, she began to make it on her own. Each day a little better. Each week a little further. Each time a little more erect. And one day, after several months of this, I saw her walking by the back windows on her way to the kitchen. She could not stand for too long so she sat on a stool and directed traffic, but she was back in the house. Associating my own well-being with Mildred's being there to take care of me was probably not a good idea, but I rejoiced that she was back in the kitchen. As most of the refinishing work was almost completed and I had moved back into the main house, I hoped that the worst, for both of us, was over.

nineteen

The Rains Down in Africa

It was a holiday weekend. It may have been Easter or it may have been a uniquely Kenyan holiday, all I recall is that it was some holiday in April. A three-day weekend. The weekends were always lonely and long for me, but a three-day weekend could be painful. There was nothing to do and no one to do it with. Karen was a family oriented town and without a family, one was all but lost. You could drop in on your friends and hang out at their house for a few hours, but I was never comfortable doing that. And what would you talk about that you hadn't talked about the day before? You could not go for a long walk, it was too dangerous, and no one would think about window shopping in Nairobi. There weren't even any newspapers or magazines to speak of. The bookstore at the Yaya Center stocked primarily textbooks, coffee table books on Kenya, and English romance novels. Browsing there might kill all of thirty minutes. And all stores were closed on Sunday.

[Yes, it was called the Yaya Center and it was a vertical mall of sorts just outside Nairobi, that was built in the early 90's. No one knew or seemed to question what Yaya meant. It was multistoried with large orange panels as decoration. Although it was built around a center atrium, the shops grew increasingly stuffy and hot as the day wore on. The architect had forgotten to build in any windows in the rear of the shops and there was no cross ventilation. When the smells emanating from the several restaurants merged with the unmoving air of the shops and the shoppers, it could get very unpleasant. There was a butchery on the ground floor that one would never want to frequent after ten AM. There was a glass sided elevator. It was the first one in Kenya and many of the local people thought this to be the eighth wonder of the modern world. Why anyone would want to get into an elevator in Kenya, land of the unannounced power cuts, was a mystery to me, but they did so at the Yaya Center. And there were working escalators at Yaya, so the reasoning for this was even more obscure. Nonetheless, the Yaya Center was a busy place. Except on Sunday and then even it was closed.]

With this long weekend looming ahead, I sent word to Graham that I was coming down to the Mara to see him. Using the method that I had had the most success with, I sent a "package" to him on one of the flights out of Wilson Airport. I would take the letter I had written and put it into a larger envelope. I would then add a T-shirt, or the like, to make it look more substantial, more important. Like a gift. I had found that if I sent a small envelope it would invariably end up in the pilot's back pocket or flight bag for a few weeks. A larger item was less likely to get tucked away. I also tried to give it to someone who knew Graham and hopefully me as well. It usually worked.

When my morning flight was landing in the Mara that Saturday, I did not to see the Range Rover Graham usually drove waiting at the airstrip. He was working for Transworld Safaris at the time and their logo, a multicolored balloon flying over a large rainbow, was plastered on the side of all the company vehicles. It could usually be seen as the plane circled for final approach. Fortunately, there were other wageni being picked up and a lodge vehicle was there to meet them. Graham was stationed at Mara Serena and, having been down there quite a few times, I was well known by most of the staff. For the twenty minutes that it took to drive from the airstrip to the lodge, I made small talk with the driver. I thought he was looking at me in a particularly odd manner and so I asked him if Graham was there. Life in the Mara was staggeringly consistent, with one day the perfect clone of the one before it. But occasionally there was some emergency that required one of the pilots to drive over to some other camp. It was at least a two-hour drive and staying for lunch was thus a necessity. After this problem was sorted out, there was enough time for a few beers before heading back. It could kill an afternoon. But this was not the case that day. Graham was at his house.

I grabbed my bag from the back of the car and headed down to the balloon house. Each camp had a separate house where the pilots lived. This afforded them some distance from the lodge itself and some privacy. (Considering the amount of sex with the clients that went on, that was a necessity.) It was also meant to be a proper home for the pilots who had their wives living with them. They were all about the same, two bedroom cement block affairs, with a kitchen and several bathrooms, but the Serena balloon house had the best view of all. It sat high on a rocky ledge that looked out over the plains. You could see for hundreds of miles and it afforded us a perfect spot for surveying all that went on in the Mara. A large part of our day could be taken up with watching the small aircraft come and go, observing the patterns of the migrating herds, tracking the annual grass fires and noting the seasonal weather patterns. It was also a great place for having a sundowner or sex under the stars.

I walked passed the kitchens and the staff quarters and took a sharp right onto Graham's verandah. There he was—sitting on a wicker chair, smoking a cigar, chatting with a woman who was sunbathing with her bathing suit top all but off. I knew instantly who she was: his wife, Pamela. Maybe it was the knot that tightened in my stomach or the way his face flinched or the look on hers. I had never even seen a picture of her and if I saw her today I would not recognize her, but I did that morning.

"What brings you here?" he snapped.

"You obviously didn't get my letter."

"Obviously not. This is Pamela. Pam, Melinda."

"Oh hi. How are you?" she actually chirped at me.

"Never better." I choked out and then turned on my heel and left. Without saying a word to her, Graham was running up the path to the lodge behind me. I no longer recall what he said, just that he was rattling on at a great rate.

I said nothing until we got up to the bar. I ordered a gin and tonic and then had a great deal to say.

What transpired next is about what you would expect: hours of tears and shouting, lots of "how could yous" and "I had no ideas" and a few more gin and tonics. He was visibly distraught, a fact that gave me some solace as I was in a weeping, hair tearing rage. This was a reality byte that I had not expected and did not want.

I knew about Pamela, I had from the beginning. I knew that

Graham had been at her house in Spain on and off for the past eighteen months. I had spoken to him there. I didn't like it, less because of where he was than the feeling that he was lying to me, but I certainly knew about it. But the line I had been fed ever since Day One was that they were "separated." They "led their own lives." I accepted this because I wanted to accept it. The key point that morning was that I believed that his being away from Kenya for the past year and a half had been the aberration and his coming back signaled that he was there to be with me. They were not a couple, we were.

Pamela made these treks to Africa every year. If Graham had not told me that himself, there's an excellent chance that every gossip in Karen surely had. But he had presented this to me in the light that she had her own friends in Africa and she was there to see them, not him. She liked to come on safari just as much as anyone else did. It was not a conjugal visit.

"So what is she doing at your house now, sunbathing with her bloody top off?" I howled. She just "popped 'round." She was staying at Governor's actually and had just come over for the weekend. He hadn't told me because he knew I would get upset. He was sparing my feelings. It was nothing.

"OK, then where is she sleeping?"

There was no good answer to that and I went off on another weeping tear. I was furious, but, more than that, I was humiliated. It was one thing to know she was in Spain and it was all fine and good for them to be 'friends,' but it was an entirely different matter to have her here. In Africa. In my territory. In HIS bed. She was his "wife."

What did that make me? The bimbo?

After hours of high drama, I said that I wanted him to get on the radio to Airkenya and find out if there was a plane coming to Serena, or any of the other camps for that matter, that afternoon. And I wanted him to get me on it. He did. Then we got in his car and drove out to the airstrip to wait for the plane. And watch the sky darken.

This was April and we were in the middle of the long rains and the chance of huge storms blowing up in a moment's notice was great. They could race across the Mara drenching everything in their path in a matter of minutes or they could just sit in one spot. The sun could be shining all around this enormous faucet that had been turned on in the clouds above. As we sat there tracking the plane making its appointed rounds at the other camps, we also tracked a thunderstorm that was heading across the plains towards us. The question was not so much would it come this way, but if it did, would it get there before or after the plane.

Before. The plane was on its way from Governors, the last stop before Serena. We were talking to the pilot on Graham's air radio, when the storm picked up speed, raced over to where we were parked and, as if deliberately planned, opened up right on our heads. There was lightening, there was thunder, there were high winds. Right on the runway. The pilot, circling nearby, took one look at that and said to Graham,

"There is no way I am landing in the middle of that. I'm outta here. Kwa Heri."

He banked his plane to the left and flew due East, back to Nairobi. Leaving Graham and me sitting there with our mouths hanging open, staring out at the deluge still falling from the skies. We knew that that was the end of the line. There were no other options. There were not going to be any more flights and it was too late to escape to another lodge to avoid this coming soap opera. There was no way out of this. I was stuck there. Graham was stuck with his wife and his mistress in the same hotel for the coming night. And we were all stuck in a lodge that was filled to capacity for this holiday weekend.

Nothing was said as we drove back to what awaited us at the lodge. The bumpy ride I would have had in that small airplane now half way to Nairobi was nothing compared to the 'fun' we were all going to have that night.

Graham managed to wrangle me a room in the hotel and then spent the entire night traipsing back and forth from his house to my room. I spent the entire night crying and I have no idea what Pamela spent the entire night doing. The only thing that happened out of the expected was when I bumped into her in the dining room (the hotel served dinner in two shifts.) She just walked up to me and in that irritating, chirpy, British fashion said, "My, you certainly have had an interesting day, now haven't you?"

I was speechless and, again, just walked away. I don't know how she was taking this, but I found it embarrassing and awkward. I had no intentions of having little bonding moments with this woman. I didn't care what kind of an "English" marriage they had, I was sleeping with her husband and, where I came from, that wasn't considered grounds for a friendly chat over cocktails. Graham seemed bordering on nauseated the whole time and as close to a screaming fit as I had ever seen him. This may not have wrinkled Pamela's starchy exterior, but it certainly rendered Graham nearly frantic. It was also the first time I had seen him upset about my emotional well being. Up until then all my howling about my feelings being stepped on was usually met with him telling me not to be so "daft." But that night he seemed truly shaken and even appeared to be worried about me. (I now think he was probably worried that I might be carrying a large knife or packing a pistol. I just might have a jealous female go at his throat should the right moment present itself. But at the time, I read his pale countenance as "love.")

We all lived through the night and I was on the morning flight back to Nairobi. I have no idea what those two said to each other (probably very little) or what happened after I left. I went back to Karen and wrote long letters to my friends recounting this tale, and explaining why it was that I had not knee-capped the man. I came up with the best rationalization for my spineless behavior and obvious willingness to accept just about anything that has ever been penned. I then repeated it over again until it was firmly etched into my brain. Then I believed it too.

Pamela left Kenya a week or so later and that was the last I heard about her for awhile. And, on the surface anyway, Graham and I went back to doing what we had been doing ever since his return. It wasn't as though nothing had happened, it clearly had, we just didn't talk about it. I tried any number of times to get some further information on just what was going on, what was his position with her, and what was to happen next. He simply refused to talk about it. I didn't know how he could refuse to talk about something that important, but he did. He would make it very clear to me that if I pushed this he would get very angry. And I backed down. Every bloody time.

But somewhere down deep, I had taken a significant hit. After that April weekend in the Mara it was hard for me to convince myself that all was well, that I was the one and only and that he was really "separated" from his wife. This was not what I had expected and certainly not what I wanted. I was hurt, I was humiliated, and I was angry. I now think it's amazing and a testimony to both my loneliness and my ability to believe whatever it is that I wanted to believe that I didn't tell him to take a hike right then. But Graham was my only really intimate relationship. I had no real close friends over there, no one who had known me in New York or well enough to stick their nose into my affairs. And probably no one who cared that much. There was no one to take me by the shoulders, shake me, and say, "Have you lost your mind?" But even if I could not admit it outloud, I knew that this relationship was a lousy one. He lied to me and he cheated on me, and yet things still went on.

twenty

Gorillas

My friends, Eleanor and Peter Nalle, made their first safari to Kenya the spring after I moved there. Travel of that ilk was not, up until then, Eleanor's usual choice, but by the time they left Africa, the success of that first safari had her conversion to a true Africa-phile well under way. Back again this year for another dose, they started their safari at the Coast. But after one week, Peter had to return to Philadelphia for some business crisis. Eleanor and son Graham stayed on.

Following in the footsteps of the master safari planner, young Winter, I did unto them as he had done unto me. I raised the bar a little higher each trip, making every safari slightly more demanding. The hours were longer, the roads rougher and the accommodations at the end of the day a bit less predictable. As long as expectations weren't too high and the surprises kept to a minimum, it usually worked out. This year we were going to track the Gorillas in Zaire. I had attempted to do this once before on my own, but had sprained my ankle on the first day out. I never saw the Gorillas. I spent the rest of that safari sitting in a tent, on a drizzly mountainside in Zaire, watching my foot swell, and swilling warm beer.

The beginning of this trip was not particularly auspicious either. Our entire first day was spent at Jomo Kenyatta Airport waiting for our flight to Rwanda to depart. We were joined by three other couples and one single man, all of whom had come from the USA, seeking great adventure in Zaire. They were, instead, stuck in Kenya's miserable excuse for an international airport for the better part of a long day. By the time we arrived in Rwanda, it was too late for the connecting puddle-hopper to the Zaire border to take off. The runway at the other end had no lights. The representative from our travel agency was encouraging us to make the rest of the trip by car. It was, he kept repeating, "Not too far." We were all tired, hungry, and anxious for this endless day of travel to be over, and this sounded a bit too vague to suit me. When asked to be more specific about the duration of this proposed car ride, he allowed that it was "about five hours." That didn't strike me as 'not too far.' Given the condition of most roads in Africa, a five-hour trip would undoubtedly turn into an eight-hour trip. We were also told that we would get some dinner "some place." It was, by then, seven PM. This was not a good plan.

I knew many people in the safari business and had heard countless times that when there was a mishap of this sort, late arrivals of planes and the like, their job was to hustle around and keep things moving and on track. I also knew that these proposed alternative plans were mere "suggestions." No where was it written that the client had to accept some mediocre, quickie solution. I proposed another plan. Why didn't we stay in Kigali that night, getting us a meal within the hour and a good nights sleep, and then catch the next day's flight to Zaire. It would require switching the reservations around a bit, but that was do-able. The tricky part was not the hotel reservations; the real issue was exchanging the permits we held to see the Gorillas.

Due to the state of near endangerment of the species, World Wildlife and CITES had requested that the various African Governments institute strict laws to protect the Lowland Gorillas. Several measures had been put into place. The first was to limit the number of people who could visit any one habituated group to eight people. Secondly, the amount of time you could spend with them was also restricted. Even if it took you five hours to find your assigned group, and this was highly possible given the mountainous terrain they favored, you were only allowed to stay one hour. It was strictly adhered to. This was for two reasons. First of all, there was the very real concern that the Gorillas would become too used to humans. Losing their fear would make them more likely to wander into the local villages in search of food. If they took to munching on the local people's crops, they might get shot at for their crimes. Then there was the risk of catching human diseases. The Gorillas immune systems were close enough to humans to make them vulnerable to our maladies. A cold, the flu, a "runny tummy" could be fatal for them.

Knowing all this, we had purchased permits for two consecutive days to increase our chances of seeing them. We had these permits months in advance because, under normal circumstances, they were always sold out. That was not the case that year. This was before the more serious problems in Rwanda erupted, but there was still enough local friction to keep most American tourists away. I had a friend in Karen who led these very trips and she had told me, just the week before, that her trips were half-empty. I was certain that we could swap our permits for different days and was obviously willing to risk it.

The three American couples from the plane elected to take the mini vans to Zaire that night. Eleanor and I and our two boys stayed in Kigali. The tall guy, Harry from Hawaii, had the good sense to agree with me about this endless drive into the African night, and joined our party. (Eleanor entertained all kinds of matchmaking schemes during that trip. None materialized.) For very different reasons than budding romances, it was an advantage to have a man with us. In Africa, it was very difficult to get any attention paid to a woman and Harry's very male presence lent us much needed clout. When he changed the wording of our desire to switch our tickets from "request" to "rather insist upon," he got the nod of recognition from our travel representative that I had been vainly seeking.

The flight the next morning depositing us near the Rwanda/Zaire border took forty-five minutes and was fairly uneventful. Neither Eleanor nor Harry, however, was a big fan of bouncing around on the African thermals in small aircraft and both were seriously green when we landed. We were met at the airstrip by a car and driver whose task it was to get us through all border formalities and deliver us safely to our hotel on the shores of the lovely Lake Kivu.

When we arrived at the Zaire customs building, a small, nondescript shack on a dusty road, we were greeted by a man in some kind of uniform. It was probably military issue, but it had seen better days. He stuck his head in the window to have a look at us and after walking around the car and exchanging a few words with our driver, went back into the customs shed. Returning in a few minutes with another chap, also dressed in some form of military garb, they talked further with our driver. After a few more exchanges, ever increasing gesticulations and strident tones, our driver informed us that we needed to get out and take all our luggage with us into the customs shed. I looked at Eleanor and she looked at me and Harry looked at us both.

"Uh oh." At the very least, this was going to be a hassle. At the worst . . . ? We dragged all our gear out of the trunk.

I have crossed many dicey borders in many strange places and been hassled on many different levels in quite a few of them. I have had both small and large amounts of contraband either in my luggage or in my back pocket, but I was never really all that frightened. I am also never completely calm until I am on my way again, well around the next bend. I did not like the feel of this.

When we got into the customs shed, basically two rooms, we were told to hand over our US passports. I get nervous sending my passport through the U.S. mail for a new visa and when the man then left the room with all three passports, I was even less pleased. We were told to open our suitcases. Eleanor and I were instructed to open up our cosmetic bags as well. Everything was looked into. As they do not speak Swahili in Zaire, I had no idea what was being said. Asking our guide didn't help, he was busy translating everything into English and looked even more uncomfortable than we did. After about half an hour of this, Eleanor and I were told to pack up our stuff and leave, without our passports. We did as we were told.

Back in the car, the boys were anxious to know what was going on. We didn't do too much to allay their fears, as we were far from comfortable with this situation ourselves. Then we waited.

Harry finally emerged about an eternity later, looking haggard. But he was carrying his bag and had all our passports in his hand. Folding his large frame into the front seat with a sigh, he slammed the car door behind him and said, "We're outta here."

Aside from just hasseling us for the sake of it, the bigger issue was money. As a visitor in Zaire, Americans were required to pay for everything with American dollars. The Zaire government was no fool, as we have all since learned, and they wanted hard currency. Harry didn't have enough. He had enough for him to be there on holiday for three days; he just didn't have enough for all five of us. Who elected Harry our guardian and the keeper of the exchequer? The customs guys. They thought we were one big happy family; a man and his two wives and matching children. I suppose it could have made sense: we were all Americans and all about the same age. Jake was blond like his mother and Graham had dark hair like his. Having several wives was common place in Zaire and Harry was a big guy, after all.

Harry told us that he had tried to explain that we had all just met and that our traveling together was purely coincidental. They didn't buy it. What finally got his point across was when he took all the pictures out of his wallet and showed them to the customs officers. "Here is my dog and here is my Mom and here is my girlfriend and me in Hawaii." No pictures of the two ladies in the car outside. No pictures of his two sons. For whatever reason, that rang true to the customs fellows. That they understood and they let him go. Of course, it would have been just as easy to ask Eleanor and me how much US currency we were holding, but that never occurred to them.

When we finally arrived at the hotel, the very inappropriately named Riviera, we learned that the other American couples had arrived in one piece. But it had taken all night. They got to the hotel about forty five minutes before they were slated to be ready to start their trek into the woods. Their day had been a long one. The Gorilla family they had been assigned to was deep into the forest and it had taken over four hours to locate them. Then another four to get back out. They were tired and didn't have too many smiles for us. I spared them the "I told you so's."

To add to their irritation, our Gorilla tracking that next day was quick and easy. After we switched our tickets, which didn't require much more than greasing a few palms, we set out the first morning and located the Gorillas in about thirty minutes. The next day it took us about four hours, but by then, we were well rested.

Before you are allowed to go off to seek the Gorillas, you are given instructions on what you may and may not do. You may not touch them, even if they get close to you or even if one of the youngsters touches you first. You must never stare them in the eyes, especially the dominant male. He is easy enough to identify as he weighs about eight hundred pounds and has a prominent streak of silver hair running down his back. He is quite obviously, the main man. Staring at any of the Gorillas is not a good idea, but staring at the Silverback, eyeball to eyeball, is a high-risk venture. He will take it as a challenge. Once challenged, being the alpha male that he is, he will feel compelled to prove himself. That will almost certainly take the form of a charge. It is usually a mock charge, but you can't really tell that until he stops. What you are told to do, in the case of a charge, is drop down into a crouch and avert your gaze. Look humble and submissive, cower and tremble. But whatever you do, don't run. If you bolt, he will take this challenge to the next level and chase you. And given that this is his territory and he is faster, bigger and more surefooted than you are, the chances of him catching you and taking a bite out of your backside are excellent.

On our second day of Gorilla tracking, we went deeper into the Zairian forest. It took us many hours to locate our Gorillas. Once located, we had been following them around for some time, always at a proper distance, waiting for them to settle down and munch on some leaves. As long as they kept swinging through the trees looking for the perfect place for brunch, we had to follow along through the thicket underneath. They never really stopped moving, but at one point they were still enough for us to attempt to get a bit closer. These are habituated, and they did permit people to come closer than a totally wild Gorilla might, but only just so close. We were all watching and peering through the underbrush trying to see the various family members when there was a horrific scream. The pounding of chest sounds and the crashing of branches and more screaming brought this massive Gorilla into view. He was in full charge, teeth bared, headed right for us.

Did Harry and Eleanor and I stop in our tracks and crouch down? Did we lower our eyes and avert our gaze? Did we do as we had been instructed to do? Not a chance. We ran. Moving as one piece, we bolted. Luckily, we tripped over each other and landed in a tangle on the ground. In a pile of Gorilla poo. We sat there staring at each other with the Silverback only a few yards away. He had stopped his charge. Not only did he have no further reason too continue, we were clearly the lesser beings, but I am sure he was on the verge of laughter. There he was standing up and scaring everyone to death and there we were piled on top of each other in a heap on the ground, sitting in a pile of his leavings.

That night we were back in Kigali. The flight back to Nairobi was, once again, delayed. At the time it was due in Rwanda, it had not even left Kenya. It would be well past three in the morning, if we were very lucky, before we got back to Karen.

Hanging around the Kigali airport was seriously tedious. It was uncomfortable and there was nothing to do. As the hours ticked by, getting progressively more disgruntled with this situation, I noticed on the departure sign that there was a plane leaving for Nairobi within the hour. Air France. It was on its way to Paris, but it was stopping in Nairobi to pick up passengers. Why don't we hop on that? The desk agent informed me that was impossible. The flight only took on passengers in Nairobi, it didn't let them off. There was no luggage facility to unload our baggage and no passport clearance either. I explained to the man that we only had carry on bags and that we were all staying in Kenya and that I was a Kenya resident. I cannot imagine what possible difference it could have made that I was a Kenya resident, but it must have. Or maybe it was my fast-talking or that I slipped some money into his hand, furthering my life of petty crime, but he actually started to consider this. It might be possible, but it would have to be cleared by the Minister of Transportation in Rwanda.

"So," I said to this chap, "Call him up."

The next thing I know we are being escorted out to the Air France jet. The other American couples, still pacing the floors in the waiting room, stared as we were waltzed out onto the tarmac. Harry could not resist the urge and he waved ever so jauntily as we traipsed past.

As we had come straight from Lake Kivu, again via small aircraft, to catch our much delayed flight, we had not had a chance to change our clothes. We were still dressed in the Gorilla poo pants. But the French Stewardesses didn't say anything and we sat on our Air France flight for the hour it takes to fly a 747 to Nairobi sipping champagne.

There was a customs person waiting for us in Nairobi and after a brief look at our passports, we cruised out of the airport. Wilson was there with my car to meet us and, after dropping Harry off at the Norfolk, drove us all back to Karen. Mildred had everything waiting and ready and we were all showered, fed and in our respective beds by midnight.

twenty-one

Home

When my house was finally finished, it was, to my eye, perfection. It sat long and low, all windows and doors. You could see from one end to the other. The floors of the halls and the kitchen were finished in rough red tiles while the main room floors were done in mvuli, a beautiful African hardwood. I had brought over some of my mother's Oriental carpets and the faded reds and blues of the rugs mirrored the richness of the wood as it darkened with use and the endless waxings Elemina insisted upon. Brass was very plentiful and inexpensive on the Coast, and I had acquired quite a few pieces. I had tiffin cans from Mombassa, planters of various sizes, candlesticks, and fireplace screens. They too were polished to a farethewell by Celestine and glowed in the afternoon light.

I had remodeled a few apartments in the past, but I had never done a whole house from the ground up. It gave me the chance to incorporate many things that I had not been able to use before. Like a New England barn ceiling. We had ripped out the ceiling in the living room all the way up to the roof, eliminating not only years of moldy pressboard and countless mouse carcasses, but all the structural support for the roof as well..The 'barn beams' were then installed as new support and painted white. The finished ceiling above them was brick red. The spot lights attached to these beams were pointed in different directions and they cast wonderful shadows on all the walls at night. The dining room ceiling had more exposed beams with the enormous bolts that held them together left visible. I had a local chap copy an Early American chandelier from a picture I had. It was not what you would call an exact replica, but I loved that it was a funky attempt.

Jake's little group of rooms was meant to mirror the main house and his sitting room also sported barn beams. The window seats in the living room and my bedroom were repeated in his sitting room as well. We had cut back a tree that blocked our view of the Ngong Hills and the light, especially in the late afternoon, as it cut across the lawn always drew me those window seats.

All my furniture from the States had initially been chosen to fit into the Winter's house and eventhough that had not come to pass, it meant that I knew exactly what was coming. We began the new house as a shell with each room designed around the furniture that would go in it. The space between the dining room windows was designed especially to show off my mother's old clock. It made the proportins of each room seem balanced and right.

There were fireplaces in the bedrooms and the living room and I had a walled in private garden off my bedroom. You stepped down a step to my bright yellow office which had a slanted ceiling, a built in 'dogs leg' desk and windows on two sides. One looked out to the driveway, so I could always see who was coming and going. The other window faced the side yard. There were many times when I walked into the living room, especially around sundown with the early evening light bouncing off the brass, and I was stopped cold in my tracks. The whole room seemed to glow. I came very close to murdering the contractor over the completion of all the work, but when it was finally finished, I was besotted with that house.

Come May, Mildred's health took a turn for the worse. Swallowing seemed to be more difficult and she complained of constantly aching joints. All she could manage was to sit outside her house with a kanga draped over her head. She looked like the grim reaper incarnate. Fearing that she was going into a rapid decline, I decided to take her to Nairobi Hospital. I knew the European community would criticize me and that it would probably cause problems with my other staff members, but I didn't care. I also knew, as she did not, that Mildred would be in for days of possibly painful tests. I would probably need to stay with her for the majority of the time. My presence would make sure that she got proper care.

Nairobi Hospital was a paying hospital and although the fees were small compared to what one is charged in the USA for hospitalization, anything other than completely free care was out of the reach of the majority of the Africans. If I were paying the bills, the doctors and the nurses would look to me for the nod.

I had only been in Nairobi Hospital once before, the night Celestine's toto's was born, and I was happy to see that it was as I remembered it: clean and well run. The "sisters" were attentive and pleasant, the doctors came when requested and the staff members were all efficient and personable. It looked just the way a small colonial hospital in the tropics and one that is supported by the European community, should look: all whitewashed stone and red tile roof. The wards were all named after famous Kenyan settlers.

After admission we were assigned to a Dr. Okello (a Luo who had been born after twins.) He was a sympathetic, competent and thorough man who taught at the Medical College in Nairobi. After several days of tests, he announced that Mildred had scleroderma. Much like lupus or polio, it attacked the connective tissues of the body. Slowly they would harden and degenerate and she would eventually die. But, he told me, it was a slow process and that steroids would help. She could actually "be quite well for some time." That phrase sounded like a polite evasion to me, but to Mildred, this was very good news. Dr. Okello started her on a regimen of medication and, as they started to take effect, she felt much better.

I tried to explain all of this to Mildred, leaving out the finality of her situation. She was happy to be feeling better and grateful to have finally been told what was wrong with her. As we checked out of the hospital, she told me that she considered herself well on the road to being cured. Dr. Okello and I had fixed her and she was going to "be better now." She came home from the hospital and insisted upon going straight up to the kitchen to cook. Acting well meant being well. She was anxious to go back to work.

Mildred health seemed to hold its own for some time, but soon the pain in her joints and the difficulty in swallowing returned. She came to me, fearful and bewildered about this reoccurrence. I tried to explain to her that what she had was a chronic condition, rather like the arthritis I have in my lower back. She knew that my back hurt from time to time and that I complained about it when doing my "ex-cise." But it also went away and I was fine for months at a time. I tried to tell her that we could make her feel better by taking dawa (*medicine*), but that the condition she had would never be completely gone. She just stared at me saying nothing. It did not dawn on me at the time, but I had said the wrong thing. She had believed that it would all go away and that she would no longer be plagued by these problems. She now knew that she would never really be cured. The belief in the future and the appearance of health were far more important to her actual well being that the medical reality.

After that Mildred lay down and gave up. None of my exhortations helped. She lay on her bed refusing to eat until she was too weak to sit up unassisted. I would go down to see her everyday, taking juice or the chocolate she loved, and tried to convince her that all was not lost. But she wasn't listening. Finally she announced that she wanted to go home to die. She wanted to go back to Kitale and get her shamba put into her son, Frederick's, name, and then "wait to see if God calls" her. As much as I begged her to stay and let me take care of her, she would not. She had made up her mind and that was all there was to it. She was very weepy about her decision, and about leaving me, but she told me that it was up to God now.

"My body is kwisha *(finished)* now Madame. There is no more body. Only my head and my talking is left."

I knew that Mildred would probably die in Kitale, and the chances were great that I would not find this out until much later. But it was what she wanted and I could not stop her.

Wilson packed up all Mildred's things and loaded them into my car to take to the railway station to ship to Kitale. Her bed and her cupboard, the afghan I had given her, pictures and mementos, and the few pots and pans that she owned were all piled into the car. When Wilson drove out the main gate, bound for the train, I sat in my front window and cried. Two days later, when the time came for Mildred herself to actually leave, the other house staff and all the Kufuma people gathered once again in the yard to say their good-byes. I was trying to be positive and kept saying that she would be back as soon as she was better. All thirty two of them stood there, a sea of grieving faces, nodding at me and saying Ndio Mama, and Kwa Heri, Mildred. Safari Salama *(peaceful journey)*, but I knew they didn't believe me. It truly now was a "Shauri a Mungu" (*God's problem)*.

I drove Mildred and Wilson down to the bus depot in Nairobi. Double-parked on a tiny side street, we unloaded the two of them and the few things they were taking with them. As they put Mildred on a stool to wait for the bus, I stuffed an envelope into her skirt pocket. It contained the money that I knew she needed to put a roof on her house in Kitale. It was all that was left for me to do. The cars were beginning to back up on the street and were all hooting their horns at my double-parking. I could not linger.

Hugging her, I said goodbye.

"Kwa Heri, Mildred."

"Kwa Heri, Madame. Asante sana."

"Si Kitu, Mama. Kwa Heri. Taonana." *(You are welcome. Good Bye. I will see you again.)*

Then she was gone.

It was hard to tell anyone in Karen how heartbroken I was over Mildred's departure. She was "just staff," after all. But Mildred had been part of my life since my first days in Africa and she meant a good deal to me. I was also mourning, once again, the loss of my mother four years before. The whole thing felt so familiar to me. Someone I cared for, and who looked out for me dies and I am left behind. I had tried to do the best I could for both of them. I understood that knowing you have tried should be of some consolation, but I always felt that I should have tried harder. "If only I had . . . "

I left Kenya for a week in New York with Jake. It was good to get out of Africa for awhile, and it was always wonderful to be with my son. Jake understood how I felt about Mildred, and with him, I could express what I was feeling, something I rarely did in Africa.

twenty-two

The Thin End of the Wedge

My next visitor to Kenya, Susan Corey, was another pal of mine from New York. We had met only a few months before I moved to Africa, but we corresponded a great deal and I had come to consider her one of my very good friends. Corey, as she was called, came out in October '90 for a two-week safari and I took her to all my usual haunts. Corey and I looked very much alike, had almost identical backgrounds, and were often taken for sisters. We also behaved towards each other as two sisters might. We laughed out loud at the same jokes, we argued vociferously when we were at odds, and we always told each other exactly what we thought. It was a no holds barred friendship.

The most salient characteristic of Corey's first week in Africa was the unusual weather. October is normally glorious in Kenya with all the Jacaranda in bloom and the temperature near perfect. But the rains were early that year and extremely heavy in the northern part of the country, especially north of Samburu where we were to spend a few days. The rain rushing down from the distant hills turned the almost dry Samburu River into a raging torrent. The resulting waves, fit for a California surfer, rolling by in front of our tent every day were something to behold. It all would have been quite amusing had we not wanted to go anywhere. When the rain stopped long enough for us to actually take a game drive the deeply viscous mud and heavily rutted tracks made for high adventure driving. I had enormous faith in the power of a four wheel drive Land Cruiser to stay upright and found all this rocking and rolling to be great fun. Corey did not. She had been in one too many car accidents in her day and slipping and sliding around in a sodden Kenyan game park, often completing full three hundred and sixty degree spins, did not amuse her at all.

As the days went by, the rain at night kept falling and the mud got so deep that all game drives were cancelled. We were stuck at Larsen's, the camp we were now confined to, for the next few days. We drank as much Gin as we played. Although it rained every day, the nights were significantly more dramatic: the rain pounding on our canvas roof could wake the dead. Every morning we stepped out of our tent to investigate the damage and see how much higher the river had risen. Anyone with any sense in Africa took the possibility of a flash flood seriously, but the folks at Larsen's took this more seriously than most. Larsen's had had its first camp, located in that very same place, albeit closer to the river, completely washed away a few years before. Luckily, the camp had not officially opened and there were no guests there that night. The banks of the river had washed away and the huge waves took everything downstream. Had there been people there, they would all have been killed. The force of the river lifts even the largest tent right out of the ground and rolls it, all zipped up for the night, over and over on top of itself until it snags on something. Furniture, tent poles, luggage, lamps, and whatever else is caught up in the turmoil, batter the individuals trapped inside. They have no chance.

The rising river and the sound of the heavy rain every night had already cost us some sleep, but on this third night, the drama factor ratcheted up a notch. The rain had been heavy, but the center of the storm had been miles away. That night it sat right above us. The thunder, rolling down from the Matthews range and crashing down along the riverbed had us levitating off our beds as it cracked over our heads. The flashes of lightening were blinding. Big storms in Kenya are frightening and always seem too close. Perhaps it's the particular lay of the land or maybe there is something about being on the Equator that makes it all seem worse than it is, but when a big thunder storm hits, it shakes the house. If you are out in a tent, it will shake your nerves just as thoroughly. The sound that night sent Corey and me diving under the covers like four-year-olds in a Disney movie. It was great fun.

The less amusing part was that not only would there be no daily game drives, there would be no driving of any sort, including our leaving Samburu at the end of our reserved few days at Larsen's. But even though we could not get out, others could get in. The Airkenya flights from Wilson could fly over the storms and they deposited their wageni at Samburu's tarmac airstrip. They arrived at Larsen's ready to take up their rightful places in their reserved tents. We had to move out. We made a brief attempt to drive out of the camp, but my car, my trusty Subaru wagon, was not a four-wheel drive. Even when the rivers receeded somewhat, it could not plow through the mud of the sand rivers. We were stuck and evicted from our billets. We were tentless.

The manager of the camp, an accommodating and resourceful Kikuyu, had a small pup tent that he offered us. He pitched it and installed camp beds and wash basins, making it as pleasant as possible. It was, granted, set up right behind the camp's public toilets, a fact that did not escape Corey's notice, but it was, more importantly, on the highest ground in camp. We would not get washed away. My concern was the strength of that little tent. The big green canvas tents, with extra fly covers and metal poles sunk deep into the ground had been straining to hold up under the weight of these downpours. If the storms were even half as ferocious as the ones we had experienced the previous two nights, that little pup tent would surely collapse. Before we turned in, I pulled my station wagon up to the rear of the tent and had some blankets put in the back. If our tent collapsed on us, we could bolt for the relative safety of my car. I found all this highly entertaining, but Corey was frightened and irritated and not in the best of spirits. Even the extra wine at dinner didn't seem to help.

The rain held off and we made it through the night. With that one dry twenty four hour spell, we had a window of opportunity to get the car out. The following morning we headed out of Samburu in convoy between two Abercrombie and Kent mini vans. They were to be our rescue team should we got stuck. Which we did, more than once. We were door handle high in mud a good deal of the time and we smashed my sump guard to pieces charging over the rocks hiding beneath the water of a running luggah. But the A and K drivers took it all in stride and pulled us out each time. Several of the male passengers lent a shoulder. Everyone got covered in mud as the wheels sprayed red sludge back over one and all. But we were laughing and into the spirit of things. Pushing cars out of the mud felt very collegiate. After a long four hours, we landed on the tarmac road in Isiolo. My car was all but destroyed, but we had made it.

I look back on many of the stunts I pulled while living in Africa with wonder. I took too many risks and did far too many fool hardy things all in the name of grand adventure. Before I moved to Kenya, I had never been one to throw caution to the wind nor had I ever taken too many physical chances. But when I lived there, I took a great many risks. And not only with my safety but also with my friends' and, worst of all, with Jake's. I shudder now to think of how, on many occasions, we were within spitting distance of serious disaster. One more punctured tire, one more hour until sunset, one less bottle of water and it would have been curtains. But we always squeaked by. So often that I came to believe that all that talk of danger was just so much Kenyan folklore. I took the threat of disaster less seriously as the years went along and I closed my eyes even tighter to obvious dangers. In many ways, it was stupid. And yet some kind of bravado, real or feigned, is necessary when living in a place like that. If you were as frightened and as cautious as you probably should have been, and if you acted on all those fears, you wouldn't last too long. And you certainly wouldn't have as much fun as I did.

The other very significant part of Corey's visit was our visit with Graham. She had met him before when he and I had passed through New York City in tandem. We had spent a lively evening with her and her boyfriend and, I assumed, that she liked him well enough.

Corey and I were ending her safari by spending the last few days in the Mara. We had been at Little Governor's for a few days and were winding things up with a night at Serena with Graham. On the drive from one camp to the other I brought up the topic of our respective plans for the upcoming Christmas holidays and I was told, with little hesitation, that he was spending Christmas in Spain. The ensuing row continued well into the night. Corey did what she could to try to calm things down, but eventually retired to her room, sparing herself witnessing what was cooking up to be emotional carnage. But, as was always the case, come sun up, I was no longer crying, the dust had seemingly settled and there was the outward appearance of calm. Graham was still going to do whatever he damn well pleased and I just had to accept it. Or not. It didn't matter what I wanted nor how I felt about it.

That scenario was not new. What was different this time was that he barely bothered with the "I'm sorrys" and the "I know you want me to do otherwise and I wish I could, but . . . " He didn't bother to lie to me about seeing his parents in UK or having to get some English flying license renewed. He just said he was going to Spain and that was that. He knew that my threats were empty and that he could get away with just about anything he wanted to. What, other than walk out on the man, could I do? And we were both pretty sure I wasn't going to do that.

All this had happened before, in lesser degrees, but this time it didn't happen in the usual African vacuum. This time there was a good friend of mine, someone who knew me when I had lived in New York, standing witness to this semi battered wife syndrome. And witnessing what I had been telling her about, in all those long afternoons and tense drives through rain and mud and whatever else Africa had handed out that week. Corey and I had been together for two weeks by then, day and night, and many of the sadder facts of Graham and my relationship had been revealed.

After that night in Serena, there was no way I could run for cover. I couldn't wait a few days until I felt better and then tell her what had happened, in a long letter back home, making it sound as palatable as possible. I couldn't cover up the enormous hurt I was feeling by writing it far nicer than it actually was. I couldn't make myself appear less subservient and stepped on than I felt. There was no possibility of spin control. She had seen it.

As we two sat at the breakfast table that next morning, Corey looked at me and said, "So . . . when did you become a fucking doormat?"

When indeed.

I protested and even went so far as to ask her where she got off talking to me like that. But what was going on between Graham and me was so obviously unhealthy that it was impossible to defend. No matter what I said, she just looked at me and kept repeating,

"Yeah, right. This is me you are talking to. I know you and this relationship sucks. He treats you like dirt."

And she was right. I knew it, she knew it and I think Graham probably knew it. It had taken years to evolve into this one-sided, 'he takes all' kind of deal, but that is what it was. He had always done whatever he wanted, whenever he wanted and, it would later become painfully clear, with whomever he wanted. There may have been a time, way back when, when he did actually consider my feelings, I certainly fed myself that little fiction, but he clearly no longer did. And whom could I blame? I had allowed this to happen. No one had held a gun at my head. Graham may have been a rat, but I had allowed myself to become what Corey so aptly called a "fucking doormat."

Corey and I returned to Karen to spend a last few days there before she went back to New York. Although she and I had had some heated words over this, I knew that she had done it out of friendship for me. I listened to her and I finally agreed that the best thing to do was to just end it. Cut him out of my life. Would I be lonely? Sure. But what was worse? More loneliness, which would not be all that unusual, or to allow this demeaning relationship to continue? There was no need to write to him or tell him, he had already left for Spain anyway, I would just be unavailable when he got back in January. Kwa heri, fella. When I put Corey on the plane for the States, I was fully resolved. My affair with Graham Elson was over. I had support and I felt stronger. No more tears.

Then Kaz came to visit.

Kaz was an American who also flew balloons in the Mara. He had been a roommate of Graham's for about a year and he and I had become good friends. Naturally, he was witness to the battles, the tears, and the sulking silences that Graham and I played out on many of the weekends I was down at Serena. He had already told me a number of times that he thought I was being taken advantage of and that I should dump the guy. He used to ask me why was it that the nice guys, which he considered himself, never got the girl? Why did the skunks and the rats and the liars, like Graham, always have a woman in tow? He would flatter me by adding, "attractive," or "a great woman in tow," but he made it clear that he thought I deserved better. I never took this to be a form of flirting with me. Kaz and I were very much a "We-Americans-against-all-these-stiff-British-types" brother-sister team.

Kaz was in Nairobi on his way to the US for his Christmas holidays and came out to Karen to see me. He usually stayed with me when he was up from the Mara. We would have dinner and drinks and a long chat. He would stay in Jake's room and that was that. We enjoyed each other's company and it would be very rude to be in

Nairobi and not stop in and see your friends in Karen. That night however, what he had to tell me ruined an otherwise good meal at Rolf's. Graham, Kaz informed me, had had some other woman staying with him down in the Mara. It was "The Stewardess," the one I had been hearing rumors about for the past three years, the one Graham so vociferously denied having seen in the past three decades. She had spent a week with him in Serena that past May. Kaz was sorry to tell me this, he knew it would hurt me, but just in case my resolve to cut Graham out of my life slipped, remember this.

Maybe Kaz should have told me this and maybe he shouldn't have. Maybe he should have told me when it happened. Maybe not. What is relevant was how shocked I was. And how hurt. I was saying I was through with that man, but the feeling of being punched in the stomach was very real. I all but threw up on the spot. I had always doubted Graham. Every cell in my body was on full "you are about to be kicked in the teeth" alert, all the time. Every minute Graham was out of my sight, I worried that he was up to something. Aside from all the rumors, my own instincts had been telling me, right from the start that this man cheated on me and lied to me. But hearing what Kaz had to say that night still shocked me. I was dumbstruck. And utterly devastated.

With that, I left for my Christmas holidays in the States.

twenty-three

Desperate Times, Desperate Measures

By the time I returned from the States, the escalating War in the Gulf was on everybody's mind. Everybody except those of us who lived in Kenya. We hadn't heard much about it. Yet. Under normal circumstances, the entire world could come to and end, never mind some little thing like a war take place, and it would probably take months before we in Kenya found out about it. But those normal circumstances were about to change. There was a new game in town: television, real television. CNN was coming to Kenya and we were all going to get to watch the Gulf War on TV.

Up until then, there had been just one local channel. It was on the air for a few hours in the evening, but there was never much to see other than grainy footage of President Moi making speeches, followed by young girls singing nationalistic songs as he shook hands with local dignitaries. There was one weather broadcast, but it was in Swahili. Although I had not bothered to take a TV with me when I first moved to Kenya, after a few months, the electronic stimulus deprivation Jake and I were suffering got the better of us and we bought a tiny, TV/VCR combination. It was locally made, barely adequate, and horribly expensive. On this mediocre machine, we were going to play the locally available videotapes.

These were videos that had been pirated from overseas and were known as "camera copies." That meant that someone had sat in the rear of a movie theatre, usually in England, pointed a small video camera at the screen, and pressed the record button. You could see people in the audience moving around in the theatre as well as hear them laughing and talking, often drowning out the sound on the screen. Some of the videos came from The United Arab Emirates, but they censored out all the good bits. The first time Jake and I saw one of these "camera copies" we could not figure out what was going on. We couldn't believe how bad they were, but we watched them. Beggars cannot be choosers.

In the coming years, there was a steady influx of better quality videos and little rental shops popped up in all the surrounding towns. Finding the newest and best video rental place and getting our "vids" for the evening ahead of us was one of the tasks Jake and I set for ourselves on our long afternoons in Kenya. (In the end, the Yaya Center was the all time winner.) I often bought tapes on my way through London; they had to be in the European format, and carried them back with me. When I finally had my container shipped over, I included a bigger multi-system set so that I could watch videos imported from England and the US. There are some movies, mostly musicals, that I have completely memorized. I watched "The Silence of the Lambs" nine times. In the four years I had been there, I had become fairly used to all this, but I was still very happy to have CNN arrive.

Before anyone was going to see anything on a television, however, antennas had to be placed on rooftops. A massive satellite dish had been installed atop a tall building in Nairobi, but the reception in Karen was still very iffy. Rain affected the reception. Wind affected the reception. I came to think that the dogs' tails wagging affected the reception. But no matter how bad the reception, having real TV was thrilling. Whereas the Kenyans had not been raised with TV, I had, and the sound of an American broadcaster's voice was right up there on the familiarity scale with peanut butter and jelly sandwiches. Along with CNN, a few other programs graced our screens that winter. A seriously mediocre Australian soap opera called "Neighbors" was shown at some strange hour, but we never missed an episode. Occasionally we would get a segment of the entertainment news. Something momentous like the Oscar nominations or the opening of a big movie in Hollywood would be on the air, but usually the eight hour time difference meant that what was programmed for USA markets was not fed to Africa. We got the Gulf War.

Another interesting spin on CNN entering Kenya was the fact that uncensored news was finally being piped into a country that had a heavily guarded press. It was never stated out loud that there was complete censorship of the news in Kenya, but there was. We all knew that if articles in the International Herald did not please the Kenyan Government, that day's papers would "go missing." Everyone wondered just how the Government was going to handle this. Would there be a ten second-delay button? If something negative were said, would it get deleted? This was essentially, freedom of the press. What would happen?

[For a few years, nothing happened, but CNN News was eventually taken off the air. Some of the non-news programming from the USA remained. Reruns of "The Jefferson's" and "The Cosby Show" made the cut, showing the more comfortable lives African-Americans had in the States The hard news was given back to KTN, Kenyan Television Network. It was now in English, but it was still only what the government wanted you to hear.]

CNN was the good news. The bad news was that the War in the Gulf had affected the tourist business. The War was happening too close to Africa, it would seem, for the average tourist to fly over the war zone. The fact that they would not be flying anywhere near Kuwait did not seem to figure into this, perception was everything. Graham once noted that the minute the Americans figured out that Libya was in Africa the whole safari business would fold up entirely. The tourist business did not fold up in '91, but it suffered a serious set back. And trouble in the tourist industry meant trouble for just about everyone. There were enough people in and around Karen making a living on some kind of spin from tourism that when safaris took a hit, they did too. That included Kufuma.

Over the past few years, the bulk of my business had shifted to making carpets for the hotels, lodges, and tented camps in Kenya. I had done bedside carpets for Governor's in the Mara, carpets for Larsen's Camp in Samburu, and carpets and wall hangings for several of the Block Hotel chain. It is an indication of my meager business skills that although it was good money and steady work, I didn't relish doing orders for the lodges because it wasn't creative enough. It took me about twenty minutes to come up with a design, usually some variation on either their logo or a simple geometric pattern, and then about three meetings with the hotel people to finalize the deal. Sometimes they wanted samples of the proposed carpets. That meant more back and forth from Nairobi with a car full of sheepy smelling carpets. Once approved, I got half the money in advance, and the wheels began to turn.

The Kufuma people would be down at the factory for the coming weeks happily spinning and weaving away, producing these relatively small carpets very quickly. It was far less time consuming to repeat the same design fifty times than to do one much larger piece. Everyday I would walk down to the factory, for my morning rounds and I could hear people singing. That was always a good sign.

"Jambo, gang." I would say to everyone.

"Jambo, Mama." I would be greeted.

We had money in the bank and orders to fill and everyone was optimistic.

So much so that, over the past year, I had hired more people to get these large orders out in a timely fashion. This was another example of what I did not know about running a business, especially in Kenya. Rather then let customers wait a bit longer for their carpets, I hired people that I would later not be able to fire, just to get it all done that much quicker.

I was not totally ignorant of the employment laws in Kenya, Bill Sr. had repeatedly told me about all the problems I could get into with the Labor Board if I didn't do things in a certain fashion. But that was years before and his lectures had to do with my house staff. I had read the pamphlet on Kenyan Labor Laws that I had inherited with Kufuma, but I obviously hadn't fully recorded the majority of it. I had almost no idea how sticky things could get if you ran into problems with your workers. Up until then, everything had been very peaceful with the Kufuma people. I gave them steady work and we seemed to be growing at a good rate. By 1991, I had forty people working for me. Kufuma was the second largest consumer of raw wool in the country (most of Kenyan's wool is exported) and everything was going great guns. Then, with the war, the bottom fell out.

There was still business from the ex-patriot community. They were paid in America or England and neither the War nor tourism affected their salaries. But that was a seasonal event. They arrived in Kenya in August, in time to settle in and get their children into school and showed up on my doorstep in September. They usually wanted something immediate and tended to buy stock pieces. We kept a large amount of stock and always repeated any carpet we sold, but that didn't require forty people.

I often got the ladies tour groups coming through the factory. Women from the American Women's Association or the British High Commission would descend on me, en masse. After the tour of the factory and my speech on how a carpet was made, I would offer them coffee and biscuits. That guaranteed that they would hang around a bit longer and perhaps buy something on the spot. They often did. But the ex-pats were not our bread and butter, the lodges were.

So, I reasoned with myself, if business is slow, let a few people go. But you can't just let people go. You can make them redundant, as they say in Africa, but that means you have to pay them severance pay for all the years they have worked for you and any unpaid leave money or housing allowances owed. I consulted with someone who knew about these things to see what I should do. I owed them for two years, right? Wrong. They had worked for Kufuma for twelve years. Some had been working there for fourteen years. They had been with the company from the beginning and every time the company changed hands, they went along with the new owner. When I bought Kufuma, I should have made sure that the previous owners made everyone redundant, paying his or her severance off, and all other monies owed. Then I could rehire everyone anew. I had not done that and now I could not afford to let them go.

The labor Laws of Kenya were created primarily for the benefit of the employee. They were formed to protect a large population of people from being exploited, and they were not only archaic, they were also wide open to interpretation. As there were too few jobs, many people were willing to work for next to nothing and it was easy enough to get around the laws and to pay below the government minimums. This was, by American standards, a piteously low wage, but the entire standard of living in Kenya could not be compared to Americas. Some people did indeed take advantage of the Africans and their unemployment situation, but that was definitely the exception not the rule.

Even if you played it straight, as I thought I had, and did everything you should be doing, the rules were still convoluted and difficult.

And should you run afoul of the law, even the Labor Board, it was downright frightening. Facing off with a government official in a land that doesn't run things according to any Bill of Rights is extremely unnerving. I wanted to avoid that. I also wanted to keep people employed. But I was running a business, for what it was worth, and even I knew that keeping forty people employed because I am a soft touch wasn't too smart.

With too many employees for the work I had to give them, I needed to come up with a new scheme to create more employment. We needed to make things that would sell to either local people or to the few tourists we had. Something different. Something labor intensive. Something high end.

Needlepoint. It took an enormous amount of time to do and sold for a huge price when completed. I had been doing needlepoint since I was fifteen and I was sure I could teach everyone how. I had taught other people in the past; my mother had been a constant student because she never could get it right, but Mildred had picked it up very quickly. She had done some beautiful pillows for the house. The Kufuma workers all read graphs and they all could knit and weave. I had books of pattern stitches, baskets full of wool and bits of canvas left over from my own endless projects (this was one of my great time killers in Africa) with which I could get them started.

After a full Sunday of making up learners kits and gathering all my materials together (the best days were the ones when I had a "project," something to actually do) I marched down to Kufuma and announced that we were going to learn to do needlepoint.

"Kushona," they said to me. Sewing.

"OK, Kushona."

I sat down on the grass with everyone gathered around me and spent the rest of the morning showing them what to do. I had drawn small boxes and triangles on each canvas square. They were to put their own initial in the center, reading the letters of the alphabet from a graph in a book I had given them. They could then fill in the rest as they saw fit. I was doing one myself as an example. They watched me for awhile, asked some questions, tried out a few things, and then turned themselves to their task. Announcing that I would be back later to check on the progress, I left them, men and women, to it. I was encouraged that they had seemingly picked this up so quickly, but was secretly hoping it would take much longer to really master. I wanted this to take more time to do. I walked around my house all that afternoon mumbling to myself, "Pole pole, gang. Let's take this slow."

The learner squares were all very good, and some were exceptional. I had never seen anyone pick needlepoint up that quickly. These people could obviously do this, but so much for taking a long time to learn the trade. We began to produce things under a new name "Kushona Tu." That is Swahili for 'Just Sew.' (or 'Just So.') I was the only one who appreciated the pun.

The other event that was looming on the horizon was the opening of a craft center that Bonnie Bishop and Sue Larsen had masterminded. Called Utamaduni, it was set in an old house in Langata, and was going to be a showcase for the best of Kenya's crafts. Bonnie and Sue hoped this would lure the tourists away from an increasingly unpleasant and dangerous Nairobi. It would be an alternative to African Heritage, the very successful African craft store in town. There would be a small restaurant and about twenty different shops in each of the rooms of the house. I had signed up for a small space where I intended to house Kufuma, but the closer we got to the opening, the more I thought that the needlepoint would do better. I hoped this would give me more exposure to the kind of people who would appreciate needlepoint and therefore be willing to pay higher prices. I also hoped, as I did with every new endeavor, that this would help me meet more people. Maybe I would meet someone to replace Graham or give me a life as busy and as exciting as I always envisioned.

In early June, I made a quick dash to the States to attend Jake's graduation from high school. I could stay only a few days as I had already been in the USA for the time that the tax man allowed me each year. I owned property in New York City and was only permitted to be in the States for thirty days a year or I would lose my non-resident status. That would mean paying New York City and State taxes. Thirty days meant thirty, not thirty-one, days. My passport was stamped and I sent copies of it to my accountants every year to prove I had not over stayed my time.

On my way back through London I made contact with a man who worked in a large needlepoint wool manufacturing company and we struck up a deal. Let's just say it was a real Kenyan kind of arrangement: lots of fast talk, palms greased, and no paperwork. You don't tell and neither will I. I got on the plane to Nairobi with three huge duffel bags full of wool and canvas that I had paid an excellent price for it. The longer I lived in Kenya the more of a petty criminal I became, but I never gave it a second thought. All I cared about was clearing customs in Nairobi. What story would I make up this time?

twenty-four

Bloody Africa

It had been six months since Mildred had left Karen, and we had been writing to each other fairly regularly. When I sent her a letter, usually hand carried by Wilson to Kitale, I would enclose, "some small, small money." I had sent her Christmas gifts, along with Jake's senior yearbook picture and she wrote back. I knew her letters were dictated in Abaluya, her native tongue, and translated into English by either her son Frederick or a nurse at the hospital, but they had the lilt of her voice and her wonderful way of putting things.

I once sent her an early draft of a story I had written about her, knowing she would enjoy that, only I had not returned her previous letter quickly enough to suit her. She wrote:

> *Dear Madame,*
> *How are you over there? I believe in Jesus name that you're still breathing in and out as usual and can communicate as always. Despite my sickness I still thank God that I am also breathing and can communicate with you.*
> *What a silence I have been expecting your missive ever since then; did you receive mine?*
> *You have been already a help to me. A close friend to me. A sister to me. Although I am weak I have faith in Jesus that despite this suffering I will get well one day.*
> *I am glad to hear your swahili. The story you wrote about my meeting with you since 1987, the fun story, was very interesting*

to me. You have a good memory.
Thank you, may God bless you so much.
Here I pen off by saying please write and say hallo to me,
Yours Sincerely,

Mildred Nzike.

And then a few months later:

Dear Melinda,
[Mildred had never called me Melinda before]
I am very gladsome when writing to you this short missive hoping that you are fine and OK.
Before I dare go any farther I want to thank you very very much for the gifts you sent me on Xmas.
I know for sure your love toward me is so great.
Briefly, I really miss you and Jake. I liked Jakes picture, he is now a man, not a boy, the chicks (cheeks) *is no longer fat.*
Although I am sick and weery I thank you so much for everything. It is my prayer that I recover and come back to make nice dishes for you dear. I wish I was there to see Coco (another new dog). *I liked my Kipele, he was a very close friend to me. I really miss him. I request that you send me a picture of Coco together with Kipele. How do you find Elemina? (*Her sister who was now working for me*) I believe she is making the house clean all around and not stealing. If she is stealing, let me know. We take her to the police. That sounds funny isn't it?*
So long as communication is available, lets not forget one another.
Yours faithfully,

Mildred Nzike.

I was at the breakfast table one morning when Celestine came in, bringing the coffee.

"Jambo, Celestine,"

"Jambo, Madame."

"Habari?"

She didn't answer with the usual quick "Mzuri." She stared at the carpet for a moment and then said, "Madame, habari mbaya sana leo.

Mildred iko kufa. Pole, Madame. Pole sana."

("The news today is very bad, Madame. Mildred is dead. I am sorry, Madame. Very sorry.")

I remember the date, June 25th. It is my mother's birthday.

Not that her death wasn't expected, I had probably known for months that she would not make it. Not in Kenya, with what she was suffering from, but I still hoped. I wanted her to "be better" as she always said she would. I hoped that one day Stephen Karanja would come to tell me Mildred was back or that she would just appear at my kitchen door one Monday morning smiling her wonderful smile. I still hoped that she would go back to running my house and my life for me. "I will make nice dishes for you, Madame." I knew it was about a thousand to one chance, but I guess I still believed that it might happen. And then she was dead.

Bloody Africa.

I have a vivid picture of Mildred, one that I never photographed. We were still living in President Moi's house and late one night, thinking I heard a noise in the kitchen, I went down to see what it was. There was Mildred, probably the cause of this noise, standing in the pantry. She was wrapped only in a kanga. No headscarf, no European house girl uniform, just a piece of the archetypal African cloth wrapped around her. Her head was shaved and neat and her skin was dark and sleek and she looked surprisingly beautiful. I had never thought of Mildred as beautiful before, but standing there, that night, in her African wrap, she was very beautiful indeed.

A letter I received from her brother Ernest sometime later.

Dear Madame,
I am very happy to have this chance of saying hallo to you.
Briefly we are fine in Kitale, except the common Tropical malaria which we are fighting.
On behalf of entire Wemali family I would like to thank you so much for your assistance, materially and financially.
Madame, I am writing to you this letter while the tears are just running down my cheeks. When I remember the love you had toward my sister, I feel you are part of our family. I know you still love us all as we also do love you dearly.
My prayer is that, "God bless your business,"

*I beg Madame if you can only offer that boy Frederick (*Mildred's son) *a job it will be a good idea. Since I know from him the assistance to the rest of his brother and sister will appear.*
If you feel like communicating with us or me (Ernest Emali) you just writte using the above given address.
I don't have much. Mine is to say, "God bless you."
Kwaheri,
Emali.

Shortly thereafter, Frederick came to live with Elemina at my house. Frederick might have been able get a job working in a garden or sweeping out a store, but I thought that his mother would want him to do more than that. Instead of a job, I thought he needed an education. Education is the only real hope for countries like Kenya and I was forever preaching at everyone in my employ that their children must be educated. I knew that Mildred would have wanted this. With me as his guardian, Frederick went back to school. He was seventeen and way behind, but being older than everyone else in his class never seemed to bother him. He lived with Elemina and I paid his school fees. It should have made me feel better to have so many of Mildred's relatives still with me, but it did not. Mildred was gone and the sadness I felt just added to the darkness of the days ahead.

twenty-five

Taonana

Graham returned to his job in the Mara in January of '91, and I did see him again. My excuse was that his mother had died the day after Christmas and that touched all my soft spots. Of course, I could have made my farewell speech as soon as his tears had dried and he was feeling better, but I didn't. We did go nose to nose about 'The Stewardess' and his answer, "Are you always such and angel?" was clearly off the point.

But whenever he arrived on my doorstep, up from the Mara for a day or two, I was so grateful for the company and the excitement he brought that I never refused him entry. It was something to do and someone to do it with and I was just lonely enough to let him stay.

In the very early months of Kushona Tu, things went surprisingly well. We sold a large number of both needlepoint kits and finished cushions to Governor's Camp and had a significant order from the Mt. Kenya Safari Club. My friends, the Craigs, bought almost every pillow I had and there were good sales at Utamaduni as well. But all too soon, things slowed down. I didn't get the reorders from the lodges that I needed. The kits were selling, but I had to employ people, not keep someone's fingers busy when they got back to the States. The smaller items, eyeglass cases, and belts, sold well enough, but my Kushona ladies could produce these so quickly, it was impossible for me to keep up.

When I started Kushona Tu, I miscalculated a number of things, the most significant being the speed with which this could be produced. I had never known anyone to be able to do needlepoint for more than two hours without getting either bored or severe eyestrain. These ladies would sit for fifteen hours straight and just sew. They were needlepointing machines and I had to pay them when it was done, not when, or if, it sold.

I tried doing bigger pieces, carpets, safari chairs in different animal "skins," and patterns from very intricate graphs, anything I could do to slow things down. It didn't work. They would just enlist the help of their sister, mother, uncle, brother, or aunt to stay on schedule. Once I walked down past my staff quarters and saw one of Nyamburra's daughters, aged six, happily sewing away at a cushion cover her mother was supposed to be doing. I understood that it was a family effort to earn more money, but all that industry was breaking my bank. Another mistake was using imported goods. Jake joined my life of petty crime when he brought me more wool on his next trip through London, but it was too difficult to get what we needed when we needed it. After six months, I knew that I was in trouble. We weren't selling enough and, with the added burden of rent to pay at Utamaduni, within a year, Kushona Tu was floundering.

And so was I.

My being alone so much of the time had taken its toll on me and in more ways than my obviously desperate behavior with Graham. I had spent the majority of my time in Africa alone, but I had always assumed it was a temporary situation. In the early months, I just accepted it. I had moved to a new country, and one would expect a period of adjustment. The sheer shock of moving to Africa had kept me off balance for some time. When I bought Kufuma, I was certain that being in business would give me plenty to do and a much-needed purpose for my days. And it did. Kufuma was a definite change for the better. It was exciting and made me feel capable and back in charge. But it did nothing for my social life. And in no time at all, Kufuma could run itself. After three years, my role was much more that of bill payer and policeman, than creative driving force.

When I met Graham, I thought that would make a significant difference. Had he worked in Nairobi and had we actually functioned as a couple, never mind had it been a decent relationship to start with, things would have been very different. But Graham was never around. As far as everyone in Karen was concerned, I was single and being single in Karen is not a social plus. When I bought my little house, I was sure that would make things feel more settled and indicate to everyone that I was there to stay. I hoped that would make me more socially acceptable. But it didn't. It did take some time to build, keeping me busy for about a year, but eventually, it was finished.

During Graham's many absences from Kenya, I dated a few other men, but nothing really clicked. I could only talk about the weather at the Coast and spare parts for Range Rovers and the fate of the rhinos in the Mara for just so long. As to women friends, I had a few, but no one I ever got close to. I tried; it just didn't seem to jell. Our backgrounds were too dissimilar. I tried entertaining. I had many parties and hosted an annual Thanksgiving Day feast for several years running. Over thirty people accepted my invitation to a sit down dinner, but the return invitations never came. I tried to be as 'Kenyan' as I could. I wanted to belong. I wanted to be thought of as one of the local folks. But I was always slightly discontent and, I guess, forever looking around to see what was coming up next to finally make things more interesting.

During my fifth year there, I could no longer deny how restless and lonely I was. I missed Jake. I missed the theatre. I wanted to be able to talk on the phone with my friends. I wanted friends. I wanted to read the New York Times on Sunday. I wanted stimulating conversations. Book stores. I had always thrived on the energy and pace of New York City, a fact that had been pointed out to me, many times, back in 1986. But I had seen moving to Africa as the ultimate adventure. How could life there ever become common place? Or dull? But once the dust I kept kicking up had settled, I could not rid myself of the feeling that it just wasn't enough. I was too isolated and alone and there was never enough for me to do.

For the very first time since I had arrived there, I started to wonder: "So, is this it? Is this the way my life here is going to be? Forever? Maybe things aren't going change all that much. Maybe this is what life in this very small town is going to be. And nothing I can come up with or organize or force into being is going to change that. Maybe this is it, old girl."

And if that were really the case, then it was not enough.

I loved Africa. I loved my house. I loved my dogs and now there were eight new puppies that Deliah, our Labrador, had deposited in the garage. How could I leave all that? How could I leave the things that I had worked so hard for, Kufuma and now Kushona Tu? Every night, sitting in the window seat in my living room, I watched as the shadows crept across the yard. The brass was all polished and shining and the woodwork glowed in the late afternoon light. My mother's furniture finally looked as if it belonged there. I could smell the roses from my garden that I had put on every table. Elemina and Celestine could be heard chatting in the kitchen, starting dinner, ironing the clothes. My dogs, released for the night by Jotham, were tearing around the back yard, racing up to the house, looking for me. It was peaceful and beautiful and comfortable and familiar and just the thought of leaving made me cry. Whenever I would go on a safari, especially up to Lewa Downs when I would sit with David Craig, staring out at the vast space that is Africa, as we watched the elephants swaying into the distance, the tug on my heart was physically painful. How could I leave this?

But safaris weren't my life. Lewa wasn't my life. My life, my very solitary life, was in Karen running those two small businesses, however badly, and dealing with the forty people I had working for me. Forty people and all their attendant problems. Sick children and bad debts. Lack of work and more bad debts. Endless requests for loans and for jobs for their relatives. Due to the necessity of having to lay people off, I finally had those problems with the Kenya Labor Board. I was in Nairobi several times a week haggling over every shilling. I had problems with the wool supplier. Problems with meeting my payroll. Problems with the lack of water when the bore hole blew up. Problems with things being stolen from the factory. The books being "fiddled."

My house was broken into one night, while I was there. I heard the glass in the living room window shatter and muffeled voices on my back patio. It was only when the outside floodlights exploded when I hit the switch, they were wet from a reecent downpour, that the thieves ran off. Although I could not prove it, I knew it was people who worked for me. There were so many car hijackings around Nairobi, that I could no longer go anywhere after dark without taking an askari with me. I felt physically threatened when out, and even unsafe when at home, something I had never before either felt or admitted to. As the months went by, it was increasingly difficult for me to handle all the things that came up everyday, especially as I was always on my own.

I didn't want to deal with the Kenya government anymore. Beyond all the hassles with the Labor Board, I was tired of the endless bribery and endemic corruption. I could afford the amount of money that was usually shelled out for petty bribes, called "chai" in Kenya, "Please Madame, can you just give me something small? For a cup of chai (tea)?" It just never stopped and it had gotten on my nerves. For the first few years in Kenya, I got a kick out of all the back alley shenanigans that went on. I had enjoyed being a gun –slinger, living in The Wild, Wild West:

" Lissen l'il lady, y'all be migh-ty careful now. You know there ain't no law south o' San Antone."

Well, there's even less law south of the Sahara. And that means there ain't no no law to protect you, American citizen or not, should things get difficult. It was scary.

I took to going down to the factory for my daily check on things at the end of the day. Mary Wambui complained that I was not hovering over everyone enough, but I was tired of having to watch over everyone so closely. I preferred to visit then. The workers had all gone home and there was no one there to corner me with their problems. Or glare at me. With the layoffs had come more jealousy and friction among the workers. There were also suspicions and a pronounced feeling of hostility towards me as well. And after the break in, my reciprocal anger towards those that I suspected was hard to hide. No one was singing any more.

But in the early evening, it was quiet and peaceful. I knew everything down there so intimately; the looms, the huge bales of raw wool, the spinning wheels, the hanks left drying in the sun, the children's toys scattered on the floor, the kangas draped over the looms. Even the way the factory smelled. I had not fully appreciated that "Kufuma" smell at first, but I had come to love the sheepy scent of the wool as it mixed with the damp ground and the odor of human effort. I could remember those first tentative days; how enthusiastic I had been and how excited. Kufuma was now one very large headache for me, but pulling away from it was still painful. And remembering those early times made me sadder still.

I would head back up the path to my house, thinking how nice it would be if I had someone waiting for me. Someone to share this with. Someone to talk to. But I knew I would sit on the patio and have a cocktail by myself. I would have my dinner alone and then either watch a video, probably for the third time, or write a letter to someone back in the States. I would go to bed early, knowing that I would get up and do it all again, just the same way, the next day. The incredible beauty of the land, the quality of the light and the smell of the rain soaked earth, no matter how magical, were never going to change that.

I began to think about going home.

One of the brighter moments of those sad months was the day I opened my front door to find Bill Sr. standing there. I had not spoken to him in over three years and yet there he was, looking at me as if he came by for tea every day. I showed him around my house and all that we were up to at the factory. He was at his most charming and told me how well I had done. I had not sought his approval, but having it meant a great deal to me. Then we sat down on the patio, had tea, and talked as we always had. There was a brief mention of the rift of the past, but we quickly agreed to let it go. Neither of us wanted to get into that again and it no longer mattered anyway.

Bill Sr. was one of the few people I could have a conversation with whose subject matter went outside the borders of Kenya. Although we never said it outloud, we both knew that it had been far better for me that I had "learned to fly" on my own. Had I stayed as attached to him as I had been, I never would have done all that I had. And, more importantly, I never would have felt as accomplished. I had managed to get along with out him for the past three and a half years, but it was wonderful to have his company again.

A good friend of mine once said that I ran off to Africa 'to find myself.' I disagree. First of all, I wasn't lost, I was in pain. My mother's death and the battle over her Will that followed had been more than I could handle. My life, both in and out of New York, was in shambles. And secondly, I wasn't that timid a little thing to start with. I ran away to Africa because I needed to and because I could. The door was open and I went through it. I thought very little about what I was doing, I just did it.

Leaving Africa, however, was very different. I thought long and hard about that decision. During my summer weeks in New York that year, I talked with my friends for hours, debating this issue. I had tried to ignore the obvious signs that I was increasingly unhappy, lonely and caught up in a very toxic relationship, but there were no compass points for me in Kenya. Being back in New York gave me the perspective I needed. I would, ofcourse, leave many things behind in Africa, but there were many things that I would take with me.

A woman visitor, after looking around the factory, once remarked, "How can you leave all you have done here? You are so clever."

Without even thinking, I shot back, "Well, I get to take that with me."

If I really was all that "clever," I could be so in New York as well.

Leaving my house may have been the hardest of all, but I finally realized that the reason I loved that house was because I had made all the choices. Of course it struck me as perfect, everything in it was to my taste. If I had done that there, I could do it again elsewhere. I could build another "house of my dreams."

I feared leaving a place that had been so formidable. I had stretched my wings daily in Kenya, taking on all sorts of challenges. While there, I had felt strong and capable. I wondered if I would lose the sense of accomplishment that I had always had.

I didn't go to Africa 'to find myself,' but while I was there, I found a strength and a resourcefulness that I had never known I had. I would keep that too.

When I returned to Karen in August, everyone knew I had decided to leave. I had stayed longer in New York than I should have, thereby giving up my tax status as a Kenya resident. By September, I had put my house and Kufuma/Kushona Tu on the market.

It took almost eight months to sell the house and the business and get everything sorted out. And I spent a good deal of that time in tears. I would sit at night, hanging on to the necks of my dogs and cry. I knew it was time to go, and I believed that I was doing the right thing, but while walking around my house and grounds, making posterity videotapes for myself, I kept repeating, "I can't believe I am leaving here."

I made tapes of my house, walking room to room, and tapes of all the gardens. I made tapes of the rain falling on the back patio, tapes of Jotham and Stephen Karanja, and endless tapes of the new puppies. The dogs featured heavily in these videos. I made tapes of everybody at Kufuma, although that was quite strained at the time.

I made tapes of Celestine's new toto, Jake *(Jack.)*

I had found Jack (I think of him as Jack) aged six months, lying in his basket in my very dark garage one day. He was wide awake and staring into the black abyss of the garage roof.

"Celestine, how long has Jack been in the garage?"

"He has been there many hours, Madame. Iko msuri (*It is good*)."

"But if he is awake, don't you think it would be better if he had something mpore interesting to look at? Other than darkness?"

"Kwa nini? (*Why?)*"

"Because his brain, his kichwa, will get bigger, kubwa sana, if he sees colors and lights. Or he could look at the trees, the miti, and the leaves. He needs mental stimulation!"

Celestine did not understand this strange theory of mine.

I asked Wilson to build Jack a little chair so that he could sit up. When it was ready, we lined it with an old quilt and set it on a stool outside the kitchen door. He could sit and watch everything that was going on around him. I dubbed Jack the King of Kenya, sitting on his throne.

I bought him a musical mobile that played Braham's Lullaby. (I spared Celestine my lecture on the value of classical music in early childhood development.) We attached the mobile to his chair and as it turned around over his head, Celestine would name the animals that dangled above him: *farasi* (horse), *mbusi* (goat), *kuku* (chicken). Jack kicked his chubby baby legs and try to grab the animals dancing over him. Celestine called the music box "Jack 's ca-ssett." (Accent on the first syllable.) I made video tapes and Jack was a happier guy.

I heard through the Karen grapevine that Graham had gone back to Spain. There had been some crisis with his wife's health and he had left to take care of her. He never said anything to me and had been gone for months by the time I heard about it.

My last safari was, appropriately enough, with Billy. He had a camp in the Mara and with a gap in his schedule, I flew down to join him there. Once again, it was just the two of us. And, my number one tent man, Wairangu. (He was impressed with all the Swahili I had learned since my NFD days.) We took long, lazy game drives, making even more video tapes. I taped a cheetah on the kill, Billy napping in the shade of his car, and all the activities in camp. We sat by the fire at night and reminisced about all the things we had done together, over the past eight years, most notably the "Safari Kubwa." No one could go to the NFD anymore and we were very pleased that we had gone when we had. We talked a great deal about my leaving; he was for it. He felt that there were just too many things that were missing from a life in Kenya. Things that you could readily have elsewhwere. If I could get out, and many people there could not, then I must do so. We knew that I had had an incredible experience, and we knew how much Africa meant to me. But he agreed with me that it was time to go.

After our few days, we took that familiar drive from the Mara back to Karen. He was off the next day with more clients and when he dropped me at my house, we just said taonana *(I will see you again).*

A few days before I was to leave, Bonnie Bishop had a farewell party for me. Everyone I knew was there, but I found much of the sentiment that evening a bit odd. I had never felt particularly embraced by the European community in Karen while I was living there, what was all this carrying on now that I was leaving? I made videotapes of that evening as well.

Home from the party, I was walking towards my front door carrying my video camera, some flowers, cards I had been given, and a plate with a large piece of cake on it. My three big dogs and Deliahs eight puppies came from behind the house and raced towards me. I had on high heels, a very rare event, and when they all circled my feet, I lost my balance and fell. I landed one step and eight inches down, on the stone walkway, squarely on top of one knee. My kneecap was broken in half.

The doctor at Nairobi Hospital wanted to put my leg in a cast for the next six seeks. That was impossible, I informed him, I had movers coming to my house the next day. I would be on a plane for New York City in three more. You can't wear a cast on a plane because your leg swells and you can't maneuver into the bathroom either. They would have to come up with something less permanent.

There were no temporary casts, all velcro and space age plastic, in Kenya. What they concocted looked like something left over from the Civil War. There was ten tons of gauze packed around my leg to keep it moderately straight, covered with yards of ace bandages. It took about thirty minutes to take it off and even longer to put back on. I learned very quickly and in a more up close and personal way than I ever wanted, why 'knee capping' is so effective. If your kneecap is damaged, you cannot move your leg. At all. It is totally incapacitating. The only good thing about my having broken my kneecap is that my leg hurt so much that I had little time left to think about how much my heart was aching. I hobbled around my house with a cane, stupid and numb on pain killlers, while the movers packed up everything I owned.

I was returning to my furnished apartment in New York City and did not need all those extra beds and assorted bits and pieces I had accumulated. I was shipping back all my mother's antiques and the pieces of Africana that I had acquired and loved, but selling much of the rest. It still took two days to pack.

The woman who bought my house, another American, had a rather unique situation. She was bringing her aged Mother, Aunt, and Uncle to Kenya to live out their final years. She felt that they would be just as happy and probably more comfortable in Africa. They would have each other, their own home in a beautiful place with a wonderful climate and as many attending staff members as needed. It would certainly be better than the alternative, a nursing home in Texas. And she could be closer to them as well. This was a huge stroke of luck for me as she needed to set up an entire new household. She took on all my house and shamba staff, much of my furniture and my dogs as well. With this arrangement, things would stay just as they had been. Only I would be missing.

As the hour for me to leave for the final flight home approached, my staff members lined up on the driveway to say goodbye. There was Stephen Karanja and wife Nyamburra, both of whom had been there since Day One. Nyamburra now worked for Kufuma as a spinner and did needlepoint on the side. There was Isaac, the first baby born on my property. He was now five. There was Wilson and Elemina, Mildred's brother and sister, who looked so much like her, and her son Frederick. He was on his way the next semester to boarding school in Nakuru to finish his schooling. (He graduated in 1997.) Jotham was next in line, proud father of two. He too had been with me since the very beginning. Celestine was next, holding Night, Fannis and Jack, my official African 'niece', and 'nephew.'

I had already settled all financial accounts with everyone, handing out salaries and severance pay, as well as the much expected "farewell" bahati *(gift)*.

All that remained was for me to hobble down the line, trying not to cry again, and shake everyone's hand.

And tell them, once again, "Taonana."